Korean

An Essential Grammar

Korean: An Essential Grammar is a concise, user-friendly guide to the basic grammatical structures of Standard Korean. Presenting a fresh and accessible description of the language, this engaging grammar is linguistically sophisticated uses clear, jargon-free explanations and sets out the complexities of Korean in short, readable sections.

Key features include:

- clear grammar explanations
- frequent use of authentic examples
- Korean alphabet used alongside McCune-Reischauer romanization system
- glossary of grammatical terms
- pronunciation guide

This is the ideal mature reference source both for those studying Korean independently and for students in schools, colleges, universities, and adult classes of all types to back up their studies.

Young-Key Kim-Renaud is Professor of Korean Language and Culture and International Affairs, and Chair of the Department of East Asian Languages and Literatures at The George Washington University. She is the author or editor of ten books including *Korean Consonantal Phonology*, *Studies in Korean Linguistics*, and *The Korean Alphabet: Its History and Structure.*

Routledge Essential Grammars

Essential Grammars are available for the following languages:

Arabic
Chinese
Czech
Danish
Dutch
English
Finnish
German
Modern Greek
Modern Hebrew
Hindi
Hungarian
Norwegian
Polish
Portuguese
Romanian
Serbian
Spanish
Swedish
Thai
Turkish (forthcoming)
Urdu

Other titles of related interest published by Routledge:

Colloquial Korean

Korean

An Essential Grammar

Young-Key Kim-Renaud

Routledge
Taylor & Francis Group
LONDON AND NEW YORK

For Ariana Sua

First published 2009
by Routledge
711 Third Avenue, New York, NY 10017

Simultaneously published in the UK
by Routledge
2 Park Square, Milton Park, Abingdon, OX14 4RN

Routledge is an imprint of the Taylor & Francis Group, an informa business

Typeset in Sabon and Gill by
Graphicraft Limited, Hong Kong

British Library Cataloguing in Publication Data
A catalogue record for this book is available from the British Library

Library of Congress Cataloging in Publication Data
A catalog record for this book has been requested

ISBN13: 978-0-415-38513-8 (hbk)
ISBN13: 978-0-415-38388-2 (pbk)
ISBN13: 978-0-203-88361-7 (ebk)

Contents

Preface

Korean: An Essential Grammar aims to fill a long-felt need, among both teachers and students of Korean, for a linguistically sound but generally accessible introductory reference grammar of the language. The book is informed by modern linguistic research and explains basic principles underlying a wide range of phenomena in Korean including the sound pattern, sentence structures, major class words (verbs and nouns), modifiers, negation, honorifics, and language protocol.

The language examples from Standard Korean are presented first in *han'gŭl*, which is followed by McCune-Reischauer romanization. Hyphens mark a grammatical boundary when they occur within a word or a sentence. When they occur next to an independent form, it indicates that the form is bound, i.e., it cannot stand by itself but must occur with some other form. An asterisk (*) indicates that the expression it is attached to is ungrammatical. Vowel length or lengthening is marked by a colon (:).

The general principle of M-R romanization is to represent a close proximation of the actual pronunciation. However, when words are broken into smaller units for clarification, basic forms rather than actual pronunciation are noted. Therefore, readers are strongly recommended to learn to read *han'gŭl*, which is much more systematic than romanization. Glosses are provided for each relevant component of a word or a sentence, and then an English translation of the whole string is provided, sometimes with a literal meaning given in parentheses ('*lit.*...'). When examples are embedded in the narrative text, romanization is given right after the Korean writing, and the two parts are always considered together as a unit and therefore are not separated by any punctuation marks. Reverse arrows indicate where the particular forms came from, and regular arrows indicate obligatory change into the following forms.

While working toward the completion of this book, I have benefited greatly from the moral support and practical assistance of various organizations and individuals. I thank the Korea Foundation and the Columbian College of Arts and Sciences of The George Washington University for their generous support of my sabbatical research. I owe a special word of gratitude to my two former deans, William F. Frawley and Diana Lipscomb, and the current dean, Marguerite Barratt, for their collegial support; my colleagues, Miok Pak and Yunkyoung Kang for having read my manuscript and provided valuable comments; my friends Lindsey Eck, Amin Y. Teymorian, and David Yoo for their fine editorial assistance; and my husband Bertrand Renaud, my daughter Nicole Renaud, and my brother Hoagy Kim for their constant support of everything I do.

I thank the University of Hawai'i Press for their permission for me to use Figure 2.1 and Figure 2.2 from *The Korean Alphabet: Its History and Structure*, edited by Young-Key Kim-Renaud and published by the UH Press (1997).

The book project took much longer than originally planned, and I am most grateful for the patience and professional assistance of the superb editorial staff at Taylor & Francis and Routledge Publishers including Sophie Oliver, Sonja van Leeuwen, Geraldine Martin, and Annamarie Kino.

List of abbreviations and notations

Abbreviations

Act = Active
Adj = adjective
Adv = adverb
AH = addressee honorification
C = consonant
Caus = causative suffix
CL = numeral classifier
Comp = complementizer
Conj = conjunctive
Conn = connective
Cop = copula
Dat = dative
Dec = declarative
Def = deferential
Det = determiner
Dim = diminutive
Emph = emphatic
Exc = exclamation
Exist = existential
Fut = future tense
G = glide
Gen = genitive
Hon = honorific
Imp = imperative
Int = interjective
Loc = locative
Mod = modifier

N = noun
Neg = negative
Nom = nominative
Nominal = nominalizer
NP = noun phrase
Obj = object
OH = object honorification
Pass = passive
Past = past tense
Pl = plural
Pol = polite
Pres = present tense
Proc = processive
Prog = progressive
Pron = pronoun
Prop = propositive
Q = question
Quot = quotative
Rel = relative
Ret = retrospective
RH = referent honorification
S = sentence
SH = subject honorification
Sing = singular
SK = Sino-Korean
SOV = subject-object-verb
SS = sound-symbolic
Subj = subject
Sugg = suggestive
Sup = suppositional
Top = Topic
V = verb, vowel
VH = vowel harmony
Voc = vocative
Vol = volitional
VP = verb phrase
w = word
WH = wh- word

Notations

< >	graphic symbols
$[\ ]_x$	grammatical category X
/ /	phonemic forms
[ ]	phonetic forms
[▶ X]	see X (cross-reference)
X / \\ Y Z	X consists of Y and Z in that order
“ ”	quotation marks
‘ ’	gloss, meaning
?	possibly ungrammatical; unacceptable
*	ungrammatical; impossible; etymological
+	combines with
σ	syllable
SPACE	word and clausal boundary
- or .	word-internal boundary
.	syllable boundary
←	derived from
→	becomes
↓	low tone/pitch
↗	rising tone/pitch
↘	falling tone/pitch
↑	high tone/pitch
$C^{\neg}$	unreleased consonant
X_1	one or more/at least one X
~	varies with
S_x	clause, sentence within a sentence
’	word-internal graphic symbol boundary

List of tables and figures

Tables

Figures

Chapter 1

Introduction: the Korean language and its speakers

A native language for some 72 million people on the Korean peninsula and a first or second language for 5 million more ethnic Koreans living in China, Japan, North America, and the former Soviet Union, Korean ranks eleventh in number of speakers among more than 3,000 languages of the world.

Korean does not have a proven close linguistic relative. Many accept that it is related to Japanese and that both belong to the Tungusic branch of the Altaic family of languages, spoken mainly in Siberia and Mongolia. Typologically, Korean and Japanese are remarkably close in syntactic, semantic, and discourse-pragmatic features. Even more strikingly, Japanese and Korean show such sociolinguistic features as grammatically encoded honorifics [▶6.8, 10.1] in a way not shared with any other languages. The two languages also are extremely rich in sound-symbolic expressions called *mimetics* that are not sporadic, arbitrary words as in most languages, but are an integral part of their respective grammars.

Korean does not belong to the same language family as Chinese and also greatly differs from Chinese in structure. However, as an important member of the Sinitic civilization and a direct neighbor to China, Korea has had a close relationship with the Middle Kingdom. A huge portion of the Korean lexicon, therefore, is based on Sino-Korean roots borrowed from classical written Chinese. Today, loanwords from Western languages, especially English, are increasingly used as a result of globalization and contact with foreign trade goods, ideas, cultures, and customs. Contemporary Korean is a descendant of the language of the Silla kingdom (57 BCE–935 CE), one of the three kingdoms that ruled over the Korean peninsula and a large part of Manchuria, which unified the peninsula in 668.

The basic Korean word order is Subject-Object-Verb. Korean is an *agglutinative* language, in which words are formed by concatenating various meaning-bearing units. Typically noun phrases or verb stems are followed by suffix-like elements. There are no prepositions, but rather postpositions. For example, noun phrases consist of nouns followed by particles indicating their relationship to other elements in a sentence such as subject, object, dative, etc. Verb stems cannot stand alone but must be followed by suffixes such as those indicating tense, aspect, mood, and the expressed attitude of the speaker vis-à-vis the interlocutor and the referent. Therefore, different word orders are possible, as grammatical markers make the basic meaning of the sentence clear. However, all modifiers must precede the words they modify.

When different roots come together, their forms often influence each other. Many sound alternations are due to universal principles governed by physical and other human characteristics. However, many other seemingly complicated pronunciation changes in Korean are explainable by three important but simple metaforces in Korean: (1) the tendency for consonants between vowels to soften; (2) the tendency for Koreans to unrelease the syllable-final consonant, i.e., retain its contact position in the mouth [▶3.4.6]; and (3) the strong nature of the utterance-initial position.

Two salient features of the Korean language are intricate systems of *honorification* and *sound symbolism*. In Korean, rather narrowly defined interpersonal relationships are grammatically coded, and a speaker cannot open his or her mouth without considering linguistic protocol. Sound symbolism is the direct or iconic representation of meaning in sounds, which categorizes the world in a Korean-specific way through sound and meaning but still follows certain natural linguistic tendencies such as certain kinds of vowels or consonants occurring with similar sounds. Vowel harmony, which used to be much more systematic in Korean, is now most productive in sound-symbolic words, also called *mimetics* or *ideophones*.

Korean is written in *han'gŭl*, a unique alphabet invented in the mid-1400s, that shows a remarkable linguistic fit between its letter forms and various phonological units of the language. Chinese script was used in writing the Korean language for two millennia, and it is still mixed with Korean script in some academic or legal documents, although writing in *han'gŭl* only recently has become the norm even in those cases.

Chapter 2

Han'gŭl, *the Korean alphabet*

Korean is written in an alphabetic system, commonly known today as *han'gŭl* ("Han [Korean, great, unique] script") in South Korea and elsewhere, but called *chosŏn'gŭl* in North Korea. This simple, yet systematic and efficient, alphabet invented in the mid-1400s is a source of great pride for Koreans. In the Republic of Korea, October 9 is celebrated as *han'gŭl* Day, a rare national day of celebration honoring a linguistic achievement. Various foreign linguists, especially specialists in writing, have noted *han'gŭl*'s many unusual qualities, calling it, for example, "one of the great intellectual achievements of humankind" (Sampson 1985: 144), "perhaps the most remarkable [script] in the world" (Ledyard 1966: 370), and "probably the most remarkable writing system ever invented" (Coulmas 1989: 118).

Han'gŭl did not evolve over a long period like most alphabets but was invented, and we know its inventor – a sage king and brilliant linguist, Sejong the Great (r. 1418–50). Furthermore, the scientific, humanistic, and philosophical principles underlying its invention are clearly recorded. The original name of the alphabet was *Hunmin chŏng'ŭm* ("correct sounds for the instruction of the people") when it was proclaimed in 1446. The proclamation, also entitled *Hunmin chŏng'ŭm* (hereinafter *HC*), was a kind of handbook for learning the alphabet; it contained explanatory treatises and examples called *Hunmin chŏng'ŭm haerye* ("explanations and examples of the correct sounds for the instruction of the people," or *HCH*). This historic publication miraculously resurfaced in 1940 after having been lost for centuries. In 1997 UNESCO voted to include it in its Memory of the World register – the first and probably the only linguistic treatise honored in this manner.

Sejong wanted to devise a writing system that would be easy for all Koreans to learn and to use, as clearly stated in his famous Preface to *HC*:

> The sounds of our country's language are different from those of the Middle Kingdom (China) and are not smoothly communicable with literary (Chinese) characters. Therefore, among my dear people, there are many who, though they have something they wish to tell, are never able to express their feelings [in writing]. Commiserating with this, I have newly designed 28 letters. I desire only that everyone acquire them easily, to make them convenient and comfortable for daily use.
>
> (trans. Kim-Renaud)

Sejong was also eager and confident that the new system would become universal. As Chŏng In-ji put it in his Postface to *HCH*:

> Though only twenty-eight letters are used, their shifts and changes in function are endless; they are simple and fine, reduced to the minimum yet universally applicable. Therefore, a wise man can acquaint himself with them before the morning is over; a stupid man can learn them in the space of ten days . . . There is no usage not provided for, no direction in which they do not extend. Even the sound of the winds, the cry of the crane, the cackle of fowl and the barking of dogs – all may be written . . .
>
> (trans. Ledyard 1966: 258–9)

2.1 Inventory of the Korean alphabet

This section gives a complete list of the Korean alphabet as used today, in dictionary order. Note that sounds vary depending on the position in which they occur, as shown in Table 2.1. English examples containing similar sounds are underscored.

2.2 Design principles of *han'gŭl* letters

Han'gŭl is an alphabet, originally composed of 28 letters, but now consisting of 14 consonants and 10 vowels (in reality, either simple vowels or diphthongs – sequences of two vowels one of which is pronounced as a glide, i.e., a [w] or [y] sound). It originally had systematic accent markers, when pitch was a significant part of the Korean language. *Han'gŭl* is unlike all other alphabets, because its letter shapes are not arbitrary but are designed to represent various characteristics of the Korean sound system.

Table 2.1 Consonants

Letter	Name	Initial	Intervocalic	Final
ㄱ	기역 [kiyŏk]	[k] baker	[g] ago	[k] book
ㄴ	니은 [niŭn]	[n] no	[n] china	[n] in
ㄷ	디귿 [tigŭt]	[t] into	[d] Sunday	[t] what
ㄹ	리을 [riŭl]	[r] radio	[r] bury	[l] cool
ㅁ	미음 [miŭm]	[m] man	[m] Thomas	[m] dam
ㅂ	비읍 [piŭp]	[p] super	[b] sober	[p] tip
ㅅ	시옷 [siot]	[s] nice	[s] nicer	[t] but
ㅇ	이응 [iŭng]	[Ø] –	[ng] singing	[ng] sing
ㅈ	지읒 [chiŭt]	[ch] inches	[j] unjust	[t] pit
ㅊ	치읓 [ch'iŭt]	[ch'] church	[ch'] church	[t] pit
ㅋ	키읔 [k'iŭk]	[k'] kit	[k'] cookie	[k] book
ㅌ	티읕 [t'iŭt]	[t'] took	[t'] guitar	[t] sit
ㅍ	피읖 [p'iŭp]	[p'] pie	[p'] import	[p] nap
ㅎ	히읗 [hiŭt]	[h] hat	[h] vehicle	[t] sit

Table 2.2 Geminate consonants (doubled letters but single sounds)

Letter	Name	Approximate pronunciation
ㄲ	쌍기역 [ssang kiyŏk]	[kk] backgammon
ㄸ	쌍디귿 [ssang tigŭt]	[tt] hot dog
ㅃ	쌍비읍 [ssang piŭp]	[pp] tapebox
ㅆ	쌍시옷 [ssang siot]	[ss] dissimilar
ㅉ	쌍지읒 [ssang chiŭt]	[tch] sweet juice, blackjack

HCH makes it clear that the alphabet Sejong created for the purpose of universal literacy was based on his sophisticated understanding of the Korean sound system. He strongly believed that native speakers have a subconscious knowledge of linguistic units, and a writing system that reflects phonological aspects of the language iconically is easier to learn and use than arbitrary symbols.

In *han'gŭl*, consonants and vowels are represented by two clearly distinguishable kinds of graphic shapes. Basic consonantal shapes are geometric and depict graphically the place and manner of articulation. Vowels also are iconically represented to express different classes according to articulatory and acoustic characteristics.

Table 2.3 Basic vowels and *y*-diphthongs (*y* + basic vowels)

Letter	Name	Approximate pronunciation
ㅏ	아 [a]	alms
ㅑ	야 [ya]	yard
		(NB: here and below, the extra short stroke represents a [y] sound.)
ㅓ	어 [ŏ]	caught, tough
ㅕ	여 [yŏ]	young
ㅗ	오 [o]	boy, tow, society
ㅛ	요 [yo]	Yosemite, yoga
ㅜ	우 [u]	two, spoon
ㅠ	유 [yu]	you
ㅡ	으 [ŭ]	book, petite, support
ㅣ	이 [i]	eat, key, pill

Table 2.4 Complex vowels with optional *w* or *y*

Letter	Name	Approximate pronunciation
ㅐ	애 [ae]	cat, ask
ㅒ	얘 [yae]	Yankee
ㅔ	에 [e]	phonetic
ㅖ	예 [ye]	yes
ㅚ	외 [oe]	quench
ㅟ	위 [wi]	queen, twig
ㅘ	와 [wa]	Hawaii
ㅙ	왜 [wae]	wagon
ㅝ	워 [wŏ]	wonder
ㅞ	웨 [we]	west

Note: 애, 에 and 외, although graphically complex, are single vowels today but originally were diphthongs ending in y, as the letter shapes show.

2.2.1 Consonants

According to *HCH*, the consonant letterforms schematically show the shapes of speech organs – such as the tongue, teeth, or mouth – articulating the sound in question.

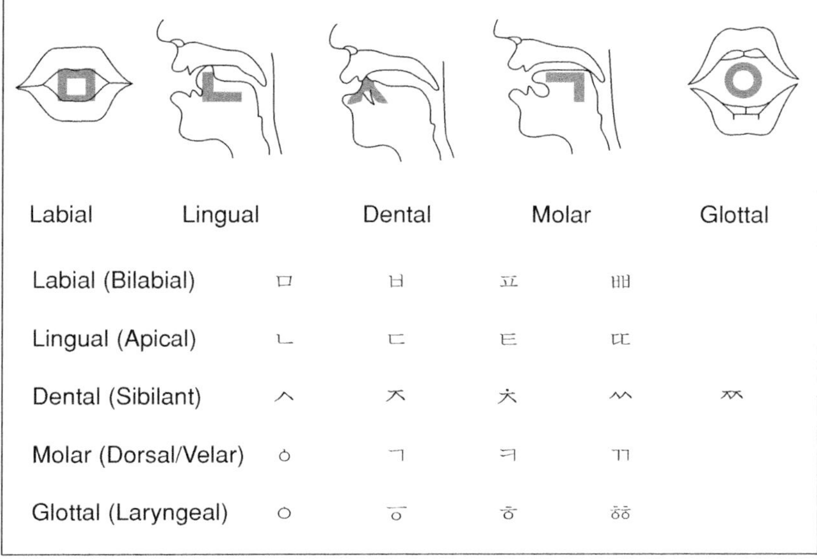

Labial
Lingual
Dental
Molar
Glottal
Labial (Bilabial) ㅁ ㅂ ㅍ ㅃ
Lingual (Apical) ㄴ ㄷ ㅌ ㄸ
Dental (Sibilant) ㅅ ㅈ ㅊ ㅆ ㅉ
Molar (Dorsal/Velar) ㆁ ㄱ ㅋ ㄲ
Glottal (Laryngeal) ㅇ ㆆ ㅎ ㆅ

Figure 2.1 The letterforms of *han'gŭl* consonants
Source: Kim-Renaud (ed.) 1997: 279

All of the original 28 letters, including the four no longer used, were arranged in categories that related shape to function. First, five basic categories of the 17 consonants were identified according to their positions of articulation, and a simple, geometrical form was designed for each one. For example, the letter <ㄴ> depicted the tongue touching the back of the teeth, <ㄱ> the back of the tongue being raised to block the air from the throat, and <ㅁ> the mouth or the lips coming together in producing the respective sounds. Figure 2.1 gives a schematic representation of articulatory positions of the five types of consonants.

Then, strokes were added to create the remaining consonant letters.

Table 2.5 Categories of consonants and the principle of adding strokes

		→	Stronger		
Labial	ㅁ /m/	→	ㅂ /p/	→	ㅍ /p'/
Lingual	ㄴ /n/	→	ㄷ /t/	→	ㅌ /t'/
Dental	ㅅ/s/	→	ㅈ/ch/	→	ㅊ/ch'/
Molar	(ㆁ /ng/	→)	ㄱ /k/	→	ㅋ /k'/
Glottal	ㅇ/ɦ/	→	ㆆ /ʔ/	→	ㅎ /h/

The result is that sounds that belong to the same category of pronunciation (the same *natural class*) all contain the identical basic form. For example, the *lingual* sounds, ㄴ/n/, ㄷ/t/, ㅌ/t'/, ㄸ/tt/, and ㄹ/l/, which are produced by placing the tongue on the ridge above and behind the teeth, all have shapes that include the basic symbol ㄴ ***n*** that represents that articulatory position. In contemporary Korean, the sound /ng/ occurs only in a syllable-final position while the small circle, zero, occurs only in a syllable-initial position when there is no initial consonant; therefore, the two symbols, ㆁ and ㅇ, have graphically merged. Both shapes still coexist, but they are no longer distinctive but perceived as only stylistic variants of the same symbol.

HCH explains that each time a stroke is added the sound becomes more severe, while the type of consonant remains the same. The design principle of "adding strokes" is based on a representation of the Korean consonantal-strength scale, which explains many phonological phenomena elegantly.

2.2.2 Vowels

The 11 vowel letters were designed according to different but equally systematic principles as the consonant letters. The vowel letters are composed of a long, horizontal or vertical stroke with one, two, or no short strokes (originally dots) attached to one side of it. At the time of their invention, the three basic vowel sounds were /ʌ/ (the vowel of English *judge*), /ŭ/ (the vowel of *good*), and /i/ (the vowel of *meet*). The symbols representing these vowels, a dot < · > symbolizing heaven, a horizontal line < — > earth, and a vertical line < ㅣ > a human being, derive, respectively, from three basic symbols in East Asian cosmology (Figure 2.2).

The remaining vowel symbols were created by combining the dot with either the horizontal or vertical line in such a way that they pair off neatly into two groups of vowels, called *yin* and *yang* (or dark and bright), thus graphically contrasting vowel letters and remarkably capturing the vowel-harmony phenomenon in Korean [▶3.3.3]. Again, symbols for vowels belonging to the same harmonic class share certain features: The dark vowels have the dots placed below the horizontal line or at the left side of the vertical line, while the bright vowels have the dots above the horizontal line or at the right side of the vertical line. In other words, when the sun or sky is above the earth or on the right side of a person, it is bright, and when it is in the opposite directions it is dark.

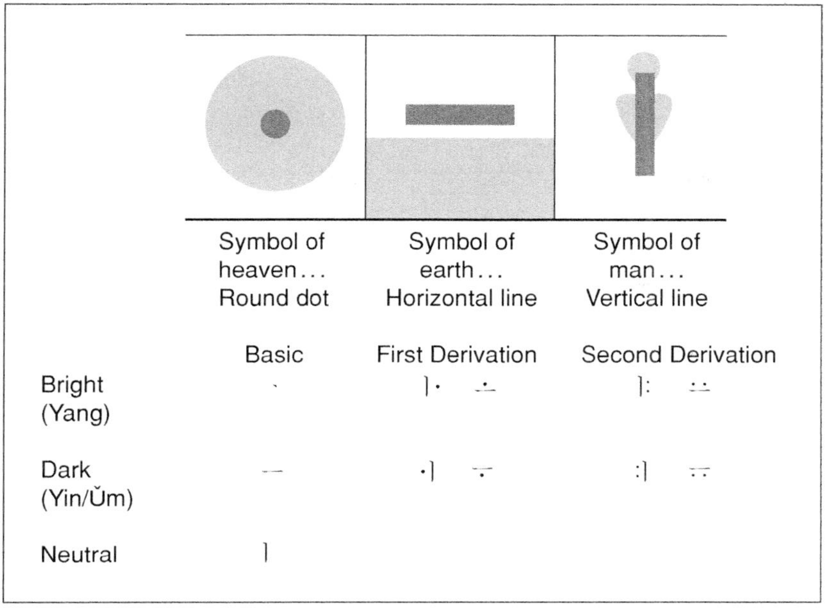

Figure 2.2 Letterforms of *han'gŭl* vowels
Source: Kim-Renaud (ed.) 1997: 280

Table 2.6 Categories of vowels and the principle of adding strokes

	First derivation	Second derivation
Yang/Bright Vowels	• + ㅡ → ㅗ	• + ㅗ → ㅛ
	• + ㅣ → ㅏ	• + ㅏ → ㅑ
Yin/Dark Vowels	• + ㅡ → ㅜ	• + ㅜ → ㅠ
	• + ㅣ → ㅓ	• + ㅓ → ㅕ

Vowels emerging from the first derivation are simple vowels, and those from the second derivation are diphthongs. Adding strokes gives vowels more weight.

Soon after the invention of the Korean alphabet, the dot was replaced by a short line, most probably for ease of calligraphy done by brush. The sound represented by a single dot disappeared from the language, and therefore the symbol is no longer in use.

The vowel-harmony principle [▶3.3.3] is strictly observed in the design of Korean letterforms. For example, when two vowels are combined to create

Table 2.7 Written forms showing Korean vowel harmony

Bright:	ㅐ ae, ㅒ yae, ㅘ wa, ㅙ wae, ㅚ oe,
Dark:	ㅔ e, ㅖ ye, ㅝ wŏ, ㅞ we, ㅟ wi, ㅢ ŭi
	(never *ㅗㅓ, *ㅗㅔ, *ㅜㅏ, *ㅜㅐ, etc.)

a complex vowel in writing, the semi-vowel or glide [w] sound is represented either by the vowel ㅗ *o* or ㅜ *u* depending on the vowel it occurs with. When the following vowel is a yang (also called *bright*) vowel ㅏ *a*, choose the bright vowel ㅗ *o* for the [w] sound. Everywhere else choose the dark vowel ㅜ *u* to represent the [w] sound. ㅣ *i* and ㅡ *ŭ*, being neutral vowels, can occur with either group. Table 2.7 shows this clearly.

2.3 Orthography

2.3.1 *Writing in syllable blocks*

The unusual nature of the Korean alphabet is also evident in how the letters are used in actual writing. *Han'gŭl* is written in syllable blocks (units that are independently pronounceable). Thus, the letters are not written on one line as in English but in clusters of letters, where consonants envelop a vowel nucleus. One important requirement is that all syllables should be more or less the same size, each fitting into an imaginary square. As a consequence, letters within a syllable are adjusted in size and in shape to fit that imaginary square proportionally. Furthermore, certain spelling conventions are established to keep syllable shapes as uniform as possible. These include the following:

1 The order of sounds in a syllable is *consonant* + *vowel nucleus* + *consonant(s)*. All alphabetic letters are written proportionally depending on their positions and also depending on how many other letters are included in an imaginary identical square area into which all elements of a syllable should fit in a given text, except when the size is altered for design purposes.
2 A written syllable is supposed to have at least a consonant and a vowel. When the syllable has no initial consonant, a circle representing zero is inserted to fill the initial position. When the vowel is complex, it wraps around the consonant, with the latter always located in the upper left corner of the imaginary syllabic box.

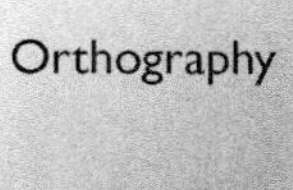

- If the vowel has a long vertical stroke, ㅏ, ㅑ, ㅓ, ㅕ, ㅐ, ㅒ, ㅏ, ㅔ, ㅖ, or ㅣ, then write it to the right of the initial consonant, as shown in Figure 2.3.

C	V

C = any consonant or ㅇ (zero)
V = any vowel with a long vertical stroke (ㅏ, ㅑ, ㅓ, ㅕ, ㅣ, ㅐ, ㅔ, ㅒ, ㅖ),
e.g., 나, 야, 더, 벼, 키, 해, 제, 이, 예

Figure 2.3 Syllables with long vertical strokes

- If the vowel has a long horizontal stroke, ㅗ, ㅛ, ㅜ, ㅠ, or ㅡ, write it below the initial consonant, as shown in Figure 2.4.

C
V

C = any consonant or ㅇ (zero)
V = any vowel with a long horizontal stroke (ㅗ, ㅛ, ㅜ, ㅠ, ㅡ),
e.g., 소, 요, 추, 큐, 그

Figure 2.4 Syllables with long horizontal strokes

- If the vowel is complex, i.e., made of a vowel + a vowel with a long vertical stroke, place it wrapping around a consonant, the latter being located at the left upper corner of the syllable block, as shown in Figure 2.5.

C	V_2
V_1	

C = any consonant or ㅇ (zero)
V_1V_2 = complex vowel where V_2 = a vowel with a long vertical stroke (ㅘ, ㅝ, ㅚ, ㅟ, ㅙ, ㅞ, ㅢ)
e.g., 과, 뒤, 쇠, 쥐, 쾌, 궤, 의

Figure 2.5 Syllables with complex vowels with long vertical strokes

- Final consonants are always written below the basic C+V unit. Even with the final consonant or consonant clusters, the overall size of the square must remain equal to that of the C-V syllable. Observe the following three syllable blocks containing final consonants, as shown in Figure 2.6.

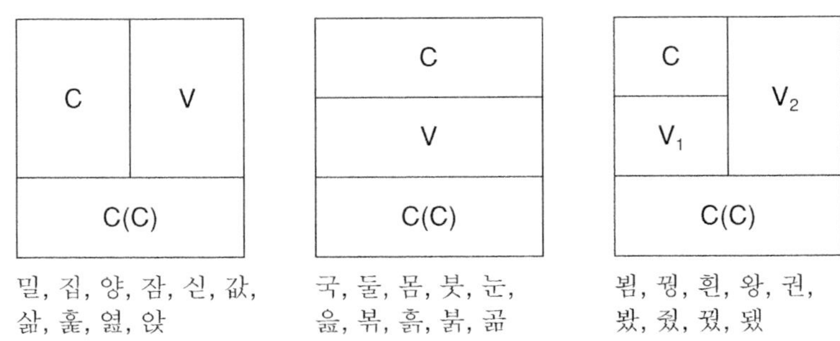

Figure 2.6 Writing syllable-final consonants or consonant clusters

This list of final consonants and consonant clusters is quite limited – Koreans do not release the syllable-final consonants and not all consonants appear in the syllable-final position. Even those that do are often altered, deleted, or simplified in actual pronunciation.

3 The stroke order is similar to that used in writing Chinese characters, i.e., from top to bottom, and from left to right. For example, the word *han'gŭl* is not written linearly as *ㅎㅏㄴㄱㅡㄹ, but written in two syllable blocks as 한글, each syllable block having the composition and order of writing, as shown in Figure 2.7.

2.3.2 *Writing words consistently*

Korean is a polysyllabic language in which various grammatical units representing the function of a word in a sentence are combined. Sounds are often affected when they are pronounced next to other sounds, as is true in almost all languages. For example, in English we can make an adjective out of the word "president" by adding the suffix *-ial*, in which case the pronunciation of the final consonant changes due to its assimilation to the following vowel and is pronounced "sh." English orthography is far from systematic, but in this case word parts are spelled the same from word to word even though their pronunciations vary. This is called morphophonemic writing, i.e., writing the basic forms (phonemes, represented essentially by the alphabetic letters) of meaningful units (morphemes) rather than their positional variations.

As expected of most agglutinative languages, parts of Korean words are more often than not pronounced differently from when they occur independently.

한 <han> 'Korean, great, one'

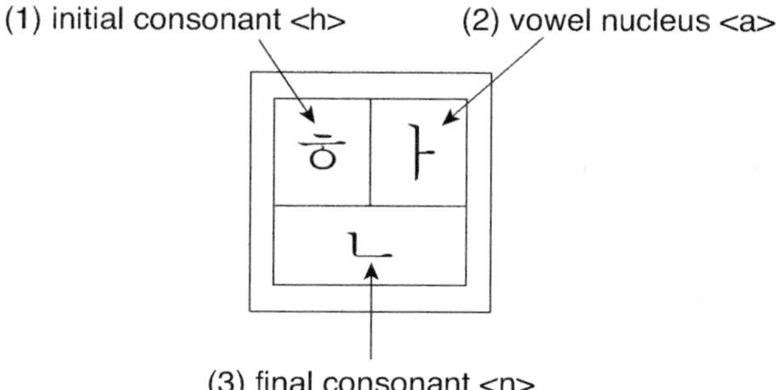

글 <kŭl> (pronounced [gŭl]) 'writing, script, composition'

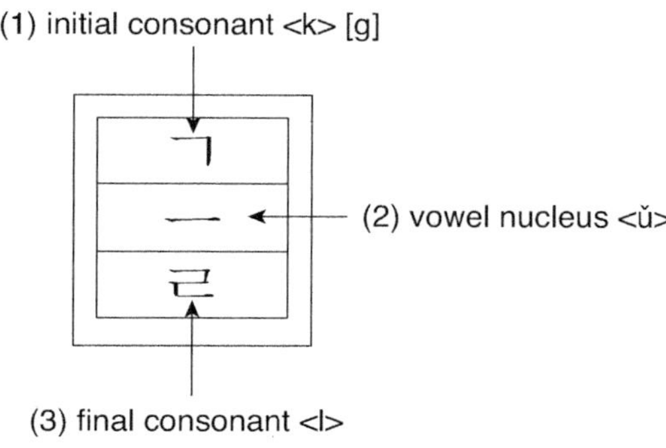

Figure 2.7 Structure of syllable block and order of elements

Korean orthography dictates that the basic forms be written, not the actual pronunciation, just as in English we write *presidential*, and not **presidenshal* or **presidensial*. *Han'gŭl* is written morphophonemically, which means it is a sound-based alphabetic system but the basic forms rather than their phonetic variations are written down. Except for alternations of which native speakers are conscious, such as vowel harmony and irregular-verb alternations, there is one spelling for each morpheme, i.e., the smallest meaning-bearing unit. For example, 'flower' is always written 꽃, regardless of the kinds of sounds that follow. That is, although the final consonant may be pronounced in many different ways depending on what sound follows it, the word is written consistently as 꽃, as shown in Figure 2.8.

꽃-이 (subj.)	[kkoch'i]	no change when followed by a vowel
꽃	[kkot]	[t] elsewhere
[*This [t] further assimilates to the following consonant as shown below.*]		
꽃-마을 ('village')	[kkommaŭl]	[m] when followed by an [m] sound
꽃-놀이 ('game')	[kkonnori]	[n] when followed by [n]
꽃-비 ('rain')	[kkoppi]	[p] when followed by [p]
꽃-도 ('also')	[kkotto]	[t] when followed by [t]
꽃-과 ('with')	[kkokkwa]	[k] when followed by [k]

Figure 2.8 Actual pronunciations of the final consonant ㅊ *ch'* in different contexts

As long as Koreans can tell that these forms are further analyzable, the basic forms will be written. However, complex forms are sometimes reinterpreted through language change as an indivisible single word, in which case the whole string is written as it is pronounced rather than showing the etymology. For example, 'pine tree' in Korean is written now as 소나무 *so-na-mu*, although it is etymologically* 솔 *sol* 'pine' + 나무* *namu* 'tree,' because it has become a name for the variety of plant rather than 'a tree of pine.'

2.3.3 *Writing direction, spacing, and punctuation*

For centuries, Koreans combined syllables into sentences without any space between words, and they wrote sentences vertically, starting from the top right corner of the page. They continued mixing in *hancha* (Chinese characters) to express Sino-Korean words even while writing in *han'gŭl*. Today, however, the Western-style of writing horizontally across a page, starting from the top left rightward, has become the norm. Koreans also have incorporated Western-style punctuation marks, including quotation marks, question marks, exclamation marks, and parentheses, etc. Writing in *han'gŭl* only is not only acceptable in any kind of writing, including academic and official documents, but seems increasingly preferable. While *hancha* is disappearing, the mixing in of roman letters when referring to some company's Western name or the initials of some politicians' names is a common practice today. Some newspapers and websites will sport some English words, but in spite of the massive use of loanwords from English and other Western languages, Koreans transliterate them into Korean when writing for print media. Observe the following excerpt from a news report on the winning performance of Yu-na Kim in an international figure-skating competition in Moscow on November 24, 2007 (http://sports.donga.com/bbs/

sports.php?id=syn_synthesis&no=5583), where all Korean transliterations of loanwords are underscored:

> 트리플 플립 (triple flip)-트리플 토우 (triple toe) 콤비네이션 (combination) 과 트리플 루프 (triple loop) 등 시니어 (senior) 데뷔 (debut) 후 가장 완성도 높은 점프 (jump) 연기였다.
> 'Her jump performance with triple flip-triple toe combination and triple loop, etc. was the closest to perfection since her debut as a senior.'

Chapter 3

Sound pattern

The letters of the Korean alphabet correspond more or less to phonemes (the smallest contrastive units that contribute to meaning differences) in the Korean sound system. The only exception is the circle **o**, which is used for both the zero (null) mark in a syllable-initial position and the syllable-final /ng/ or [ŋ] sound as in English *sing* [▶2.2.1]. Because there is such a close fit between the Korean alphabet and the phonemes of Korean, *han'gŭl* can be used for phonetic notation.

3.1 Sound units

Korean has 19 consonants, eight vowels, and two glides or semivowels /w/ and /y/. Syllables and accentual units play a significant role in the Korean sound system.

3.1.1 *Consonants*

A consonant is a sound produced by completely closing the vocal tract or passing air through a narrow opening in it. In Korean, consonants are not independently pronounceable and cannot form a syllable by themselves. It is useful to categorize Korean consonants by place and manner of articulation, as shown in Table 3.1.

Consonants are broadly categorized into *obstruents* and *sonorants*. Obstruents are sounds produced when the airflow is completely stopped (stops like /p/, /t/, /k/) or escapes through a narrow opening (fricatives like /f/, /s/) in the vocal tract. Sonorants are produced when air flows out with little or no obstruction though the mouth, the nose, or both. Sonorants include sounds such as vowels, nasals, and liquids. In general they are *voiced*, i.e., pronounced with the vocal cords close together and vibrating.

Table 3.1 Korean consonants

Manner			Place: Labial	Dental	Palatal	Velar	Glottal
Obstruent	Stop	Tense	ㅃ /pp/	ㄸ /tt/	ㅉ /tch/	ㄲ /kk/	
		Aspirated	ㅍ /p'/	ㅌ /t'/	ㅊ /ch'/	ㅋ /k'/	
		Lax/Plain	ㅂ /p/	ㄷ /t/	ㅈ /ch/	ㄱ /k/	
	Fricative	Tense		ㅆ /ss/			
		Lax/Plain		ㅅ /s/			ㅎ /h/
Sonorant	Nasal		ㅁ /m/	ㄴ /n/		ㅇ /ŋ/	
	Liquid		ㄹ /l/				

In most languages, obstruents are usually paired, one group being voiced, the other voiceless. For example, in English, counterparts such as *p:b*, *t:d*, *k:g*, *s:z*, and so on are differentiated by whether or not they are voiced. Touching your neck area, you will feel your Adam's apple vibrating when you pronounce sounds such as [b] and [g], but not [p] and [k].

In Korean all obstruents are voiceless. Korean completely lacks the voiced series, *b*, *d*, *g*, *z*, and is unusual in that there are three different kinds of obstruents differentiated by degree of aspiration and tenseness: lax (ㅂ *p*, ㄷ *t*, ㅈ *ch*, ㄱ *k*), heavily aspirated (ㅍ *p'*, ㅌ *t'*, ㅊ *ch'*, ㅋ *k'*), and tense (ㅃ *pp*, ㄸ *tt*, ㅉ *tch*, ㄲ *kk*). Tense consonants are produced by tightly constricting the vocal cords; heavily aspirated consonants, by widely opening them. Lax stops are gently articulated with the vocal cords slightly open. The three-way distinction among Korean stops is shown in Table 3.2.

Aspirated consonants are a little like English stops in word-initial positions such as the *p* sound in *pack*, *t* in *tissue*, and *k* in *kiss*. The vocal cords are

Table 3.2 Three-way distinction among Korean voiceless stops

Lax/Plain C	Aspirated C'	Tense CC
방 pang 'room'	팡 p'ang '(sound of explosion)'	빵 ppang 'bread'
달 tal 'moon'	탈 t'al 'mask'	딸 ttal 'daughter'
자 cha 'Sleep!'	차 ch'a 'It's cold.'	짜 tcha 'It's salty!'
개 kae 'Fold it!'	캐 k'ae 'Dig it!'	깨 kkae 'Break it!'

wide open and articulation is forceful. Tense consonants are also strongly articulated, but tenseness is achieved by squeezing the vocal cords and keeping the closed position longer than usual.

Aspirated and tense obstruents are harder or "stronger" than lax consonants because they are produced with extra effort in the vocal tract. Learning this three-way distinction can be a challenge for learners of Korean as a second language. Tense and lax consonants may sound almost identical because they have no strong aspiration. On the other hand, the lax series is moderately aspirated in initial position and, to foreign ears, corresponding aspirated and lax consonants are not as easily distinguishable either. Research has shown that cues in the length of the vowel follow the three types of stop consonants. A vowel is longer after tense stops, intermediate after lax stops, and shortest after aspirated stops. As a matter of practice, pay attention to the vowels that immediately follow these consonants.

In English, not all stops are heavily aspirated. English stop sounds are unaspirated and rather tense when following an *s* sound as in *spoon*, *still*, or *scope*. So, one can imagine an [s] before pronouncing a tense stop in Korean. Here is another way to look at it. The *d* in *hot dog* is actually pronounced like the Korean tense [tt]. So, when trying to pronounce a tense consonant, imagine another identical consonant except for voicing preceding it. For example, say *up* first in your head, before the syllable *beat*, and say the sequence faster and faster, and finally make the first vowel very weak or not pronounced at all, although imagined. You will get the tense [pp] sound that you want. There is no doubt that this kind of imagined or subconscious gemination was in the mind of the inventor of the alphabet in designing the geminate letter shapes for tense consonants.

Korean sonorants are all the vowels and nasal consonants, ㅁ /m/, ㄴ /n/, and ㅇ /ng/, where the air escapes through the nose, and the liquid consonant, ㄹ /l/, where the sound escapes through the sides of the tongue. Sonorants in Korean, as in most languages, are voiced.

Fricatives are like stops, but their distribution is different. There is no strongly aspirated series, but, as with the stop series, the lax (or plain) *s* is slightly aspirated.

3.1.2 Vowels

Articulation in vowels is not as clear as that in consonants. Different vowels are distinguished by three articulatory characteristics: tongue height, frontness and backness, and lip rounding, as shown in Table 3.3.

Table 3.3 Korean vowels

Front-backness	Nonback		Back	
Lip-rounding	Unrounded	Rounded	Unrounded	Rounded
Tongue height				
High	ㅣ /i/	ㅟ /wi/ [ü]	ㅡ /ŭ/	ㅜ /u/
Mid	ㅔ /e/	ㅚ /oe/ [ö]	ㅓ /ŏ/	ㅗ /o/
Low	ㅐ /ae/		ㅏ /a/	

The vowels ㅔ /e/, ㅐ /ae/, ㅟ /wi/ and ㅚ /oe/ are now single units, even though they are graphically complex showing their origin in diphthongs. ㅟ /wi/ and ㅚ /oe/ are rounded front vowels that are pronounced [ü] and [ö], like the two German vowels. Rounded front vowels are universally less common and are supposed to be less natural and require more effort to produce. For this reason, these two vowels are resplit in Standard Korean into two sounds, [wi] and [we] respectively, especially when they are not preceded by a consonant, as shown in Table 3.4.

3.1.3 *Semivowels (glides)*

A glide, sometimes called a semivowel, is like a vowel but cannot form a syllable nucleus by itself. It is pronounced closely together with a main vowel, forming a diphthong together in a syllable. In Korean there are two semivowels, /w/ and /y/, which start at the vowel positions of /u/ and /i/, respectively, and glide into the position of the following vowel. Graphically, too, a *w*-glide is written as a small <u> or <o> harmonizing with the yin

Table 3.4 Pronunciation of front rounded vowels in Standard Korean

M-R romanization	In initial position	After a consonant
/wi/	위 [wi] 'upside'	뒤 [tü] 'backside'
/oe/	외 [we] 'outside'	괴 [kö] 'box'

or yang category of the following vowel. For example, when the following vowel is < ㅓ >, the *w*-glide is written with <ㅜ>, and if the following vowel is < ㅏ >, then it is written with <ㅗ>, as seen in <ㅘ> and <ㅝ>. The vowel < ㅣ >, being neutral, can either have <ㅗ> or <ㅜ> preceding it, as seen in <ㅚ> or <ㅟ>.

The *y*-glide is represented as an extra short line (originally a dot) in the vowel nucleus. Thus, the vowels ㅏ, ㅓ, ㅗ, ㅜ when preceded by a *y*-glide are written ㅑ, ㅕ, ㅛ, ㅠ, respectively.

Most glides are on-glides in Korean in the sense that they precede the vowel they glide into. One exception is the *y*-off-glide that follows the vowel ㅡ /ŭ/, as in 의사 *ŭisa* 'doctor,' which is pronounced [ŭysa]. Even here, it is really a diphthong, and the first part *ŭ* remains in a word-initial position and the second part *i* remains in a non-initial syllable. For example, 의사 *ŭisa* is often pronounced as [ŭsa], and 한의 *hanŭi* as [hani].

Korean thus has true complex vowels and diphthongs. The semivowel *y* can precede any vowel with the exception of the unrounded high vowels, /i/ and /ŭ/. Thus there are ㅑ *ya*, ㅕ *yŏ*, ㅛ *yo*, and ㅠ *yu*, but no such diphthongs as **yi* and **yŭ*. The semivowel /w/ can precede any vowel except the three back vowels, /o/, /ŭ/, and /u/. So, the diphthongs **wo*, **wŭ*, and **wu* are not allowed. That is why Koreans have a hard time pronouncing English words such as *wood*. Korean semivowels can only precede, never follow, a vowel except in the syllable ㅢ *ŭi* [ŭy], where the semivowel *y* follows the vowel *ŭ*. So, when Koreans pronounce foreign words containing vowels with off-glides like English *tie*, *boy*, and *tow*, they will break the diphthongs into two syllables – [t'a-i], [po-i], and [t'o-u], respectively.

The list of diphthongs in Korean is shown in Table 3.5.

Table 3.5 Korean diphthongs

Tongue height	Front-backness			
	Nonback		Back	
High	ㅢ /ŭi/	ㅟ /wi/		ㅠ /yu/
Mid	ㅞ /we/	ㅚ /oe/ [ö] or [we]	ㅕ /yŏ/	ㅛ /yo/
Low	ㅙ /wae/, ㅒ /yae/		ㅑ /ya/	

Vowels are broadly categorized as yang (or *bright*) and yin (or *dark*). Yang vowels are pronounced with a more open mouth (lowered jaw) than yin vowels. Hence, the young vowels in the shaded areas of Tables 3.3 and 3.5 occupy the lowest position in each of the vertical vowel spaces.

3.1.4 The syllable

The Korean syllable can consist of only the medial, optionally preceded by one consonant, and followed by one or two consonants. Any consonant can occupy the initial, also called syllable-onset, position, except for ㅇ /ng/. No off-glide is allowed except in ㅢ /ŭi/, pronounced [ŭy]. The final, also called the *coda*, may have up to two consonants in writing, but in actual pronunciation only one consonant is allowed in the final position due to the Korean requirement to unrelease the final [▶3.4.6].

A zero (or circle) sign is written when nothing occupies the initial position. This is generally thought as an aesthetic effort to achieve a harmonious syllable shape. This makes good sense. However, there is also a linguistic reason. An "optimal" syllable has the shape CV, and here is a clear interpretation that the minimal syllable shape is CV; when there is nothing to occupy the C slot, a zero is written. When you see forms such as 아 ***a***, 오 ***o***, 우 ***u***, 이 ***i***, just remember that the initial has no sound value.

Han'gŭl writing shows the basic form of each meaningful unit [▶2.3.2]. The structure of the written syllable is not always identical to that of the spoken syllable because of two principles that cause syllables to change their structures in actual pronunciation from their underlying structures:

1 The principle of *liaison* The final consonant of a syllable slides into the next syllable that starts with a vowel within a word. That is, when a syllable ending with a consonant is followed by a syllable starting with a vowel, that consonant is pronounced as if it is the initial sound of the next syllable. For example, in the string 몸-이 *mom-i* 'body-Subj' the noun 몸 *mom* 'body' is written with the final consonant ㅁ [m] representing the basic shape of the word; but when it is followed by a vowel-initial subject particle forming a word together, the final consonant ㅁ [m] becomes the initial consonant of the next syllable, thus filling up the unoccupied consonantal space. The underlying syllable structure 몸이 *mom.i* is thus changed to a different structure of 모미 *mo.mi* in actual pronunciation. This is called *resyllabification*.

2 The principle of unreleasing syllable-final consonants Koreans do not release the oral contact of a syllable-final consonant immediately after articulation. Unreleasing the final consonant means that double consonants are not allowed in syllable final position in spoken Korean, because unless the oral contact position is quickly released the following consonant cannot be articulated.

3.1.4.1 *Resyllabification (liaison) rule*

When the syllable-final component consists of a consonant cluster and is followed by a vowel-initial syllable, then the two consonants are split into two different syllables. This *resyllabification*, a liaison phenomenon, may be schematized as follows:

Korean liaison rule
V (C) C.(G)V → V (C).C(G)V

The following examples show how the final consonant is carried over to the next syllable:

샘이 /saem-i/ is syllabified/pronounced	as 새미 [sae.mi]	'the source-Subj'
짧아 /tschalp-a/	as 짤바 [tschal.ba]	'(X) is short'
값이 /kaps-i/	as 갑시 [kap.si]	'the price-Subj'
눈으로 /nun-ŭro/	as 누느로 [nu.nŭro]	'the snow-by means of'
국에 /kuk-e/	as 구게 [ku.ge]	'in the soup'

3.1.4.2 *Written and spoken syllable structures*

The two different syllable (σ) structures in contemporary Korean can be summarized by Figures 3.1 and 3.2, where parentheses indicate optionality.

3.2 Rhythmic and intonational patterns

Standard Korean is neither a tone language like Chinese, a pitch-accent language like Japanese, nor a stress language like English, where accent variations can change the meaning of a word.

However, all languages have rhythmic and intonational aspects, called *prosody*, which determine the meaning of a unit larger than a word.

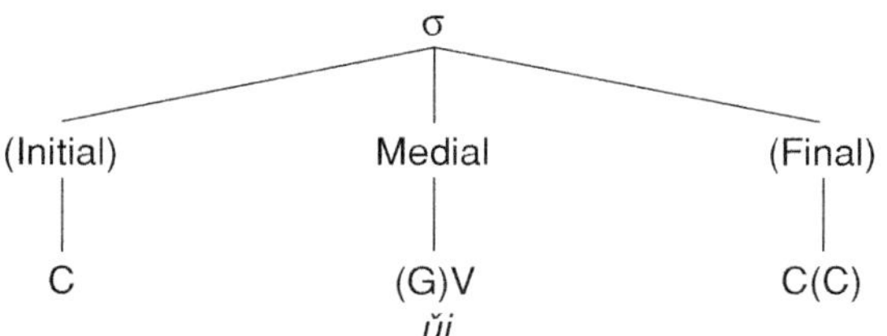

Conditions:
1. Initial ≠ ng
2. if the V = i, then G ≠ y [no **yi* sequence]
3. if V = ŭ, u, o, then G ≠ w [no **wŭ*, **wu*, **wo* sequences]
4. CC = *ps, ks, nc, lp, lp', lt', lk, ls, lh, lm, nh*

Figure 3.1 Written syllable structure

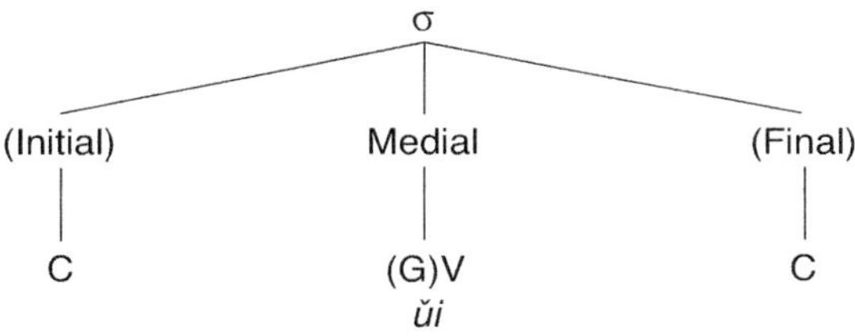

Conditions:
1. if the V = *i*, then G ≠ *y* [no *yi sequence]
2. if V = *ŭ, u, o*, then G ≠ *w* [no **wŭ*, **wu*, **wo* sequences]
3. no **ng* in word-initial position

Figure 3.2 Spoken syllable structure

In Standard Korean, a common intonation pattern of a sentence is a sequence of rising tones for each word except for the last word:

Table 3.6 A common intonation contour in Standard Korean

(미나는(↑))	(어제(↑))	(부산으로(↑))	(이사갔어요.(↓))
mina-nŭn	ŏje	pusan-ŭro	isa-ka-ss-ŏyo
Mina-Top	yesterday	Pusan-to	move-Past-Dec/Pol
'Mina moved to Pusan yesterday.'			

The tonal pattern of each word can differ across dialects in Korean. For example, in the Chŏnnam dialect, each word has a falling tone.

Table 3.7 Variation on a theme: Meaning according to the intonation contour

Intonation contour on the final syllable	Sentence type	Pronunciation	Meaning
Low (↓):	Statement	그래 kŭrae↓	'That's right.'
	Request	그래 kŭrae↓	'Do so!'
Falling (↗ ↘):	WH-question	뭘그래? Mwŏl gurae↓	'What's the issue?'
High (↑):	Yes-no question	그래 kŭrae↑	'Is it true?'

The tone pattern of each word in a sentence-medial position does not change the meaning of a sentence. But the tone pattern of the sentence-final word, especially the tone on the last syllable of the sentence, which is called a boundary tone, determines the type of sentence, e.g., a statement or a question. For example, if a sentence ends in a low tone, thus showing a falling contour from the preceding syllable, it is a statement. If a sentence ends in a high-low (= falling) tone, thus showing a falling contour on the last syllable itself, it is a WH-question. If a sentence ends in a high tone, thus showing a rising contour from the preceding syllable, it is a yes-no question. In Table 3.7, the tone on the last syllable of 그래 *kŭrae*, '(something) is so' or '(someone) does so,' illustrates this contrast.

The boundary tone of a sentence also determines the pragmatic meaning of a sentence and delivers the emotion or the attitude of the speaker. For example, a low-high-low (= rising-falling) sentence-final tone can convey *insistence*. For example, in 그거 그냥 버려! *kŭgŏ kŭnyang pŏryŏ* 'Just throw it away!,' if the last syllable 려 *ryŏ* is produced with a low pitch, it conveys ordering someone to throw something away, but if produced in a low-high-low (= rising-falling) pitch with a lengthened last syllable, it shows that the speaker is *insisting on* or *emphasizing* his or her order (e.g., 그거 그냥 버<u>려어</u>↗ ↘ *kŭgŏ kŭnyang pŏ<u>ryŏŏ</u>*), whereas if the last syllable shows a high-low-high-low (falling-rising-falling) contour with further lengthening of the syllable (버<u>려어어</u> *pŏ<u>ryŏŏŏ</u>*), it would convey *annoyance*.

Intonation can also change the meaning of a sentence by changing the grouping of words and the sentence-final tone. For example, (영이(↑))(어디에 갔니)↗ ↘? *Yŏng-i ŏdi-e kass-ni?* means 'Where did Yŏng-i go?' but (영이(↑))(어디에(↑))(갔니)↗? *Yŏng-i ŏdi-e kass-ni↗?* means 'Did Yŏng-i go anywhere?' (Jun and Oh 1996). Here, the sequence of words in the two sentences is exactly the same but the grouping of words is different, as cued by the intonation contour. If 어디에 *ŏdie* ends in a high tone and 갔니 *kass-ni* begins with a low tone, it follows that those two words belong to different intonation groups. (It has been shown that beginning learners of Korean as a second language have difficulty in producing the distinct intonation contours appropriate to each meaning.)

Phonologists have shown that Koreans often create complex pitch contours to express extra meaning such as a falling-rising-falling terminal intonation contour that carries other emotional and attitudinal meanings, but more research is needed to find a simple mechanism to find the core meaning of a simple contour from which different interpretations can be deduced depending on the context and situation.

3.3 Characteristics of the Korean vowel system

3.3.1 *The weak vowel 으 (ŭ)*

The unrounded, high back vowel, 으 /ŭ/, which sounds like the vowel in English *good*, is the weakest and the most unstable of all Korean vowels. The vowel /ŭ/ is easily deleted whenever it meets another vowel and occurs in a weak or non-initial position in casual speech and, most importantly, when it is the first vowel of a suffix following a stem-final vowel, as in 가 *ka* + 으면 *ŭmyŏn* → 가면 *kamyŏn* 'If (someone) goes.'

When a vowel is needed to break an impermissible consonant cluster, /ŭ/, as the weakest of all vowels, is inserted, as in 크리스마스 /k'ŭrisŭmasŭ/ 'Christmas.'

3.3.2 *Vowel length*

For older speakers of Seoul Standard Korean, vowel length contributes to differences in meaning. Today, however, vowel length as a distinctive feature is almost completely gone. Korean orthography stopped marking pitch accents, some of which indicated vowel length, soon after the invention of the alphabet. This orthographic convention, which probably reflected ongoing language change as well as dialect mixing, contributed to the disappearance of vowel length as a distinctive unit in contemporary Korean, where vowel length is used mainly in exaggerated or emphatic expressions. Emphatic vowel lengthening is predictable and typically occurs in the first syllable of a word, as seen in the following examples (where vowel lengthening is marked by a colon):

Emphatic vowel lengthening

정말	정:말	
chŏngmal	chŏ:ngmal	'in truth'
쪼끄만	쪼:끄만	
tchokkŭman	tcho:kkŭman	'small'
대단해요	대:단해요	
taedanhaeyo	ta:edanhaeyo	'It's tremendous.'

3.3.3 *Vowel harmony*

Restrictions on compatibility among different kinds of vowels within a given unit is thought to have been rigorous in earlier Korean, but due to several historical changes, the vowel harmony (VH) principle has come to be restricted only to certain environments. However, it is still an important aspect of the Korean sound system. Understanding the VH principle will help you realize that the same kind of mechanism is at work in different parts of the grammar, one involving sound-symbolic (SS) vocabulary and the other in a verb conjugation.

3.3.3.1 *Vowel harmony and sound symbolism*

VH is most saliently applied in sound-symbolic (SS) words, in which Korean is very rich. The vowels ㅣ *i*, ㅔ *e*, ㅟ *wi*, ㅡ *ŭ*, ㅓ *ŏ*, and ㅜ *u* form a harmonic group, traditionally called "dark" or yin (음 *ŭm* in Korean) vowels, while ㅐ *ae*, ㅚ *oe*, ㅏ *a*, and ㅗ *o* form the other set, termed "bright" or 양 yang vowels. Within an SS word, vowels must be all bright or all dark except that the vowels ㅣ *i* and ㅡ *ŭ* are neutral in non-initial syllables and may co-occur with either dark or bright vowels. Furthermore, each harmonic group carries a particular, systematic connotation that all Korean speakers recognize. Bright vowels usually correlate with the diminutive connotation, giving the impression of smallness, brightness, and shallowness; and dark vowels convey an impression of size, depth, and darkness. Compare the following pairs of SS words that carry the same basic meaning with bright and dark connotational contrasts:

Vowel harmony in sound symbolic vocabulary

Dark		**Bright**		**Meaning**
지껄	chikkŏl	재깔	chaekkal	'talkative'
뗑그렁	ttengŭrŏng	땡그랑	ttaenggŭrang	'tinkling'
뀌쥐쥐	kkwijwijwi	꾀죄죄	kkoejoejoe	'shabby'
슬쩍	sŭltchŏk	살짝	saltchak	'stealthy'
뻘겋	ppŏlgŏh	빨갛	ppalgah	'red'
꾸기적	kkugijŏk	꼬기작	kkogijak	'crumpling'

3.3.3.2 *Vowel harmony in verb conjugation*

VH is applied systematically in the alternation of suffixes beginning with the vowel 어 *ŏ*-. For example, the very prevalent past tense marker, -었 *ŏss*, becomes -았 *ass*, starting with a yang vowel, when the last syllable of the preceding verb stem has the yang vowel 아 *a* or 오 *o* [▶2.2.2]. Observe the following pair:

1 잡았다.
chap-ass-ta.
catch-Past-Dec/Plain
'X caught Y.'

2 접었다.
chŏp-ŏss-ta.
fold-Past-Dec
'X folded Y.'

> *Note:* The -어 *ŏ* initial endings follow the VH rule only when it follows a verb stem directly. Observe the following example, in which the past tense marker -었 *ŏss* applies the VH rule, but not the subsequent sentence ender -어요 *ŏyo* because the second ending does not follow a verb stem immediately.
>
> 잡았어요.
> chap-ass-ŏyo (←chap-**ŏss-ŏyo**).
> catch-Past-Dec/Pol
> '(X) caught (Y).'

3.4 Characteristics of the Korean consonantal system

3.4.1 *Consonantal strength and sound symbolism*

Consonants are also categorized into different sound-symbolic groups according to their strength scale. In general, the more complete the closure,

Table 3.8 Consonantal groups according to their strength

↑ Stronger						
Tense	ㅃ pp	ㄸ tt	ㅆ ss	ㅉ tch	ㄲ kk	
Aspirated	ㅍ p'	ㅌ t'		ㅊ ch'	ㅋ k'	ㅎ h
Plain	ㅂ p/b	ㄷ t/d	ㅅ s	ㅈ ch/j	ㄱ k/g	
Sonorant	ㅁ m	ㄴ n		ㄹ l/r	ㅇ ng	

the stronger the consonant. So, sounds produced with more obstruction and with more force in the speech organ are stronger than those that are pronounced with less or no obstruction and with relaxed muscles. Table 3.8 shows the consonantal strength scale.

The nasals and liquids are the softest resonating consonants and carry a 'gentle, airy, and relaxed' connotation, while voiceless stops like *k* and *p* carry an 'abrupt' meaning. This contrast is well exemplified by the following pair, both of which express a hitting sound:

땅 ttang (sound of a gong)
딱 ttak (sound of an arrow hitting a target)

The sound of a gong with a resonating aftertone is expressed with a nasal consonant, ㅇ *ng*, and the abrupt ending of the sound of the arrow hitting a target with a stop consonant, ㄱ *k*.

Among the obstruents, the three-way phonetic distinction corresponds to a systematic three-way differentiation in meaning. The lax consonant is the gentlest of all. The strongly aspirated series connotes a sense of roughness, explosion, strength, and power. The tense series gives a tight, dense, and intense connotation. The three related words below show the three-way sound and meaning differences and correspondences:

감감하다	kamgam-ha-ta	'It is dark; X is in the dark (generally lost).'
캄캄하다	k'amk'am-ha-ta	'It is dark and spooky (hopeless).'
깜깜하다	kkamkkam-ha-ta	'It is pitch dark (completely ignorant).'

The Korean alphabet expresses consonantal strength remarkably. So the gentlest consonants carry the basic forms of the pertinent group, and letter forms for stronger sounds are made by adding more strokes.

3.4.2 *Intervocalic voicing*

In a word-initial position, Korean plain or lax stops (ㄱ *k*, ㄷ *t*, ㅂ *p*, ㅈ *ch*) are slightly aspirated and voiceless, i.e., pronounced with air passing through the slightly open glottis. That is why Koreans have a hard time pronouncing the initial voiced stops [b], [d], and [g] in such English words as *ball*, *do*, and *get*, pronouncing them as [pol], [tu], and [ket], respectively. However, Koreans have no problem pronouncing medial [b], [d], or [g] in such words as *symbol*, *ado*, or *slogan*. That is because in Korean, plain stops weaken in a "softening" environment, i.e., when they are surrounded by vowels or sonorant consonants such as ㅁ /m/, ㄴ /n/, ㅇ /ng/, and ㄹ /l/. Plain stops are produced with relaxed vocal cords, so they are prone to vibration when surrounded by voiced, sonorous sounds such as vowels, nasals, and liquids that are produced with the vocal cords vibrating. This is a kind of assimilation of lax stops to a surrounding sonorous environment. Herein this kind of consonant softening will be called *intervocalic weakening*. The lax consonants ㅂ /p/, ㄷ /t/, ㅈ /c/, ㄱ /k/ are thus weakened to their sonorous counterparts, [b], [d], [j], and [g]. For example, 담 *tam* (meaning 'wall') is pronounced [tam], but in a compound noun such as 돌담 /tol-tam/ [toldam], it is pronounced [dam]. This is an automatic change, and native Korean speakers do not perceive a contrast between *tam* and *dam*, just as most native English speakers do not know the *t* in *top* and the *t* in *stop* are pronounced differently.

The following examples show how lax consonants are pronounced differently depending on location.

p > b

밥	/**pap**/	[**pap**]	'boiled rice'
보리밥	/**p**oli-**pap**/	[**p**ori**bap**]	'rice mixed with barley'

t > d

다	/**ta**/	[**ta**]	'all'
맏	/ma**t**/	[ma**t**]	'the eldest'
맏아들	/ma**t**-a**t**ŭl/	[ma**d**a**d**ŭl]	'the first son'

ch > j

죽	/**ch**uk/	[**ch**uk]	'porridge'
콩죽	/k'ong-**ch**uk/	[k'ong**j**uk]	'bean porridge'

k > g

공	/**k**ong/	[**k**ong]	'ball'
새 공	/sae-**k**ong/	[sae**g**ong]	'new ball'

Strongly aspirated stops (ㅋ *k'*, ㅌ *t'*, ㅊ *ch'*, ㅍ *p'*, ㅅ *s*) and tense stops (ㄲ *kk*, ㄸ *tt*, ㅉ *tch*, ㅃ *pp*, ㅆ *ss*) are not conducive to voicing and resist significant weakening even when they occur intervocalically. Note that the dental sibilant ㅅ *s* is actually a lax consonant, much more lax than the

English [s], but it does not weaken even in a softening environment because it is slightly aspirated:

시인	/**si**-in/	[**si**in]	'poet [*lit.* 'poetry-person']'
한시	/han-**si**/	[han**si**]	'Chinese poetry'

3.4.3 ㄹ *l*-weakening

Intervocalic weakening also applies to the sonorant consonant ㄹ /l/. In an intervocalic position ㄹ /l/ is weakened to [r], which is a flap sound produced with the tip of the tongue touching the back of the upper teeth lightly and quickly, i.e., pronounced with much less firm oral contact than [l]. For example, 말 /mal/ 'word' is pronounced [mal], but when it is followed by a vowel, e.g., the subject marker 이 /i/, the /l/ is pronounced [r]:

l > r

말이	/ma**l**-i/	[ma**r**i]	'language-Subj'

This *l*-weakening occurs even if an [h] intervenes between the two vowels. In other words, ㅎ *h* is invisible in this process or just considered part of the vowel it occurs with.

말해	/ma**l**-**h**ae/	[ma**rh**ae]	'Speak!'

The intervening [h] is also often deleted or inaudible, although it leaves a trace in the surrounding sounds [▶3.4.4].

3.4.4 ㅎ *h*-weakening

The weakest and softest of all consonants, ㅎ *h*, is further weakened in a sonorous environment. Korean [h] is weakened between voiced sounds, as is the case in many languages. For example, [h] in English *vehicle* weakens to the point of complete deletion. In Korean, /h/ is deleted when it is surrounded by soft sounds (sonorants) including vowels, *m*, *n*, *ng*, and *l*, except in very careful speech. However, rather than being simply deleted, the /h/ leaves its trace by slightly devoicing the surrounding sounds or by a little break (glottal stop). For example, 말해 *mal-hae* 'Speak!' is pronounced [marhae] in careful pronunciation but in fast speech it is [marae], in which the surrounding sounds [r] and [ae] are slightly devoiced (pronounced with an open glottis). The common expression, "안녕하세요" *annyŏnghaseyo* 'Hello' (*lit.* 'Are you well?') is pronounced [annyŏnghaseyo] in careful speech but [annyŏng'aseyo] in fast speech, where the [h] is either completely deleted or shows its trace as a brief break [▶10.3].

The ㅎ *h* sound, having no point of contact in the oral cavity, is "unreleased" by taking the most spontaneous or natural position of the tongue touching the upper part of the oral cavity, which is that of [t] [▶3.4.6.2]:

히읗 /hiŭh/ [hiŭt˺] 'the letter *h*'

Verb-final [h] is deleted obligatorily when followed by a vowel, regardless of the kind of speech style or speed:

괜찮아요.	/kwaench'an**h**-ayo/	[kwaench'anayo]	'It is all right.'
좋아요.	/cho**h**-ayo/	[choayo]	'It is fine/good.'

3.4.5 Aspiration

When the consonant ㅎ *h* is preceded or followed by a stop sound, i.e., ㅂ *p*, ㄷ *t*, ㅈ *ch*, or ㄱ *k*, the [h] sound is absorbed into the stop sound and the two are pronounced together as an aspirated consonant, i.e., ㅍ *p'*, ㅌ *t'*, ㅊ *ch'*, or ㅋ *k'*. In this environment, the wide glottal opening associated with the [h] sound causes aspiration. Here are some examples:

굳히다	/ku**t-h**i-ta/	[ku**t'**ida] → [kuch'ida]	'harden'
좋지	/cho**h-ch**i/	[cho**ch'**i]	'isn't it good?'
어떻게	/ŏttŏ**hk**e/	[ŏttŏ**k'**e]	'how'
적합하다	/chŏ**kh**a**ph**ata/	[chŏ**k'**ha**p'**ada]	'to be appropriate'
어떻든	/ŏttŏ**ht**ŭn/	[ŏttŏ**t'**ŭn]	'however it is'
좋다	/cho**ht**a/	[chot**t'**a]	'to be good'
쌓다	/ssa**ht**a/	[ssat**t'**a]	'to pile up'
끊다	/kkŭn**ht**a/	[kkŭn**t'**a]	'to cut'
복합	/po**k-h**ap/	[po**k'**ap]	'compound'
입학	/i**ph**ak/	[ip'hak]	'admission (to school)'
입히다	/i**ph**ita/	[i**p'**ida]	'to clothe, dress (someone)'
굽히다	/ku**ph**ita/	[ku**p'**ida]	'to bend'
좋지	/cho**h-ch**i/	[chot**ch'**i]	'isn't it good?'
맞히다	/ma**chh**ita/	[mat**ch'**ida]	'to hit (on the mark), fit'

3.4.6 *Unreleasing of syllable-final consonants*

A stop sound is produced by blocking the oral tract, as noted earlier. Languages differ in the way these stop sounds are released once the oral occlusion is made in a syllable-final position, called the *syllable coda*. For example, in French one hears a clear release burst. In English, releasing is optional. In some other languages, including Korean and Thai, final stops are always unreleased, unless they occur just before a vowel.

3.4.6.1 *Unreleasing of stop consonants*

In Korean unreleasing of all consonants not followed by a vowel or a diphthong is very strictly observed. Consonants at the end of a syllable retain oral contact after articulation, unless they are followed by a vowel or a diphthong. The vowel is particularly important when distinguishing between the three-way contrast in stops. The important cues for special features such as degree of aspiration and tenseness are in the time it takes from when the consonant is articulated to the beginning point of the vowel articulation. When there is no vowel, the cues are lost. From the articulatory point of view, all glottal activity ceases as soon as oral contact is made, which causes all three types of stops to sound the same. In order to pronounce a word-final consonant, just retain the position of the oral contact for a while.

In the following examples, as in other cases where unreleasing is the focus of the discussion, unreleased consonants are indicated by the symbol ˺:

수집	/suchip/	[sujip˺]	'collection'
자국	/chakuk/	[chaguk˺]	'trace'

For complex historical reasons, not all consonants appear in syllable-final position. Therefore, although the Korean consonantal system is quite rich, only seven consonants ([p˺], [t˺], [k˺], [m˺], [n˺], [ng˺], and [l˺]) may actually occur at the end of a syllable. The unreleased consonants, which are weakened at the end of a syllable, are prone to further changes and get easily assimilated to the following sound. At the same time the heightened air pressure coming from unreleasing causes strengthening of the following sounds. The next sections concern some consequences of syllable-final unreleasing, which provide a simple explanation for a large part of seemingly complex Korean consonantal alternations. Here are some examples of stop neutralization:

p*, *p'*, *pp* > *p (in reality no syllables end in *pp*)

집	/chip/	[chip˺]	'house'
앞	/ap'/	[ap˺]	'front'

t*, *t'*, *tt* > *t (in reality no syllables end in *tt*)

맏	/mat/	[mat˺]	'the eldest'
낱	/nat'/	[nat˺]	'each, individual'

ch*, *ch'*, *tch* > *t (in reality no syllables end in *tch*)

잦	/chach/	[chat˺]	'be frequent'
돛	/toch'/	[tot˺]	'sail'

k*, *k'*, *kk* > *k

묵	/muk/	[muk˺]	'ink stick'
부엌	/puŏk'/	[puŏk˺]	'kitchen'
꺾	/kkŏkk/	[kkŏk˺]	'break'

Finally, a discussion about the palatal stops is necessary. Palatal stops (*ch*, *ch'*, *tch*) are actually affricates, i.e., consonants which begin as a stop (*t* in the case of Korean) and then release as a fricative (*s*). Naturally, when there is no release, the fricative portion is absent. The result is that all distinctions between dental stops and palatal stops are canceled, as they are all pronounced as an unreleased [t˺].

3.4.6.2 *Unreleasing of fricatives*

Fricatives (ㅅ *s*, ㅆ *ss*, ㅎ *h*) are sounds produced through a narrow opening in the vocal tract. Because unreleasing requires oral contact, the closest, most natural and neutral oral contact position of [t˺] is used to achieve unreleasing, as shown below:

옷	/os/	[ot˺]	'clothes'
못과	/mos-kwa/	[mot˺-kwa] ⇒ [mokkwa]	'nail and'

The *s*-unreleasing is a quintessentially Korean phenomenon with no dialectal variation. In fact, when Korean speakers hear an unreleased [t] sound in foreign words, they assume its underlying form is [s], as in the following pairs of English loanwords:

컷	/k'ŏs/	[k'ŏt˺]	'(hair)cut'
컷을	/k'ŏs-ŭl/	[k'ŏsŭl]	'(hair)cut-Obj'
힛	/his/	[hit˺]	'hit'
힛에	/his-e/	[hise]	'at the hit'

When Koreans hear an [s] sound in a syllable-final position, they assume an underlying vowel following it to make that sound pronounced as an [s] and not as a [t]. For example, the following foreign words will have a vowel following them:

키스	/k'issŭ/	[k'issŭ]	'kiss'
한스	/hansŭ/	[hansŭ]	'Hans'

The ㅎ *h* changes to a [t] sound for the same reason, but only after aspirating the following lax consonant. For example, 좋다 /choh-ta/ is pronounced [chott'a] in careful pronunciation. The consonant /t/ following *h* becomes an aspirate consonant [t'], before the *h* sound is unreleased as a [t]. This *t* is deleted in normal-speed speech.

So, what looks like a very unusual phenomenon of massive neutralization of consonants in the syllable-final position – that all dental and palatal obstruents, ㄷ *t*, ㅌ *t'*, ㄸ *tt*, ㅈ *ch*, ㅊ *ch'*, ㅉ *tch*, ㅅ *s*, and ㅆ *ss* as well as ㅎ *h* are all pronounced as an unreleased [t˺] and are indistinguishable from each other – is nothing but a consequence of unreleasing them. Observe the following examples (in actuality, there are no syllables that end in *tt* or *tch*):

맏	/mat/	[mat˺]	'the eldest'
끝	/kkŭt/	[kkŭt˺]	'end'
낮	/nach/	[nat˺]	'daylight'
꽃	/kkoch'/	[kkot˺]	'flower'
깃	/kis/	[kit˺]	'collar'
있	/iss/	[it˺]	'exist'
놓	/noh/	[not˺]	'put down'

3.4.6.3 *Simplification of syllable-final consonant clusters*

A written Korean syllable may have up to two consonants in the final position [▶2.3.1]. In reality, however, only a very small portion of the Korean vocabulary has consonant clusters in the syllable-final position. This is again a historical consequence of the Korean characteristic of unreleasing consonants at the end of the syllable, which still affects the few extant consonant clusters.

When syllable-final consonant clusters are followed by a vowel, they are split into two different syllables by the liaison rule [▶3.1.4.1], and both consonants are pronounced. When there is no vowel following the consonant cluster, only one of them gets pronounced. In short, a "homeless" consonant has to be dropped, and the question is which one becomes homeless. Which one gets deleted is largely the function of unreleasing the entire syllable coda.

1 When the first member of a consonant cluster has complete oral closure, e.g., ㅂ *p*, ㄱ *k*, ㄴ *n*, the articulation stops there, as the point of oral contact is retained for a while. One cannot make another oral contact to produce the second consonant without releasing the first one. So only the first consonant of the cluster will be pronounced, and the second consonant will be deleted. Here are some examples:

ps* > *p

값	/ka**ps**/	[ka**p**˺]	'price'
값도	/ka**ps**-to/	[ka**p**˺to] → [kap˺tto]	'price also'
값이	/ka**ps**-i/	[ka**psi**]	'price-Subj'

ks* > *k

몫	/mo**ks**/	[mo**k**˺]	'share'
몫보다	/mo**ks**-pota/	[mo**k**˺poda] → [mok˺ppoda]	'than the share'
몫을	/mo**ks**-ŭl/	[mo**ksŭ**l]	'share-Obj'

nch* > *n

앉게	/a**nch**-ke/	[a**n**-ke] → [ankke]	'Sit down, please [to a Junior]'
앉아	/a**nch**-a/	[a**nja**]	'Sit down!'

2 When the first member of the consonant cluster is an [l] sound, the following consonant may or may not be pronounced. It is because when articulating the [l] sound, oral contact is made with the tongue tip touching the back of the teeth but the sides of the tongue are open. Therefore, near coarticulation of two contact points in the mouth in careful pronunciation is possible when the first consonant is [l]. So, Koreans can pronounce such final clusters as *-lk*, *-lp*, and *-lm*. However, if the second consonant has the same point of articulation as the [l] sound, there is no way a speaker can articulate another sound on the same spot.

- When the consonant *l* is followed by a consonant that is pronounced at a different part of the oral cavity, then both may be pronounced. In case of reduction, it is the more completely closed stop sound that is kept:

lC > C

삶이	/salm-i/	[salmi]	'life-Subj'
삶조차	/salm-choch'a/	[salmjoch'a] ~ [samjoch'a]	'life even'
맑아	/malk-a/	[malga]	'It's clear [Plain].'
맑소	/malk-so/	[malkso] ~ [makso]	'It is clear [Plain-Pol]!'

In the case of *-lp* or *-lp'* clusters, there is some variation. Some dialects such as those of Chŏlla and Ch'ungch'ŏng reduce this cluster to the unreleased [p], but in Standard Korean both consonants are pronounced in slow speech or it is the [l] sound that is kept when the reduction happens:

넓어	/nŏlp-ŏ/	[nŏlbŏ]	'It is wide.'
넓다	/nŏlp-ta/	[nŏlptta] ~ [nŏl-tta]	'It is wide.'
읊으니	/ŭlp'-ŭni/	[ŭlp'ŭni]	'as one recites (a poem)'
읊고	/ŭlp'-ko/	[ŭlpkko] ~ [ŭlkko]	'one recites and'

- In the case of the clusters *-lt'* or *-lt* (< *-ls*), the second consonant is dropped because, unless the first consonant *l* is released, near co-articulation of the two consonants at the same point is impossible. Observe the following examples:

lt' > l

핥아	/halt'-a/	[halt'a]	'Lick it!'
핥네	/halt'-ne/	[hal-ne] ~ [halle]	'X is licking it!'

lt (<ls) > l

돐	/tols/	[tol]	'first birthday'
돐도	/tols-to/	[toldo]	'first birthday, too'

Consonant-cluster simplification is a direct consequence of unreleasing the final consonantal unit of the syllable. While unreleasing can cause this kind of weakening of the syllable-final position, it has the role of strengthening the following position, as will be shown in the next section.

3.4.7 Tensing of plain stops

A lax obstruent becomes tense when following an obstruent, since that obstruent is unreleased because no vowel follows. The heightened oral pressure built up during the extended closure (nonrelease) of obstruents causes tensing of the following consonant:

입구	/ip-ku/	[ip˺kku]	'entrance'
잡담	/chap-tam/	[chap˺ttam]	'chit-chat'
옆방	/yŏp-pang/	[yŏp˺ppang]	'next-door room'
학과	/hak-kwa/	[hak˺kkwa]	'(academic) department'
미국사람	/mi-kuk-sa-lam/	[miguk˺ssaram]	'American person'
족보	/chok-po/	[chok˺ppo]	'genealogy (*lit.* clan-annals)'
쑥돌	/ssuk-tol/	[ssuk˺ttol]	'granite (*lit.* mugwort-stone)'
먹자	/mŏk-cha/	[mŏk˺tcha]	'Let's eat! [Plain]'
닫고	/tat-ko/	[tat˺kko]	'close and'
웃다	/us-ta/	[ut˺tta]	'laughs'
집새	/chip-sae/	[chip˺ssae]	'between houses'
협정	/hyŏp-chŏng/	[hyŏp˺tchŏng]	'agreement, pact'

Therefore, in this position, lax and tense consonants become indistinguishable:

앞-가지	/ap'-kaji/	[ap˺kkaji]	'front branch'
앞-까지	/ap'-kkaji/	[ap˺kkaji]	'up to the front'

Pronouncing the tense stop in this environment should not be a problem for English speakers, as a similar tensing phenomenon exists in English, such as in the pronunciation of *cheap guy*, where the /g/ is pronounced tense when /p/ is unreleased. In conversation, it will be simple to tell whether [kkaji] means 'branch' or 'up to' from the context.

Syllable-final nasals (ㅁ *m*, ㄴ *n*, ㅇ *ng*) and lateral (ㄹ *l*) are also unreleased, but its effect is minimal, as the air escapes either through the nose or the sides of the tongue, despite the nonrelease.

선생	/sŏnsaeng/	[sŏnsaeng˺]	'teacher'
김	/kim/	[kim˺]	'seaweed'
눈	/nun/	[nun˺]	'eye'

3.4.8 두음법칙 *Tuŭm pŏpch'ik* *(Law of Initials)*

The consonant *l* in a word-initial position is pronounced [n]. However, word-initially, a sequence of *ni* or *ny* is avoided in Korean, as the *n* sound, including one derived from *l*, drops before [i] or [y]. Koreans call this the 두음법칙 *tuŭm pŏpch'ik* or 'Law of Initials.' That is why so many family names that start with the plain [i] sound in Standard Korean today are Romanized as *Lee, Rhee,* and less frequently as *Lie* or *Leigh*.

Just as in the case of vowel harmony, Korean speakers are well aware of this positional variation in pronunciation, and South Korean orthography dictates writing the actual pronunciation, i.e., ㅇ <zero> or ㄴ <n> in that position, as in:

이승만	<yi-sŭngman>	[isŭngman]	'Syngman Rhee'
노태우	<no-t'aeu>	[not'aeu]	'Roh Tae-woo'

3.4.8.1 ㄹ *l-nasalization*

As stated above, the consonant ㄹ /l/ is pronounced as [n] in word-initial position or after a consonant. In Korean, an /l/ is pronounced as an [l] only in a syllable-final position, when it is unreleased. It is weakened to a tapped [r] between vowels, as in Spanish or some British dialects. Initially, /l/ is strengthened to a nasal sound, /n/, which is pronounced at the same point of articulation. What happens is that the lateral /l/ sound, with the air escaping through the sides of the tongue while contact is made at the tip of the tongue, becomes a complete stop but the sonority is kept by making it a nasal sound /n/, which has the air escaping through the nose instead. Typically the initial position is a phonologically strong one and this is a kind of strengthening phenomenon. *l*-nasalization also applies to the position following an unreleased consonant, which is typically a strengthening environment. Observe the following examples:

a.	난향	**n**an-hyang	[**n**anhyang]	'fragrance of orchid'
	양난	yang-**n**an	[yang**n**an]	'Western orchid'
	군자란	kuncha-**l**an	[kunja**r**an]	'prince orchid'
b.	노인	**n**o-in	[**n**oin]	'an old person'
	양노원	yang-**n**o-wŏn	[yang**n**owŏn]	'senior citizens' home'
	초로	ch'o-**l**o	[ch'o**r**o]	'early senior years'
c.	내일	**n**ae-il	[**n**aeil]	'tomorrow'
	장래	chang-**l**ae	[chang**n**ae]	'future'
	미래	mi-**l**ae	[mi**r**ae]	'future'
d.	누각	**n**u-kak	[**n**ugak]	'high pavilion'
	옥루	ok-**l**u	[ong**n**u]	'Jade Pavilion'
	경회루	kyŏng-hoe-**l**u	[kyŏnghoe**r**u]	'Kyunghoe Pavilion'
e.	노상	**l**o-sang	[**n**osang]	'street peddler'
	대학로	taehak-**l**o	[taehang**n**o]	'College Avenue'
	을지로	ŭlchi-**l**o	[ŭlchi**r**o]	'Ŭlchi Avenue'

f. 기류 ki-**l**yu [ki**r**yu] 'air current/stream'
유랑 ← 뉴랑 **l**yu-**l**ang [yu**r**ang] 'wandering, roaming, floating'
격류 kyŏk-lyu kyŏk-**n**yu [kyŏng**n**yu] 'a torrent, a violent current'

3.4.8.2 *Initial* ㄴ *n-drop*

As stated above, the Korean sound system is averse to words that start with a sequence of *ni* or *ny*. In a word-initial position an ㄴ *n*, including one originating from ㄹ *l*, is dropped when followed by an *i* or *y* (second short stroke next to a short stroke in a vowel) sound in South Korean orthography. Compare the following forms:

a. 남녀	<nam-**nyŏ**>	[namnyŏ]	'male(s) and female(s)'
여자	<**yŏ**-cha>	[yŏja]	'female'
b. 이유	<**i**-yu>	[iyu]	'reason'
무리	<mu-**li**>	[muri]	'unreasonableness'

The Law of Initials has existed in Korean for some time and old loanwords follow it systematically, as in such Catholic names as 누가 *nuga* for 'Luke,' and other common loanwords such as 나성 *nasŏng* (< *la-sŏng*) for 'Los Angeles.'

> *Note*: The avoidance of a *ni*- or *ny*- cluster in word-initial position has resulted in language change such as coexisting variant forms of saying 'yes' in Korean:
>
> | | |
> |---|---|
> | 녜 [nye] | extremely careful speech (a little subservient) |
> | 네 [ne] (y-drop) | respectful and the most common |
> | 예 [ye] (n-drop) | previously dialectal but increasingly used also in Seoul as a deferential style |

However, the Law does not apply with more recent loanwords, as the following examples demonstrate:

리뷰	/libyu/	[libyu] ~ [ribyu]	'review'
라스베가스	/lasŭbegasŭ/	[lasŭbegasŭ] ~ [rasŭbegasŭ]	'Las Vegas'
롤링스톤	/lollingsŭt'on/	[lollingsŭt'on] ~ [rollingsŭt'on]	'Rolling Stone'
뉴스	/nyussŭ/	[nyusŭ]	'news'
니콜	/nik'ol/	[nik'ol]	'Nicole'

In South Korea, some families have recently opted to pronounce their Sino-Korean names in a way closer to the original Chinese and have started to spell their names in *han'gŭl* with ㄹ *l*, e.g., 로 *lo*, 류 *lyu*, 라 *la*, etc., instead of showing the actual pronunciation, 노 *no*, 유 *yu*, 나 *na*, etc., respectively:

리의도	<ri-ŭito>	/li-ŭi-to/	[iŭido]	'Yi Ŭido'
류승국	<ryu-sŭngguk>	/lyu-sŭng-kuk/	[yusŭngguk]	'Yu Sŭngguk'

North Korean spelling takes into account their standard pronunciation that maintains the original ㄹ *l* or ㄴ *n* sound in the word-initial position. This aspect is one of the major distinguishing factors between spelling in North and South Korea. Compare:

North Korea	**vs.**	**South Korea**	
로동 rodong		노동 nodong	'labor'
료금 ryogŭm		요금 yogŭm	'charge, fee'
리해 rihae		이해 ihae	'understanding'
려행 ryŏhaeng		여행 yŏhaeng	'travel'
녀성 nyŏsŏng		여성 yŏsŏng	'woman'
니승 nisŭng		이승 isŭng	'this world'

3.5 Compound boundary phenomena

When two words of a major class such as nouns combine to form a new word together, this is called a "compound." Koreans consider a compound basically a single word, but there is an unconscious effort to keep the components' identities separate by making sure the second member word is not weakened.

3.5.1 *Unreleasing of consonants before a compound boundary*

When uttering compound words, Korean speakers (subconsciously, of course) are careful to mark the boundary between the two components so that the second word is not weakened. For example, when the first word ends with a sonorant (a vowel, a nasal or a lateral), the following lax consonant would have normally become voiced. In order to prevent this and other forms of weakening, there is an effort to block the usual liaison, through unreleasing of the final sound of the first component word.

In compound words, the boundary between the two components has some aspects of a word boundary. So, the final consonant of the first word is unreleased. However since the two components are pronounced with no break between them, the intervocalic voicing rule applies if the second word starts with a vowel. Note, however, that unreleasing applies first and then intervocalic voicing:

부엌앞	/puŏk'-ap'/	→ [puŏk˺-ap˺]	→ [puŏgap˺]	'front of the kitchen'
옷안	/os-an/	→ [ot˺-an]	→ [odan]	'inside of the clothes'
숳오리	/suh-oli/	→ [sut˺-ori]	→ [sudori]	'male duck'
몇월	/myŏch'-wŏl/	→ [myŏt˺-wŏl]	→ [myŏdwŏl]	'what month (*lit.* how many months)'
끝없다	/kkŭt'-ŏps-ta/	→ [kkŭt˺-ŏp˺-ta]	→ [kkŭdŏpta]	'X is endless.'

3.5.2 사이시옷 *saisiot* (*epenthetic s*)

When the final sound of the first word of a compound is a sonorant, it is not possible to unrelease it without inserting a consonant. In this case, the most spontaneous and neutral stop /t/ is invoked. However, Koreans analyze it as having originated from an /s/ sound, and for that reason it is called an "epenthetic *-s*" or "Bindungs-*s*" (borrowing the German expression):

김밥 /kim-pap/ → /kim-t-pap/ → [kim-ppap] 'laver roll'

Note that the sequence *mt* is simplified to a single consonant *m* after tensing the first /p/ sound, as two consonants cannot occupy the syllable-final position.

When the first component of a compound ends with a vowel, the Bindungs-*s*, or rather the inserted consonant *t*, is retained. The inserted *s* changes depending on the following sound:

치맛바람	chimapparam (← [ch'imat˺-param] ← ch'ima 'skirt' + s + param 'wind')	'female influence'
시냇물	sinaemmul (← [sinaet˺-mul] ← 시내 sinae 'creek' + s + 물 mul 'water')	'creek water'
촛대	ch'ottae (← [ch'ot˺-tae] ← 초 ch'o 'candle' + s + 대 tae 'stand')	'candlestick'
콧노래	k'onnorae (← [k'ot˺-norae] ← 코 k'o 'nose' + s + 노래 norae 'song')	'humming'

바닷가	pada-t-ka (← [patat˺-ka] ← 바다 pada 'sea' + s + -가 ka 'shore')	'seashore'
빗소리	pissori (← [pit˺-sori] ← 비 pi 'rain' + s + 소리 sori 'sound')	'the sound of rain'

Because the compound is pronounced as one unit, the epenthetic *t* is softened to [d] as in the following:

(우-ㅅ-옷>) 웃옷 /u-s-os/ → /ut˺-ot˺/ → [udot˺] 'top garment'

Korean speakers are conscious of this so-called Bindungs-*s* phenomenon and, as this example shows, the consonant *s* (ㅅ) is written in as the most common source for an unreleased [t˺] that is understood to come from an underlying /s/. So, in writing, an epenthetic *s* is inserted only after a vowel. If the first noun ends in a (voiced) consonant, the trace of the epenthetic *s* is shown only in the tensing of the following lax consonant in pronunciation:

물고기	mulkkogi (← mul 'water' + s + kogi 'meat')	'(live) fish'
안방	anppang (← an 'inside' + s + 방 pang 'room')	'master bedroom [previously the main room in the lady's quarters]'
김밥	kimppap (← kim 'dried seaweed' + s + pap 'rice')	'seaweed-rolled rice'
장국	changkkuk (← chang 'sauce' + s + kuk 'soup')	'soup with bean-paste sauce'
손수건	sonssugŏn (← son 'hand' + s + sugŏn 'towel')	'handkerchief'

3.5.3 *Epenthetic* ㄴ *n*

An epenthetic nasal *n* is inserted when the first noun ends with a consonant and the second noun starts with an –*i* or –*y* sound. This is a kind of back application of a historical rule, which deleted a word-initial *n*- before an –*i* or –*y* sound. Note that the inserted *n* undergoes the usual sound alteration depending on what it follows (e.g., *ln* → *ll*):

막일	mangnil (← mak 'rough' + n + il 'work')	'manual labor'
앞이	amni (← ap' 'front' + n + i 'tooth')	'front tooth'
실험용	sirhŏmnyong (← sirhŏm 'experiment' + n + yong 'use')	'for experimental use'
서울역	sŏullyŏk (← sŏul 'Seoul' + n + yŏk 'station')	'Seoul station'

식용유	sigyongnyu (← sigyong 'for consuming' + n + yu 'oil')	'cooking oil'

3.6 Assimilation rules

When a sound meets another sound within a given unit, one or both of them often undergo change. One of the most common alternations is assimilation, i.e., one sound becomes like the one next to it partially or completely. Assimilation is the most common, indeed a universal, phonological phenomenon, because it is very much conditioned by the physical conditions of speech production.

3.6.1 *Nasal assimilation*

A syllable-final consonant is often nasalized when the following syllable begins with a nasal, especially in fast speech. What actually happens is simple. A consonant preceding a nasal consonant is unreleased as usual, and then the nasal tract is opened prematurely in anticipation of the upcoming nasal sound, making the unreleased stop a nasal stop. Here are some examples:

한국말	/han-kuk-mal/	[hangungmal]	'the Korean language'
감사합니다	/kam-sa-hap-ni-ta/	[kamsahamnida]	'Thank you.'
학문	/hakmun/	[hangmun]	'scholarship'
국내	/kuknae/	[kungnae]	'domestic'
혁명	/hyŏkmyŏng/	[hyŏngmyŏng]	'revolution'
믿는	/mitnŭn/	[minnŭn]	'believing'
밥내	/pap-nae/	[pamnae]	'smell of boiled rice'
잇몸	/itmom/[inmom] (→ [immom])		'gum'
젖내	/chŏtnae/	[chŏnnae]	'baby (milk) smell'
빛나다	/pich'-na-ta/	[pinnada]	'shine, shines'
부엌문	/puŏkmun/	[puŏngmun]	'kitchen door'
밭매다	/pat'maeta/	[panmaeda]	'weed the garden/field'
앞모습	/ap'mosŭp/	[ammosŭp]	'front appearance'

3.6.2 *Lateral assimilation*

Whenever ㄴ *n* and ㄹ *l* come together in any order, they are pronounced as a double [ll]:

편리	/p'yŏn-li/	[p'yŏlli]	'convenience'
진리	/chin-li/	[chilli]	'truth'
본래	/pon-lae/	[pollae]	'by nature'
원래	/wŏn-lae/	[wŏllae]	'originally'
달나라	/tal-nala/	[tallara]	'moon world'
별나라	/pyŏl-nara	[pyŏllara]	'star world'
칠년	/ch'il-nyŏn/	[ch'llyŏn]	'seven years'

Native speakers of English should be careful to pronounce [l] twice. In American English even when the spelling shows two *l*s they are pronounced as a single consonant, as in a word such as *silly* or *hollow*. When pronouncing double *l*s in Korean, imagine saying two *l*s in an expression like "Call loud!"

3.6.3 *Palatalization*

Dental stops become palatal in front of the vowel /i/ or glide /y/, both of which are pronounced in the palatal area. This phenomenon occurs only when there is a grammatical boundary between the two sounds, e.g.:

같이	/kat'-i/	[kach'i]	'in the same manner/together'
맏이	/mat-i/	[maji]	'the eldest'

Note that in a word such as 어디 *ŏdi*, which is not divisible into smaller meaningful elements, there is no palatalization.

In the case of *s*, palatalization applies even within a word. Therefore, the sequence *si* is pronounced [shi].

시간	sigan	[shigan]	'time'
한식	hansik	[hanshik]	'Korean style'
씨	ssi	[sshi]	'seed'

Chapter 4

The sentence

A sentence is a combination of words satisfying the grammatical rules of a language, which ought to express a thought that can stand by itself.

A sentence in written Korean is a sequence of words that ends with a period (full stop), question mark, or exclamation mark. In written Korean, there is no capitalization, i.e., no distinction between upper and lower case letters, as seen in languages using the Latin alphabet, e.g., *N* and *n*, or related alphabets such as Greek and Cyrillic. Words are separated by spaces in written Korean, but only in artificially slow speech do they correspond to pauses in spoken Korean. In spoken discourse, cues such as intonation, pause, and even some gestures might be helpful in distinguishing a sentential unit. Observe the following paragraph from Lee O. Young's essay "한국인이여, 한국을 이야기 하자" *han'guginiyŏ, hangugŭl iyagi haja* ('Koreans, let's talk about Korea'), quoted in the original *han'gŭl*:

> 어떻게 해서 이렇게 되었습니까? 물질적 굶주림을 없애려다가 불행히도 정에 굶주린 사람이 많아졌다면, 이제부터 여러분 젊은 세대들이 할 일은 이 정에 굶주린 사람들에게, 이 외로운 사람들에게 정을 나누어 주어야 할 때가 왔다는 것입니다. 여러분들이 무엇인가를 할 때가 온 것입니다. 그것이 여러분의 정의요, 새로운 욕망이요, 미래를 만들 열정의 구실점이 되어야 할 것입니다.

It is not difficult to identify sentential boundaries, even when looking only at this Korean text. The long paragraph has only four sentences – all extended sentences, but each consisting of simple clauses.

The first step toward mastering Korean grammar, therefore, is to understand how Korean sentences are constructed. For English speakers, it is helpful to note some salient features of Korean sentences that may look strange at first but are based on some very simple principles. Here are the *top 10 points to remember*:

1 The basic word order in Korean is *Subject-Object-Verb*.

When we observe the action or status of the physical world, which we may call *event*, there is a focal point. This focal point is called *subject*. A subject is a noun or a noun phrase, denoting a person or a thing – animate or inanimate, concrete or abstract – or a group of people or things. The *predicate* denotes something about the subject of the sentence, such as an action or condition.

A verb is a key element of a predicate. A verb or a verbal expresses processes or conditions that evolve around the subject. Some verbs are directed at another noun or a noun phrase, called an *object*, as well.

The Korean equivalent for the English sentence, *Inho buys oranges*, is:

인호가 오렌지를 산다.
inho-ka orenji-lŭl sa-n-ta.
Inho-Subj orange-Obj buy-Pres-Dec/Plain

Note: Korean is a "*head-final*" language. The essential item or the "head" in every major grammatical category comes at the end of its unit. The verb is the essential element in a sentence and therefore appears at its end.

2 Korean is an *agglutinating language*. Verbs are inflected and must be followed by *suffixes* representing tense, aspect, mood, and honorific endings indicating various speech styles. Nouns, pronouns, and other parts of speech have *particles* attached to them that indicate their grammatical role within a sentence. For example, in the above sentence, the name *Inho* is given as *Inho-ka*, with the *ka* marking *Inho* as the subject. The word *orange is* given as *orenji-lŭl*, with the *lŭl* marking *orange* as the object. The verb *buy* is given as *sa-n-ta*, with *sa* indicating 'buy,' and *n* marking *sa* as present tense while *ta* is a plain declarative ending.

3 Korean is a *topic-prominent language*. Any part of the sentence can become a topic of the sentence by adding the ending *-nŭn* (*-ŭn* after a consonant) [▶8.5.2.3]. In the following, example (ii) is the topicalized counterpart of example (i).

(i) 인호가 오렌지를 산다.
inho-ka orenji-lŭl sa-n-ta.
Inho-Subj orange-Obj buy-Pres-Dec/Plain
'Inho buys oranges.'

(ii) 인호는 오렌지를 산다.
inho-nŭn orenji-lŭl sa-n-ta.
Inho-Top orange-Top buy-Pres-Dec/Plain
'(As for) Inho(, he) buys oranges.'

4 Korean verbs are not marked for grammatical person, gender, or number. Thus there is no agreement in such categories between the predicate and the subject of the sentence, as seen in the English sentences, "***He is** a lawyer*" and "***I am** a professor.*" These sentences, when rendered in Korean, are 그 사람은 변호사이다 *kŭ saram-ŭn pyŏnho-sa-i-ta* and 나는 교수이다 *nanŭn kyosu-i-ta*, which have the same verb ending, -이다 *i-ta*.
5 Most crucially, sentences convey the speaker or writer's expressed attitude toward the hearer or audience. In English different levels of politeness can be indicated mainly by using paraphrases, such as "Would you mind buying some stamps for me?" Korean also has polite sentences of this type, but the most striking aspect of Korean grammar is its elaborate honorific system, which grammatically encodes the speaker or writer's attitude to his or her relative interpersonal status and (formal vs. informal) situation [▶6.8 and 10].
6 Items that context makes clear are frequently dropped, rather than being referred to by a pronoun such as 'she,' 'he,' and 'they.' For example, while pointing at a pile of oranges on a cart to a friend, one could simply say *sa-n-ta* ('buys'), meaning 'I am buying them.'
7 For nouns and other elements, grammatical markers on words allow them to appear *in different orders* within a sentence without changing the basic meaning of the sentence, with the only requirement being that the verbs appear at the end. So, the two sentences *Kisun-i orenji-lŭl san-ta* and *orenji-lŭl Kisun-i san-ta* are both translated into English as 'Kisun buys an orange (*or* oranges).'
8 There are *no articles* in Korean such as *a*, *an*, or *the* in English. Compare the following English sentences (with articles) with their Korean equivalents (which have no article):

English	Korean	
a. 'The mailman came here.'	우체부가	왔다.
b. 'A mailman came here.'	우체부가	왔다.
	uch'ebu-ka	wa-ss-ta.
	mailman-Subj	come-Past-Dec/Plain

9 Korean *does not distinguish between plural and singular nouns* [▶8].

English	Korean	
a. 'I read a book.'	책을	읽었다.
b. 'I read books.'	책을	읽었다.
	ch'aek-ŭl	ilk-ŏss-ta
	book-Obj	read-Past-Dec/Plain

Korean is a *numeral classifier* language, which employs classifiers together with numerals in describing and counting objects in the world [▶8.2.8].

10 All *modifiers (determiners, nouns, relative clauses, etc.) precede the words they modify* [▶9.1]. Again, this is because in Korean the most important item in every major grammatical category tends to occur at the end of the unit.

a. 그 학생. 'that student'
kŭ haksaeng.
that student

b. 한국 사람. 'Korean'
han'guk saram.
Korea person
[Korea = noun used as a modifier]

c. 한국어를 공부하는 학생. 'a student who studies Korean'
han'gugŏ-lŭl kongbuha-nŭn haksaeng.
Korean-Obj study-Mod student

4.1 Simple, compound, and complex sentences

Sentences are made up of *clauses*. A clause is a fundamental grammatical structure, and tells what someone or something is doing or being. A clause is a group of related words containing a subject and a verb, unlike a *phrase*, which is a group of related words that do *not* contain a subject–verb relationship, such as *after dark* or *coming home* or *having graduated from the university*. A clause is a sentence-like construction.

Sentences can be simple, compound, or complex, depending on the number and the interrelationship of their clauses.

4.1.1 *Simple sentences*

A simple sentence is a sentence that contains an independent clause. That is, one that neither is followed by another clause nor has a clause embedded in it:

a. 인호가 오렌지를 샀다.
inho-ka orenji-lŭl sa-ss-ta.
Inho-Subj orange-Obj buy-Past-Dec/Plain
'Inho bought oranges.' [Declarative]

b. 인호가 오렌지를 샀니?
inho-ka orenji-lŭl sa-ss-ni?
Inho-Subj orange-Obj buy-Past-Q/Plain
'Did Inho buy oranges?' [Interrogative]

c. 인호야 오렌지를 사라.
inho-ya orenji-lŭl sa-la.
Inho-Voc orange-Obj buy-Imp/Plain
'Inho, buy oranges!' [Imperative]

d. 인호야 오렌지를 사자.
inho-ya orenji-lŭl sa-cha.
Inho-Voc orange-Obj buy-Prop/Plain
'Inho, let's buy oranges!' [Propositive]

4.1.2 *Compound sentences*

Two or more clauses can be combined, one after the other, to form a sentence together, which is called a compound sentence. A compound sentence is a sentence that contains more than one main clause. These clauses must be linked by a coordinating conjunction or a semicolon. A compound sentence has a structure such as the following:

인생은 짧고 예술은 길다.
[[insaeng-ŭn tchalp-ko]$_{S1}$ [yesurŭl-ŭn kil-ta]$_{S2}$]$_{S}$.
life-Top (be)short-Conj art-Top be long-Dec/Plain
'Life is short and art is long.'

4.1.3 *Complex sentences*

A complex sentence is a sentence that contains one independent clause, as do all sentences, and at least one dependent or subordinate clause. In

English, subordinate clauses often begin with a subordinating conjunction such as *however*, *although*, *even though*, *because*, or a relative clause such as *who*, *which*, *that*; but in Korean, the conjunctives and modifying endings appear at the end of subordinate clauses. A complex sentence in Korean has the following schema, where *NP* ('orange') is modified by S_1 ('[which] a friend sells'):

인호가	친구	가	파는	오렌지를	산다.
[inho-ka	[[ch'in'gu-	ka	p'a-nŭn]$_{S1}$	orenji]$_{NP}$-lŭl	sa-n-ta]$_S$.
Inho-Subj	friend	Subj	sell-Mod	orange-Obj	buy-Pres-Dec/Plain

'Inho buys the oranges his friend sells.'

4.2 The elements of a simple sentence

There are three core elements that form a simple sentence: *subject*, *object*, and *predicate*.

4.2.1 Subject

A subject is a noun or noun phrase around which an event revolves. An event is broadly defined as a process or a condition of the world. The subject is the word or phrase that the sentence or clause tells about. As in English, the subject in a Korean sentence can be identified by asking a question beginning with 'who,' 'what,' or 'which.' A subject is typically a noun phrase followed by a subject marker (Subj), sometimes called a "particle." There are two variants for the Subj form: When it follows a vowel-final noun, the suffix is -가 *ka*. (In practice it is always pronounced [g], which is reflected in M-R romanization.) When the Subj follows a consonant-final noun, the suffix is -이 *i*.

Subject Markers
C-i
V-ka

인호가	오렌지를	산다.
inho-ka	orenji-lŭl	sa-n-ta.
Inho-Subj	orange-Obj	buy-Pres-Dec/Plain

'Inho buys oranges.'

집이 크다.
chip-i k'ŭ-ta.
house-Subj big-Dec/Plain
'The house is big.'

인호가 기순에게 편지를 썼다.
inho-ka kisun-ege p'yŏnji-lŭl ss-ŏss-ta.
Inho-Subj Kisun-to letter-Obj write-Past-Dec/Plain
'Inho wrote a letter to Kisun.'

In Korean, the subject usually appears at the beginning of the sentence. However, it is more easily identified by a specific form that indicates its role as a subject [▶8.5.1.1].

4.2.2 Object

A grammatical object is a noun or noun phrase in a predicate construction which is affected by the action of a verb. The object marker (Obj) is attached to the end of the object noun, and the noun-Obj sequence is pronounced as one word. There are two variants for the Obj form. When it follows a vowel-final noun, the suffix is -를 *lŭl*, and when the Obj follows a consonant-final noun, it is -을 *ŭl*.

Object Forms
C-ŭl
V-lŭl

In Korean the direct object usually comes after the subject. However, because of the presence of markers, the word order can be changed to suit other purposes. For example, a direct object may be put at the beginning when it is the focus of the sentence:

기순이 오렌지를 산다. vs. 오렌지를 기순이 산다.
kisun-i orenji-lŭl sa-n-ta.
Kisun-Subj orange-Obj buy-Pres-Dec/Plain
'Kisun buys oranges.'

아민이 한국말을 배웠다. vs. 한국말을 아민이 배웠다.
amin-i han'gukmal-ŭl paew-ŏss-ta.
Amin-Subj Korean-Obj learn-Past-Dec/Plain
'Amin learned Korean.'

짐이 한국 뉴스를 듣는다. vs. 한국 뉴스를 짐이 듣는다.
chim-i han'guk nyusŭ-lŭl tŭt-nŭn-ta.
Jim-Subj Korea news-Obj listen to-Pres-Dec/Plain
'Jim listens to Korean news.'

4.2.3 Predicate

A predicate is the portion of a clause, excluding the subject, that expresses something about the subject. Korean is a *head-final* language, which means that the most important information occurs at the end of a linguistic unit. The predicate is the nuclear element of a simple sentence. Within the predicate the verb is the core element, and determines to which type a sentence belongs.

There are four different types of predicates: *action verbs*, *stative verbs*, *noun + copula*, and *existential*.

4.2.3.1 Action verbs

Verbs denote activity or process. When a verb requires only a subject, it is called *intransitive*. When it requires a subject and a direct object, it is called *transitive*. When it requires a subject, direct object, and indirect object (dative), it is called *ditransitive* [▶6.1]. Here is an example:

인호가 미나에게 편지를 썼다.
inho-ka mina-ege p'yŏnji-lŭl ss-ŏss-ta.
Inho-Subj Mina-Dat letter-Obj write-Past-Dec/Plain
'Inho wrote a letter to Mina.'

4.2.3.2 Stative verbs

What is expressed by the sequence *be* + adjective in English is expressed with just a *verb* in Korean. We call such verbs *stative* or adjectival verbs. A stative verb requires only a subject. Unlike English adjectives, which require a copula, Korean stative verbs do not. English speakers are warned to resist the temptation to add the copula 'be' to stative verbs [▶6.2.2]. Here is an example:

인생이 짧다.
insaeng-i tchalp-ta.
life-Subj short-Dec/Plain
'Life is short.'

4.2.3.3 *NP + copula*

Noun + 이다 *i-ta* acts as a verb that means '...am/is/are noun.' Noun + 이다 forms a single unit in the sense that the two items are written together with no space in between and are pronounced without a pause between them. The noun in this case is not the subject of the sentence but is a part of the verb-like construction [▶6.2.3]. Here is an example:

부인이	미국	사람이다.
puin-i	miguk	saram-i-ta.
wife-Subj	America	person-Cop-Dec/Plain

'His wife is an American.'

4.2.3.4 *Existential verbs*

Existential verbs include:

Affirmative	있다 iss-ta
Negative	없다 ŏps-ta

Existential verbs are used in two different constructions.

1 Existential construction
Existential verbs indicate the existence or absence of an object including humans, animals, and abstract ideas. For example:

다마스커스에	한국	식당이	있어요?
tamasŭk'ŏsŭ-e	han'guk	siktang-i	iss-ŏyo?
Damascus-Loc	Korea	restaurant-Subj	Exist-Q/Pol

'Is there a Korean restaurant in Damascus?'

2 Possessive construction
Existential verbs are used to indicate possession. The basic structure is:

(NP-Dative) NP-Subj Exist

This structure uses the subject marker for a possessed item, even though in its English equivalent it is an object of the verb. In other words, the Korean sentential structure for saying 'X has Y' is 'To X Y exists.' Observe this example:

[나-에게] 지금 돈이 없어요.
na-ege chigŭm ton-i ŏps-ŏyo.
me-Dat now money-Subj not Exist-Dec/Pol
'I don't have money now.' [*lit.* '(To/for me) money does not exist.']
[▶6.2.4]

4.3 Basic sentence patterns

Five broad types of sentences can be diagrammed as follows (all with the polite, informal declarative sentence–verb ending, -어요 *ŏyo*):

a. **NP V$_{\text{intransitive}}$**

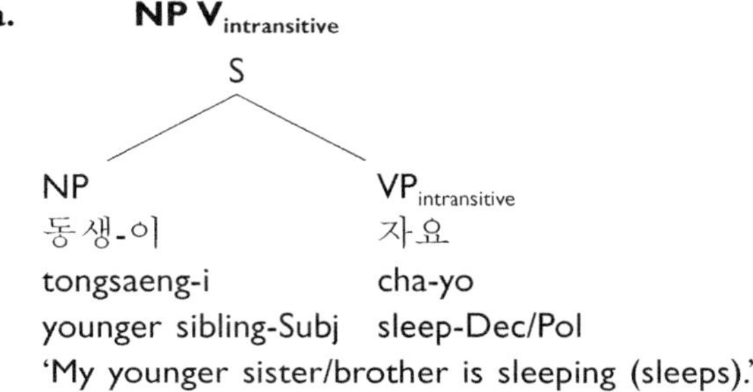

동생-이 자요
tongsaeng-i cha-yo
younger sibling-Subj sleep-Dec/Pol
'My younger sister/brother is sleeping (sleeps).'

b. **NP V$_{\text{stative}}$**

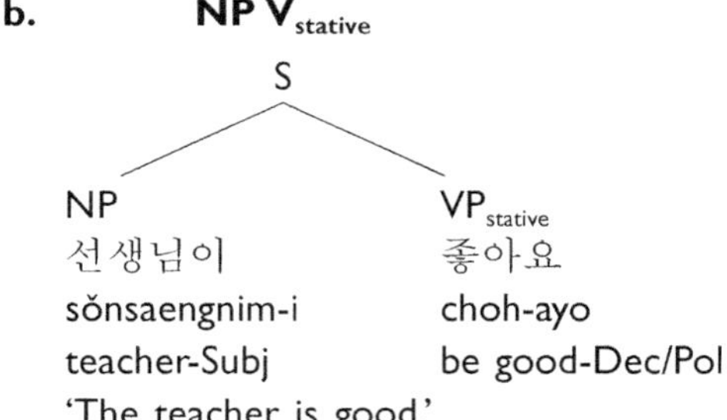

선생님이 좋아요
sŏnsaengnim-i choh-ayo
teacher-Subj be good-Dec/Pol
'The teacher is good.'

c. **NP$_i$ NP$_i$ Copula**

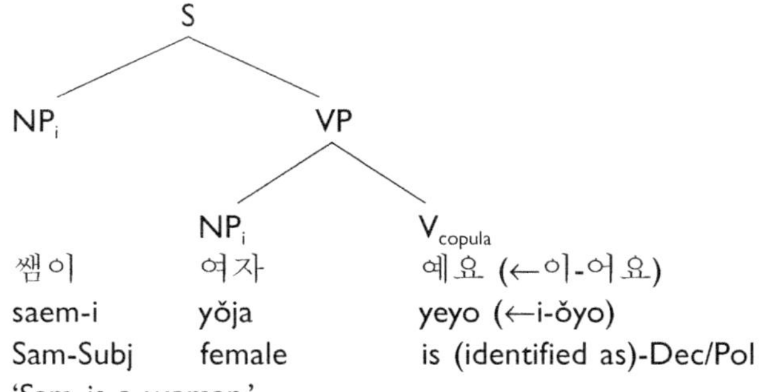

쌤이 여자 예요 (←이-어요)
saem-i yŏja yeyo (←i-ŏyo)
Sam-Subj female is (identified as)-Dec/Pol
'Sam is a woman.'

d. **NP NP $V_{transitive}$**

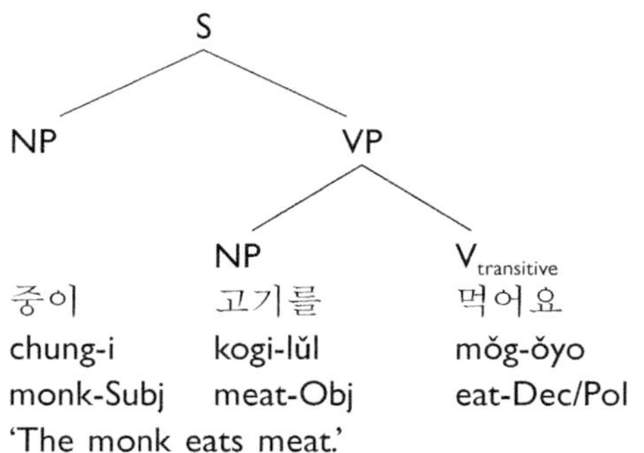
S
NP
VP
NP
$V_{transitive}$
중이 고기를 먹어요
chung-i kogi-lŭl mŏg-ŏyo
monk-Subj meat-Obj eat-Dec/Pol
'The monk eats meat.'

e. **NP NP NP $V_{transitive}$**

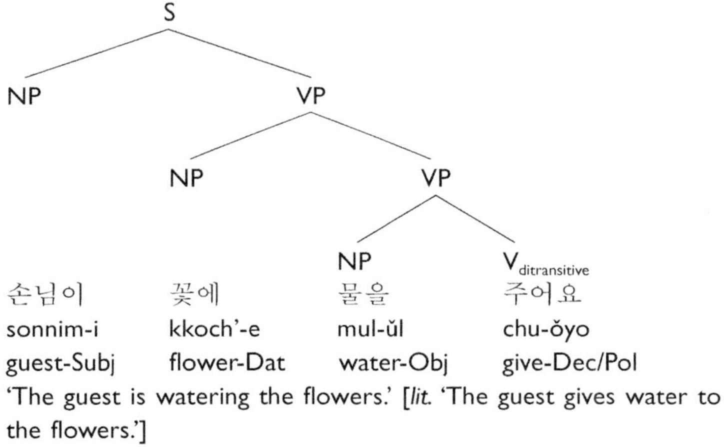
S
NP
VP
NP
VP
NP
$V_{ditransitive}$
손님이 꽃에 물을 주어요
sonnim-i kkoch'-e mul-ŭl chu-ŏyo
guest-Subj flower-Dat water-Obj give-Dec/Pol
'The guest is watering the flowers.' [*lit.* 'The guest gives water to the flowers.']

Although the only strict requirement is that the verb should be at the end of a sentence, the usual order of phrases within a sentence is as follows:

Korean Word Order
time adverbial – place adverbial – subject noun phrase – dative noun phrase – manner adverbial – object noun phrase – verb

어제 학교에서 수지가 유진에게 기꺼이 미아를
ŏje hakkyo-esŏ suji-ka yujin-ege kikkŏi mia-lŭl
yesterday school-Loc Suji-Subj Yujin-Dat willingly Mia-Obj
소개했어요.
sogaehae-ss-ŏyo.
introduce-Past-Dec/Pol
'Yesterday, Suji willingly introduced Mia to Yujin at school.'

Korean does not have prepositions. All grammatical relations and other functional relations that would be expressed using prepositions, subordinating conjunctions, and coordinating conjunctions in English are indicated by the use of postpositional particles. Because of marking by a postposition, the subject can occur elsewhere than at the beginning of a sentence:

기순에게 인호가 편지를 썼다.
kisun-ege inho-ka p'yŏnji-lŭl ss-ŏss-ta.
Kisun-Dat Inho-Subj letter-Obj write-Past-Dec/Plain
'Inho wrote a letter to Kisun.'

4.4 Sentence type classified by function

4.4.1 *Declarative (Dec)*

A declarative sentence makes a statement.

나는 오늘 바쁩니다.
Na-nŭn onŭl papp-ŭpni-ta.
me-Top today be busy-Dec/Def
'I am busy today (deferential style).'

4.4.2 *Interrogative (Q)*

An interrogative sentence asks a question and is indicated by a question mark in writing. In English, the word order changes in a question sentence. In Korean, all one needs to turn a declarative sentence into a question sentence is to choose the right sentence ender, e.g., -까 *kka* instead of -다 *ta*. Compare the following yes-no question with the example given in section 4.4.1:

학생들이 오늘 바쁩니까?
haksaeng-tŭl-i onŭl papp-ŭpnikka?
students-PL-Subj today be busy-Q/Def
'Are students busy today?'

In English, the WH-words (*who*, *what*, *which*, *when*, *where*, and *how*) are moved to the front and the auxiliary verb *do* is inserted in a WH-question sentence, as in "*What did you eat for lunch?*"

In Korean, WH-questions are simple to form. Just put a WH-word in the usual spot in a declarative sentence:

점심에 무엇을 먹었어?
chŏmsim-e muŏs-ŭl mŏk-oss-o?
lunch-Loc what-Obj eat-Past-Q/*panmal*
'What did you eat for lunch?'

> *Note*: WH-words often double as indefinite pronouns ('someone,' 'anyone,' 'something,' 'anything,' 'sometime,' 'somewhere,' 'somehow,' etc.). Koreans regard the two categories of words as essentially the same in that they both are unknown and unspecific. So, the sentence just mentioned:
>
> 점심에 무엇을 먹었어?
>
> is ambiguous when written down without a proper context; but in spoken Korean the intonation contains cues that clearly distinguish the two kinds of sentences: In a WH-question, the intonation is falling as in an English WH-question ("*What did you eat?*") and the WH-word (*what*) gets a slight accent (especially its first syllable) and the last syllable of the sentence also gets a little accent in order to create a falling pitch. In a simple yes-no question, the indefinite word (*something*) receives no accent and the sentence has a rising sentential intonation.
>
> 점심에 무엇을 먹었어?↘ 'What did you eat at lunch?' [WH-Q]
> 점심에 무엇을 먹었어?↗ 'Did you eat something at lunch?' [Yes-No Q]

4.4.3 *Imperative (Imp)*

An imperative sentence commands an action. In English it is often indicated by a lack of subject, although 'you' is implied. In Korean, the subject can be more commonly used in imperative sentences, as shown below (in two different speech styles):

오늘은 수지가 가라!
onŭl-ŭn suji-ka ka-ra!
today-Top Suji-Subj go-Imp
'Today, Suji (should) go!'

선생님께서 먼저 타십시오!
sŏnsaengnim-kkesŏ mŏnjŏ t'a-si-psio!
teacher-subj/Hon first get on (a vehicle)-Imp/Def
'Teacher, you ride first.'

4.4.4 *Propositive (Prop)*

A propositive sentence invites others to do something together with the speaker. This type is closely related to an imperative sentence. As in the case of an imperative sentence, the subject can occur with propositive sentences.

우리 토요일에 골프 치자.
uri t'oyoil-e kolp'ŭ ch'i-ja.
us Saturday-Loc golf hit-Prop
'Let's play golf on Saturday.'

4.4.5 Exclamatory (Exc)

An exclamatory sentence conveys an exclamation, and usually the (exclamatory) punctuation is indicated.

불이야
fire-Cop-Exc
'Fire!'

Note: In addition to the sentence types discussed above (i.e., declarative, interrogative, imperative, propositive, and exclamatory), the Korean literature introduces promissives (e.g., 내일 또 오마 *naeil tto oma* 'I promise to be here again tomorrow'), permissives (가렴 *karyŏm* 'Go if you want to'), premonitives (다칠라 *tach'illa* 'Be careful not to get hurt'), optatives (용서해 주소서 *yongsŏhaeju sosŏ* 'Please forgive me'), and apperceptives (벌써 갔군 *pŏlssŏ kasskun* 'Oh, he's already gone'). However, there is a debate on whether they are independent sentence types of their own and hence, no agreement among linguists regarding the exact number of sentence types in Korean has been established (*cf.* Sohn 2001).

4.5 Voice

Sentences are either *active*, *passive*, or *causative*. What distinguishes the three types is *voice*, which indicates the relation between the subject of the sentence and the action expressed by the verb. For example, "*Koreans eat kimch'i*" uses the active voice; "*Kimch'i is eaten by Koreans*," the passive; and "*A mom is feeding her child kimch'i*," the causative. In the active sentence, the agent ("Koreans") of the verb is the subject. In the passive sentence, the logical object or patient ("kimch'i") of the verb occupies the subject position, and the agent ("Koreans") is put after the preposition "by." In the causative construction, the agent ("a mom") is the subject, which causes the object ("child") to do something.

Here are examples of the different types of sentences:

Active 사자가 토끼를 먹는다.
saja-ka t'okki-lŭl mŏnk-nŭn-ta.
lion-Subj rabbit-Obj eat-Pres-Dec/Plain
'A lion is eating a rabbit.'

Passive 토끼가 사자에게 먹힌다.
t'okki-ka saja-ege mŏk-hi-n-ta.
rabbit-Subj lion-Dat is-Pass-Pres-Dec/Plain
'A rabbit is eaten by a lion.'

Causative 사자가 새끼에게 토끼를 먹인다.
saja-ka saekki-ege t'okki-lŭl mŏk-i-n-ta.
lion-Subj cub-Dat rabbit-Obj feed-Caus-Pres-Dec/Plain
'A lion is feeding her cub a rabbit.'

4.5.1 *Active voice*

An active sentence is one in which the agent of the action expressed by the verb is the subject. The verb can be either transitive (*eat*) or intransitive (*sleep*), as shown in the following examples.

동생-이 자요.
tongsaeng-i ch-ayo.
younger sibling-Subj sleep-Dec/Pol
'My younger sister/brother is sleeping.'

미나가 김치를 먹어요.
mina-ka kimch'i-lŭl mŏk-ŏyo.
Mina-Subj kimch'i-Obj eat-Dec/Pol
'Mina is eating *kimch'i*.'

4.5.2 *Passive voice*

In Korean passive sentences, the logical object of the verb becomes the grammatical subject as in English, but the agent takes the dative marker -에게 *ege* and its variants with the meaning of 'to…,' as if the action is given or imposed on the agent.

The active verb is then replaced by the matching passive verb in a passive sentence, which is either inherently passive or passivized through suffixation

[▶6.4.1]. Compare the two corresponding sentences in active and passive forms in Table 4.1:

Table 4.1 Structures of active and passive sentences

Active			Passive		
Subj	Obj	Verb	Subj	Dat	Verb
NP_1-Subj	NP_2-Obj	V_{active}	NP_2-Subj	NP_1-Dat	$V_{passive}$

Here are some sample sentences:

Active 경찰이 도둑을 잡았다.
kyŏngch'al-i todug-ŭl chap-ass-ta.
police-Subj thief-Obj catch-Past-Dec/Plain
'The police caught the thief.'

Passive 도둑이 경찰에게 잡혔다.
todug-i kyŏngch'al-ege chap-hy-ŏss-ta.
thief-Subj police-Dat catch-Pass-Past-Dec/Plain
'The thief was caught by the police.'

In Korean, passivization in general is not very common and is a recent development in the language. When passive and causative suffixes are attached, the expanded verb stems become passive and causative stems, respectively, and they appear in dictionaries as independent verb stems [▶6.4.1].

In Korean, agentless passives (e.g., "The house was sold" rather than "The house was sold by a friend") are more common than passives with the agent specified, with some of them idiomatic, and having no real corresponding active sentences:

큰 옷이 잘 팔려요.
k'ŭ-n os-i chal p'al-ly-ŏyo.
big(size)-Mod clothes-Subj well/a lot sell-Pass-Dec/Pol
'Larger-sized clothes sell well [*lit.* are sold well].'

이 소설이 많이 읽혀요.
i sŏsŏl-i manhi ilk-hy-ŏyo.
this novel-Subj in great quantity read-Pass-Dec/Pol
'This novel is popular [*lit.* is read a lot].'

고기-가 안 잡혀요.
kogi-ka an chap-hy-ŏyo.
fish-Subj Neg catch-Pass-Dec/Pol
'(We have) no luck fishing.' [*lit.* 'Fish are not caught.']

잘 안 들려요.
chal an tŭl-ly-ŏyo.
well Neg hear-Pass-Dec/Pol
'I can't hear you.' [*lit.* 'You are not heard well.']

Koreans today are using passive sentences more and more, partly as a result of their familiarity with Western languages such as English in which passivization is a productive process. Because passive suffixes are not freely used for all verbs, an increasingly common means of passivization is by the use of the auxiliary verb -어 지 *ŏ chi* with the inchoative meaning of 'turn/become...':

내-가 달걀을 너무 삶았어요.
nae-ka talgyal-ŭl nŏmu salm-ass-ŏyo.
I-Subj egg-Obj too much boil-Past-Dec/Pol
'I over-boiled the eggs.'

달걀-이 너무 삶아졌어요.
talgyal-i nŏmu salm-a-chi-ŏss-ŏyo.
egg-Subj too much boil-Pass-Past-Dec/Pol
'The eggs got over-boiled.'

The verb or verbalizing suffix -하 *ha* 'do' is changed to -되 *toe* 'become' in a passive construction. Compare the active and passive sentences shown in Table 4.2.

Table 4.2 Active and passive sentences

Active	Passive
식사를 제공**했**다 siksa-lŭl chegong-hae-ss-ta meal-**Obj** offer-do-Past-Dec 'X provided the meal.'	식사**가** 제공**되**었다 siksa-ka chegong-doe-ŏss-ta meal-**Subj** offer-become-Past-Dec 'The meal was provided (by X).'

4.5.3 *Causative*

In causative sentences, there are two agents: one agent making another agent act the way the verb expresses. Compare the active and causative sentences in Table 4.3:

Table 4.3 Active and causative sentences

Active		Causative	
딸이	결혼**했**다.	딸을	결혼**시켰**다.
ttal-**i**	kyŏrhon-hae-ss-ta.	ttal-**ŭl**	kyŏrhon-sik'i-ŏss-ta.
daughter-**Subj**	marriage-do-Past-Dec	daughter-**Obj**	marriage-order-Past-Dec
'X's daughter got married.'		'X got X's daughter married.'	

The causative verb is either short, i.e., formed simply by adding causative suffixes, which are very similar to passive suffixes, or long, i.e., formed by adding the expression, -게 하 *ke ha* 'do so that…X (cause X).' Compare the following sentences:

Active	애기가	약을	먹어요.	
	aegi-ka	yag-ŭl	mŏg-ŏyo.	
	baby-**Subj**	medicine-Obj	take-Dec/Pol	
	'The baby is taking the medicine.'			
Short causative	엄마가	애기에게	약을	먹여요.
	ŏmma-ka	aegi-ege	yag-ŭl	mŏg-y-ŏyo.
	mom-**Subj**	baby-Dat	medicine-Obj	feed-Caus-Dec/Pol
	'A mom is feeding medicine to the baby.'			
	[Mom makes the baby do X; the baby does X.]			
Long causative	엄마가	애기에게	약을	먹게해요.
	ŏmma-ka	aegi-ege	yag-ŭl	mŏk-ke-hae-yo.
	mom-**Subj**	baby-**Dat**	medicine-Obj	eat-Caus-Dec/Pol
	'A mom is making her baby take medicine.'			
	[Mom makes it happen that the baby does X.]			

There is a slight difference in meaning between the two kinds of causatives: the short form is direct, the long, indirect. The short form, 먹이다 *mŏgi-ta*, indicates the action of directly feeding someone, and the long form, 먹게 하다 *mŏk-ke-ha-ta*, simply indicates causation of someone to do something (e.g., by facilitating the event with some kind of help).

Chapter 5

Words

Korean words can be divided among various parts of speech. There are four major classes of words: *verbs*, *nouns*, *modifiers*, and *particles*. Verbs comprise *action*, *stative*, *copulative*, and *existential* verbs. Nouns comprise proper and common nouns, pronouns, and numerals. Modifiers are those words that add information to that conveyed by nouns or verbs. Particles make the function of a noun within a sentence or a phrase explicit. Table 5.1 shows some examples for each class of words.

Table 5.1 Korean parts of speech

Word class	Part of speech	Examples
Verb	Action verb	읽 ilk- 'read,' 배우 paeu- 'learn,' 운동하 undongha- 'exercise'
	Stative verb	좋 choh- 'be good,' 바쁘 pappŭ- 'be busy,' 급하 kŭpha- 'be urgent'
	Copula	-이 i- '[equational] be'
	Existential verb	있- iss- 'exist, have,' 없 ŏps- 'not exist, not have'
Noun[a]	Proper noun	서울 sŏul (Seoul), 삼성 samsŏng (Samsung), 김수아 Kim Sua
	Common noun	봄 pom 'spring,' 강아지 kang'aji 'puppy,' 어머니 ŏmŏni 'mother'
	Pronoun	나 na 'me,' 너 nŏ 'you,' 우리 uri 'us'
	Numeral	하나 hana 'one,' 백 paek 'one hundred,' 만 man 'ten thousand'
Modifier	Prenoun	새 sae 'new,' 헌 hŏn 'worn out,' 몇 myŏch' 'how many'
	Adverb	잘 chal 'well,' 아주 aju 'very,' 빨리 ppalli 'fast,' 많이 manhi 'a lot'
Particle	Particle	-이 i [Subj], -을 ŭl [Obj], -에게 ege [Dat], -는 nŭn [Top], -에 e [Loc]

[a]All loanwords are considered nouns regardless of their original part of speech in the source language.

Most Western languages mark the function of major units in a sentence by means of word order, prepositions, auxiliary verbs, or affixes; Korean indicates function mainly with one or more suffixes attached to those units. Thus, a word usually contains more than what looks like a word in Western languages.

Korean forms words by combining simple words or word components without alteration. Suffixes are added to a *word stem* (basic part of a word). Suffixes attached to a verb stem indicate items such as *tense* (past, present, or future), *aspect* (action complete, repeated, or continuing), and *speech protocol* (marking the expressed relative status of the person addressed or referred to from the speaker's point of view, and the degree of formality or intimacy). Endings attached to a noun mark the noun's function in the sentence (subject or object) as well as in a larger context (focus, topic).

For English speakers, it is helpful to note some features of Korean words that may look esoteric at first glance, but are actually quite transparent. First consider the structure of words.

5.1 Korean word (w) structure

Words are key elements in larger grammatical units such as verb phrases (VPs) and noun phrases (NPs). Every word contains a major component that carries the core meaning, called the *stem*.

A stem consists of one or more roots. The two most important kinds of stems in Korean are verb stems and noun stems. Verbs include not only action verbs but also copulas ("be" verbs) and stative (also called "adjectival") verbs [▶6]. Nouns include not only common nouns, but also proper nouns, numerals, pronouns, and some "defective" or bound nouns called 의존명사 *ŭijonmyŏngsa*, whose meaning can be completed only in combination with a preceding modifier [▶9.1.1].

In a word, a stem is followed by an ending. In the case of a noun stem the ending may be deleted, especially when the context makes its grammatical function in the sentence clear. However, in the case of a verb, the ending is obligatory. The basic structure of a word (w), therefore, is as follows:

Structure of a Korean Word (w)

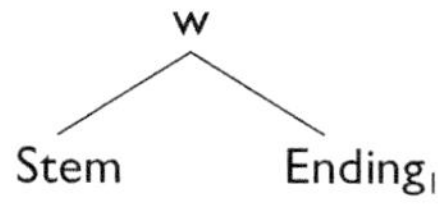

As the diagram shows, a verb stem must have at least one ending. In written Korean, words are generally separated by spaces. In slow speech these spaces more or less correspond to pauses. However, some bound nouns act as endings (postpositions) of the preceding word. The two parts act as a unit and are pronounced without a pause between them. Therefore, phonological phrase boundaries are not always the same as word boundaries.

A list of stems and endings is called *vocabulary*. Although, strictly speaking, words and lexical (dictionary) forms are not quite the same, "word" is used ambiguously to refer to dictionary forms as well as the "w" units described above.

Korean vocabulary is extremely rich, due first of all to a massive borrowing from classical Chinese, which was the standard means of written communication for a millennium before and even after the invention of the Korean alphabet in the mid-fifteenth century. In addition, Korean vocabulary owes its highly generative nature to some very productive vocabulary-building mechanisms that make coinage of neologisms common and respectable, such as creating new words by combining Sino-Korean roots, creating nuanced variations of words using the vowel-harmony rules, and manipulation of the consonantal strength hierarchy in sound symbolism.

Korean vocabulary can be classified in various ways depending on which characteristics are considered.

5.2 Word classes by structural characteristics

Korean words can be broadly categorized according to: (1) whether or not they can stand alone; and (2) whether they are of native or non-native origin.

5.2.1 Bound stems: Verbs

All verbal forms are bound in the sense that they can never stand freely but must co-occur with at least one ending. Therefore, as a conventional practice, the plain sentence ender, -다 *ta*, is attached to the verb stem even in citations and in dictionaries. To get the base form, simply drop that final -다 *ta*. For example, the basic form of the verb 'see' in the citation form, 보-다 *po-ta* 'sees,' is 보 *po-*. To conjugate the verb, add endings to 보 *po-*, but never say just 보 *po-* even when you want to repeat that part as a sentence fragment to make it clear. Otherwise people will not have a clue what you are talking about.

5.2.2 Free-standing stems: Nouns and adjectives

A noun or a nominal usually has a particle attached to it. However, nouns can be free standing, especially as their particles are often deleted when their grammatical functions are predictable from other cues.

Adverbs are free standing but can be attached to particles delimiting their meaning in particular ways. However, sound-symbolic vocabulary items, which are a subset of adverbs, may only stand alone and cannot be followed by any particles.

5.3 Word classes according to their origin

With today's unbridled borrowing from Western languages in South Korea in addition to the continued, prolific use of Sino-Korean (SK) roots for new words, it is difficult to estimate even approximately the ratio among various types of vocabulary in Korean. But according to Ho-min Sohn (2006: 44), about 65 percent of Korean words are SK words and 5 percent loanwords; only about 30 percent are of native Korean origin. 우리말큰사전 *Uri-mal k'ŭn sajŏn* ('Great Korean-language dictionary,' 1991), compiled by the 한글학회 *Han'gŭl Hakhoe* ('Korean Language Society'), possibly the most comprehensive dictionary published to date, contains among its entries 74,612 words of native origin, 85,527 Sino-Korean words, and 3,986 loanwords (Lee and Ramsey 2000: 136).

It is well known that language borrowing and language change often result in creating different classes of vocabulary in natural languages. Korean has borrowed many words from various other languages through contact with foreign cultures and languages – especially through Koreans' long use of written, classical Chinese – and demonstrates four lexical layers, two native and two from foreign sources (Cho 1999/2001).

5.3.1 Native Korean vocabulary

Two distinct segments of native vocabulary play different roles both in basic meaning and productivity. One is *sound-symbolic vocabulary* and the other is *non-sound-symbolic native vocabulary*.

5.3.1.1 Sound-symbolic (SS) vocabulary

One of the most salient features of the Korean language is the presence of sound symbolism that iconically and directly represents meaning in sounds. Words in the SS vocabulary, which are also called "mimetics," "ideophones," "impressionistic words," "expressives," and "phonoesthetics," include but are not limited to words manifesting onomatopoeia. As a matter of fact, onomatopoeia, called 의성어 *ŭisŏngŏ* [*lit.* 'sound-imitating words'] constitutes only a small part of the SS vocabulary, in comparison with the other subset called 의태어 *ŭit'aeŏ* [*lit.* 'appearance-imitating words'], which includes a whole range of expressions from visual and other sensory images to the feelings they evoke.

In English and other Western languages, sound symbolism is limited to onomatopoeia, and even there the choice is rather arbitrary, but in Korean both vowels and consonants can be varied intentionally to produce different nuances in meaning. These effects are achieved through the vowel-harmony (VH) principle and consonantal-variation phenomena.

Basically, in SS words, the vowels *i*, *e*, *wi/ü*, *ŭ*, *ŏ*, *u* (ㅣ, ㅔ, ㅟ, ㅡ, ㅓ, ㅜ) form a harmonic group called "dark" or yin (Korean *ŭm*) vowels, and the vowels *ae*, *oe*, *a*, *o* (ㅐ, ㅚ, ㅏ, ㅗ) form the other set, called "bright" or yang vowels. *i* and *ŭ* are neutral in non-initial syllables and may co-occur with either dark or bright vowels [▶3.3.3.1]. Table 5.2 presents two pairs of words with connotational differences caused by different choices of vowels:

Table 5.2 Dark and bright vowels in sound symbolic sets of words

SS Vocabulary		
Dark/Yin	**Bright/Yang**	**Meaning**
뗑그렁 ttengŭrŏng	땡그랑 ttaengŭrang	'clanging'
줄줄 chuljul	졸졸 choljol	'flowing'

In the case of the pair *chuljul* ~ *choljol*, the former belongs to the dark or yin group, denoting a massive, strong manner of falling water, while the latter belongs to the bright or yang group, expressing a diminutive, or even cute, leisurely flow of water. The 'flowing' applies not only to water, but also one person following another, tears, fluency (of recitation), etc.

The consonants within the pair may also be slightly altered to express different degrees of intensity, e.g.:

출출 ch'ulchu'l 촐촐 ch'olch'ol 'gushing'

with an added nuance of the situation being 'rough' in addition to the meaning carried for the yin and yang vowels. Korean speakers are conscious of different consonantal strength, which is clearly indicated in the *han'gŭl* system. Because of the emotive aspect of SS vocabulary, various degrees of intensity of meaning are thus expressed by manipulating the consonantal strength, especially in obstruents [▶3.4.1].

VH is thought to have been applied quite rigorously in the earlier stages of Korean until the fifteenth century, but it has gradually decayed mainly because of various reasons. One is the massive borrowing from Chinese, which, unlike most of the Altaic languages, shows no vowel harmony. It is thanks to the free-standing nature of the SS vocabulary that VH seems to have survived most clearly within it, and to a large extent consonantal variation as well.

Because of the almost infinite possibilities of creating new words based on these vocalic and consonantal manipulations, Korean is extremely rich in SS vocabulary, and its full extent cannot be ascertained.

5.3.1.2 *Non-sound-symbolic native vocabulary*

Almost all grammatical markers such as particles and sentence enders have native Korean forms. In fact, these are what make Korean Korean. That is why, even when Koreans were writing only in Chinese before the invention of *han'gŭl*, they made many efforts to transcribe these grammatical markers phonetically. Even today, when a sentence is filled with other loanwords, if it has a Korean ending the sentence is definitely understood to be Korean, as the following example shows:

A Korean sentence filled with English loanwords

미스 코리아는 이미지가 슈퍼모델이다.
misŭ k'oria-nŭn imiji-ka syup'ŏ moder-i-ta.
Miss Korea-Top image-Subj supermodel-Cop-Dec/Plain
'Miss Korea gives the impression of being a supermodel.'

Native vocabulary items are generally thought to give an intimate, informal, and sometimes innocent or childlike impression compared to Sino-Korean words. In a newly fashionable revival of things Korean since the 1980s, people have been giving their children names completely made of Korean roots such as 하늘 *hanŭl* 'sky,' 슬기 *sŭlgi* 'wisdom,' 한누리 *hannuri* 'one (or big) world,' etc., but some people, when they grow up, choose to change their names to more traditional names composed of two SK roots because they feel their name sounds too childish for an adult.

However, this is not a transient trend as large banks, companies, grocery chains, brand names, and even political parties are now choosing names that are completely native sounding, such as 한아름 *hanarŭm* 'an armful,' 하나은행 *hana ŭnhaeng* 'Bank One,' 처음처럼 *ch'ŏŭmch'ŏrŏm* 'like the beginning,' and 열린우리당 *yŏllin uridang* 'Uri Party [*lit.* Our Open Party].' However these are random samples, and neologisms based on pure Korean roots are quite insignificant in number, amounting to practically nothing when compared to those based on Sino-Korean roots.

It is noteworthy that the VH rule does not apply systematically to word stems that are purely Korean but not sound-symbolic. Thus, in many pure Korean words, vowels of different harmonic classes co-occur, e.g., 바구니 [paguni] 'wicker basket,' 사투리 [sat'uri] 'a dialect, accent,' 아버지 [abŏji] 'father,' 매우 [maeu] 'very,' 다물- [tamul-] 'close (lips),' and 넉살좋- [nŏksalcoh-] 'be brazen,' etc.

VH does apply, however, in the alternation of *ŏ*-initial suffixes, which have to harmonize with the last syllable of the preceding stem, e.g., 먹-어 *mŏg-ŏ* 'Eat!' vs. 막-아 *mag-a* 'Block it!' It happens that most verb roots are native Korean vocabulary, because loanwords are always analyzed as nouns in Korean. It may not be a coincidence that VH applies in this environment where two very closely pronounced native roots meet. While most nouns and other independent forms have gradually stopped observing VH rules, first starting with Sino-Korean words and expanding to cover the whole group membership, the final sound of verb stems continues to apply VH in choosing which first vowel to use in the suffix. The reason that the last syllable of the verb stem counts is most probably because so many verbs are based on a verbal noun, a large proportion of which are based on Sino-Korean roots, with a structure of N + 하 *ha* 'do.' But the last syllable of a verb is almost always of Korean origin.

5.3.2 *Vocabulary of foreign origin*

By the fifteenth century, when *han'gŭl* was invented, the Korean vocabulary contained words borrowed from various foreign languages, including Manchu and Mongolian. However, the vast majority of the Korean vocabulary originated from classical literary Chinese, which Koreans used for well over a thousand years until the invention of the Korean writing system and continued to do so well into the twentieth century, although its use is drastically reduced today. The majority of the Korean vocabulary is Chinese in origin, precisely because neologisms are most often based on Sino-Korean roots.

As in most modern speech communities, however, new words in Korean are constantly being created by the force of their changing social, cultural, and academic environment. Since the Korean War, loanwords have come mainly from Western languages, predominantly English.

All loanwords are analyzed as nouns, whatever the parts of speech assigned to them in their original languages – for example, the loanword 드라이브 *tŭraibŭ* 'driving' from the English verb 'drive' may carry an object particle, -를 *lŭl*. In order to form a verb out of a noun, the verbalizing suffix -하 *ha* is attached to the loanword, e.g., 키스-하 *k'isŭ-ha* [*lit.* 'do kiss'].

5.3.2.1 *Sino-Korean (SK) vocabulary*

Items of Sino-Korean vocabulary (SKV) are, to be sure, of foreign origin. However, the Korean pronunciations of Chinese characters are not Korean approximations of Chinese sounds but originate from a system codified in rhyming dictionaries and rhyme tables that developed following the Korean sound patterns. The meanings of SK roots also derive from those found in classical Chinese, but they too have evolved in Korean ways. Therefore, Koreans have appropriated Sino-Korean, called 한자 漢字 (*hantcha*), as their own in spite of their Chinese origin. SKV should not be considered "loanwords" just as the Latinate vocabulary and neologisms found in English are not. Although the absolute majority of Korean words are SKV, only about 10 percent of the so-called "basic vocabulary" is thought to come from Chinese (Martin 1992: 94). SK words differ from typical loanwords in fundamental ways.

First of all, SK roots have become so nativized that even those Korean speakers who do not know any Chinese characters at all understand SKV, except when the words are newly coined academic, legal, or other learned terms. For example, there is no Korean speaker who does not know the word 선생 *sŏnsaeng* 'teacher,' written 先生 in Chinese. The same is true for 시간 *sigan* 'time,' written 時間 in Chinese. In fact, the most natural Korean proper names, including almost all personal names and names of organizations, and even kinship terms, are Sino-Korean based. Take, for example, 학교 *hakkyo* 'school,' written 學校 in Chinese, and 형 *hyŏng* 'elder brother,' written in Chinese as 兄.

Because such massive Sino-Korean vocabulary has been created based on Chinese borrowings, Korean speakers and even dictionaries misuse Chinese characters for certain pure-Korean vocabulary items, especially nouns. For example, some dictionaries give a Chinese character 箸 for Korean 저 *chŏ* 'chopsticks,' because the Korean pronunciation of the Chinese character for 'chopsticks' happens to be pronounced the same nowadays; but this is actually an error because historical records show the Korean word and the Chinese character were not pronounced the same in earlier periods. In fact about 90 percent of the basic vocabulary – including body parts such as 'eye' and 'mouth,' natural phenomena like 'sun,' 'moon,' and 'sky,' and sensory experiences such as 'warm' and 'yellow' – seems to be native to Korean (Martin 1992: 94).

As in the case of all loanwords, all SK words are nouns. Most new words are made by combining an SK root with one or more additional SK roots. This process is extremely productive. Let us consider one example. One of the most often used SK roots is 일 一 /il/ '(number) one.' The following is only a handful of what seems like an endless list of SK compound words made of this root and another SK root.

동일시 同一視 tong-**il**-si	'regarding...as the same'
만일 萬一 man-**il**	'if (once in ten thousand times)'
유일 唯一 yu-**il**	'being unique'
제일 第一 che-**il**	'the first'
통일 統一 t'ong-**il**	'unification'
일가 一家 **il**-ga	'relative, family member'
일등 一等 **il**-tŭng	'first rank'
일생 一生 **il**-saeng	'one's lifetime'
일체 一切 **il**-ch'e	'(at) all, everything'
일방 一方 **il**-bang	'one-sided, lopsided'
일시 一時 **il**-si	'(at) the same time'
일심 一心 **il**-sim	'(in) wholeheartedness'
일약 一躍 **il**-yak	'(at) a single bound'
일정 一定 **il**-chŏng	'what is established/uniform/invariable/predictable'
일보 一步 **il**-bo	'one step'

This list, furthermore, is not a closed one. For example, one could make a new word by combining this root with another SK root, 범 犯 *pŏm*, meaning 'crime' in the context of 전과일범 (前科一犯 *chŏnkwa ilbŏm*) 'prior [criminal] record of one crime.' This expression 일범 *ilbŏm* may not be listed in a dictionary, but there is no educated Korean who would not understand it. In fact, chances are this word has been used routinely, although not found in most dictionaries.

Another example is the SK root 천 天 *ch'ŏn* meaning 'sky, heaven.' In an East Asian context, 'heavenly mandate' carries a special meaning and it is often evoked to refer to what is natural, expected, authentic, and therefore good beyond a human's grasp.

우천 雨天 u'-**chŏn**	'rainy weather'
청천 青天 ch'ŏng-**ch'ŏn**	'blue/clear sky'
천직 天職 **ch'ŏn**-jik	'a (heaven-endowed) vocation, a calling'
천재 天才 **ch'ŏn**-jae	'genius (heaven-endowed talent)'
천연 天然 **ch'ŏn**-yŏn	'being natural' [*lit.* 'as God gave it']
천적 天敵 **ch'ŏn**-jŏk	'born enemy'
승천 乘天 sung-**ch'ŏn**	'ascension to heaven'

One of the most famous neologisms based on 천 天 *ch'ŏn* is the title of a lovely poem by the late Ch'ŏn Sang-byŏng, 歸天 (귀천 *Kwich'ŏn* 'Back to Heaven'). Interestingly, the word has a Chinese order putting the verb *kwi* before the object *ch'ŏn*. Another famous poem by Hwang Chin-i, Korea's adored sixteenth-century kisaeng poet, 벽계수 *pyokkyesu* 'Blue Stream,' contains SK words showing a Chinese word order of putting the verb before the object. Here are two examples from this poem:

一到滄海 (일도창해) il**to**ch'anghae 'once having reached the wide ocean,' in which the verb *to* occurs before the object *ch'anghae*.

滿空山 (만공산) **man**'gongsan 'filling the empty mountain,' in which the verb *man* occurs before the object *gongsan*.

Koreans prefer creating new vocabulary based on SK roots because SK roots generally consist of one syllable with a clear, independent meaning and the process is highly economical compared to using native words that tend to be polysyllabic.

We have seen that a great number of SK words are not really true borrowings, i.e., adaptations of foreign words with the perceptually closest native equivalents, but in fact Korean words created by Koreans using literary Chinese roots; in a similar way new words are created on the basis of Latin or Greek roots in English.

However there are also many true loanwords from Chinese in Korean, from Koreans' study of the great Chinese classics. These words, borrowed centuries ago, have undergone Korean sound changes, and often semantic changes as well. Some examples that give the impression of being native vocabulary but are actually Chinese borrowing include the following:

붓 put ← 筆 (필 SK p'il) 'writing brush'
먹 mŏk ← 墨 (묵 SK muk) 'ink (stick)'

Some other words traditionally thought to be completely Korean but now strongly hypothesized to be Chinese loanwords include:

무늬 munŭi ← 文 (문 SK mun) 'pattern'
글 kŭl ← 契 (계 SK kye ← Ancient Chinese *k'ear) 'writing'

Here also are some examples of SK words coined by Koreans based on Chinese characters but now considered native:

사냥 sanyang ← 山行 (산행 SK sanhaeng 'going to the mountain') 'hunting'
부처 puch'ŏ ← 佛體 (불체 SK pul-ch'e 'Buddha's body') 'Buddha'
썰매 ssŏlmae ← 雪馬 (설마 SK sŏlma 'snow horse') 'sled'

Aside from a few historical linguists, virtually no Korean speakers associate these nativized loanwords with their original Chinese characters, and write them only in *hangŭl* even when writing in mixed script.

Koreans have completely taken SK roots as their own, creating new vocabulary freely based on them. SK words undergo the usual Korean sound alterations, such as intervocalic weakening [▶3.4.2]. However, SK words occupy their own stratum, as some sound alterations seem to apply only to this sector of vocabulary. For example, in a specific environment where two SK roots combine to make a word stem, if the last consonant of the first root is [l], its adjacency tenses the first consonant of the second root if it is either a dental or a palatal plain obstruent, [t], [ch], and [s], as the following examples show:

발달 發達 pal-tal [palttal] 'development (charge-through)'
실존 實存 sil-chon [siltchon] 'existence (fruit/reality-existence)'
일생 一生 il-saeng [ilssaeng] 'one's lifetime'

This kind of tensing does not occur in the case of other lax consonants ([p] and [k]), which simply undergo the usual Korean phonological weakening applicable in any sonorant environment:

발굴 發掘 pal-kul [palgul] 'excavation (discover-dig)'
실기 實技 sil-ki [silgi] 'practical skill'
일부 一部 il-pu [ilbu] 'one part'

As is the case with foreign loanwords in any language, SK words are considered more obscure, less personal, more formal and dignified, and more scholarly and scientific. When common native vocabulary coexists with SK words, it is the SK words that often sound more pompous and also outdated, as is frequently the case in many other languages.

편지 p'yŏnji	서한 書翰 sŏhan	'a letter'
시골집 sigoltchip	촌가 村家 ch'on'ga	'a house in the countryside'
딸 ttal	여식 女息 yŏsik	'a daughter'

Sometimes both SK and pure Korean forms are put together in a quasi-redundant way, but the effect is to mitigate the aloof, formal feeling of SKV. Thus a purely Korean word may be attached to a SK word redundantly, e.g., 팔월 (八月) 달 *p'arwŏl-tal* 'the month of August,' where *p'arwŏl* already means 'the eighth moon' and *tal* 'moon' is attached.

5.3.2.2 Loanwords

Koreans have had contact with many peoples and languages besides Chinese throughout their long history. Chinese characters were embraced by Koreans as their own out of appreciation for the entire Sinitic civilization and tradition, of which they felt themselves, and wanted to remain, an important part. Loanwords from other languages, however, were usually mere adaptations of foreign words for more practical purposes and out of necessity. Koreans thus borrowed from the languages of occupying groups including the Mongols, Manchus, Jurchens, Japanese, and finally Russians in North Korea and Americans in South Korea. Loanwords from the languages of Korea's northern neighbors are not numerous, but Japanese and English loanwords deserve attention.

As Koreans came into especial contact with Japan and the United States over recent years, the number of loanwords from these two sources has become considerable. However, their reception by Korean speakers is quite different. The so-called "language purification movement" – *Kugŏ Sunhwa Undong* in South Korea and *Mal Tadŭmki Undong* in North Korea – seems to eschew Japanese loanwords in favor of seeking truly native Korean-only vocabulary.

Loanwords are pronounced as native words as a general rule, but there are a few exceptions.

In non-Chinese loanwords:

1 Initial-*l* nasalization does not occur, e.g., 라디오 *radio*, 'radio,' 로맨스 *romaensŭ* 'romance,' 립스틱 *ripsŭt'ik* 'lipstick.'
2 The *ni-/ny-* sequence in the initial position is allowed, as in examples such as 니켈 *nik'el* 'nickel,' 니코틴 *nik'ot'in* 'nicotine,' 니힐리즘 *nihilijŭm* 'nihilism,' 뉴스 *nyusŭ* 'news.'
3 Certain sounds that are not in the Korean sound inventory may be observable, at least as a variation, in loanwords such as 포토 *p'ot'o* ~ *fot'o* 'photo,' 와이프 *waip'u* ~ *waifu* 'wife,' 러브스토리 *robusŭt'ori* ~ *rovusŭt'ori* 'love story.'

5.3.2.2.1 Japanese loanwords

In premodern times, Koreans benefited from their geographical proximity to China and Korean elites were eager and proud to be part of the great Sinitic civilization. Koreans in turn would be conveyors of culture and technology to the Japanese, their neighbors on the other side of the peninsula, who greeted them also with respect and curiosity. Mahāyāna Buddhism was officially introduced from Korea to Japan in the sixth century, along with a gilt-bronze sculpture of Buddha and several volumes of Buddhist scriptures.

Most importantly from a linguistic point of view, Koreans introduced and taught Chinese characters to the Japanese, and by the eighth century many Korean scholars were teaching Chinese in Japan. The 구결 *kugyŏl* (written as 口訣 in Chinese), a sound-based writing system developed by Koreans simplifying Chinese characters to help in the reading of Chinese texts, was influential in the development of the Japanese *katakana* writing system.

More recent history, however, put Japan in very close, although unwanted, contact with Korean life, and Japanese influence on Korean language and culture has become significant in a completely different way. In the late nineteenth century, Japan's emergence as an ambitious power changed the whole picture of East Asia. Japan colonized Korea from 1910 until 1945, during which the Japanese attempted to eradicate the Korean racial identity by suppressing its traditions and even its very language.

As Koreans during this era grew up bilingual, many Japanese loanwords became almost second nature to them. However, after independence, Koreans tried to extirpate anything that resembled Japanese from their language. Therefore, many formerly quotidian Japanese terms have been replaced by translated Korean names, although older people still may find these neologisms artificial. Here are some examples:

Japanese Loanwords			Calques or Loan Translations		
다꾸앙	takuan	→	단무지	tanmuji	'pickled radish'
와리바시	waribashi	→	나무 젓가락	namu chŏtkkarak	'wooden chopsticks'
스시	sŭshi	→	초밥	ch'obap	'sushi'

Many Western loanwords that have been imported through Japanese with Japanized pronunciation, and for that reason sound too Japanese, are also being replaced by Korean-style readings of foreign words. For example, a word such as 빵 *ppang* 'bread' from Portuguese *pão* remains in the language because it was already Koreanized in pronunciation and sounds more Korean than Japanese. However, certain other words that sounded clearly Japanese were replaced by words with Korean-sounding pronunciations:

Western loanwords in Japanese pronunciation			in Korean pronunciation
도락구	torakku	→	트럭 t'ŭrŏk 'truck'
센치	sench'i	→	센티멘탈 sent'iment'al 'sentimental'
핀토	p'intto	→	핀트 p'intŭ 'focus (erroneous reading of English point)'
렌토겐	rent'ogen	→	뢴트겐 roent'ŭgen (name of its inventor W. K. Röntgen) 'x-ray' or 방사선 pangsasŏn [*lit.* 'radiological ray']

Many borrowings, including grammatical and idiomatic expressions, escaped the Korean campaign for eradication; these are mainly Sino-Japanese (SJ) forms based on Sino-Japanese roots that can easily be considered Sino-Korean. Most of these SJ words were coined by the Japanese for nontraditional objects and ideas and were adopted by the Chinese also. In most cases Koreans were not aware that these were coined in Japan; as long as they could be considered Sino-Korean, Koreans seem to have embraced them as their own. Here are some examples:

신문	新聞	sinmun	'newspaper'
입구	入口	ipkku	'entrance'
할인	割引	harin	'discount'
잡지	雜誌	chapji	'magazine'
철학	哲學	ch'ŏrhak	'philosophy'
화학	化學	hwahak	'chemistry'

5.3.2.2.2 Loanwords from Western languages

Koreans' contact with the West first started through the Chinese, especially in the eighteenth century, when Koreans took an interest in the Roman Catholic Church and religion. Loanwords from that period are somewhat removed from the original pronunciation, as we can see in such examples as 마태 *mat'ae* 'Matthew,' 누가 *nuga* 'Luke,' 바오로 *paoro* 'Paul,' 방지거 *pangjigŏ* 'Francisco,' and 요한 *yohan* 'John.' These are now used mainly as Christian names by Korean Catholics. These and other words whose pronunciation is equally remote from the original are replaced by something deemed to approximate it more closely to the Korean ear:

상항(桑港) sanghang → 샌프란시스코 saenp'ŭransisŭk'o 'San Francisco'
나성(羅城) nasŏng → 로스앤젤레스 rosŭ aenjelesŭ 'Los Angeles'
화성돈(華盛頓) hwasŏngdon → 워싱턴 wŏsingt'ŏn 'Washington'
법국(法國) pŏpkuk/ 불란서 (佛蘭西) pullansŏ → 프랑스 p'ŭrangsŭ 'France'

These changes had nothing to do with rejecting the loanwords, but in fact were efforts to bring them closer to their original pronunciation.

Korea's recent tumultuous history has seen unprecedented involvement by the United States in the life of Koreans politically and socially. First, during the 1880s American missionaries were at the helm of social reform by educating women and training doctors in modern medicine. The United States occupied Korea briefly after its liberation from the Japanese, and soon after the Korean War (1950–53) broke out, in which the U.S. was a major defender of South Korea. Then there were the American Peace Corps volunteers sent to help in postwar reconstruction during the 1960s.

In spite of strong protest from ardent language-purification activists, the tide of globalization has thus arrived. One only has to pick up a newspaper or a magazine to realize that now the great majority of trademarks and everyday expressions are loanwords, most of them from English. It is actually difficult to find a sentence without any English or other Western-language loanwords. Consider the following examples from the home page of just one daily newspaper's website:

*다운로드	taullodŭ (←taunlodŭ)	'download'
*디지털 스토리	tijit'ŏl sŭt'ori	'digital story'
*로그인	rogŭin	'log in'
리얼 메이크업	riŏl meik'ŭŏp	'natural-looking (real) makeup'
리필	rip'il	'refill'
*사이트	sait'ŭ	'site'
서비스	sŏbisŭ	'service'
*서치엔진	sŏch'i enjin	'search engine'
스타줌인	sut'ajumin	'star zoom in'
스포츠렌즈	sup'och'urenjŭ	'sports lens'
*스폰서 링크	sup'ŏnsŏ ringk'ŭ	'sponsor link'
월드와이드	wŏldŭwaidŭ	'worldwide'
*웹 사이트	wep sait'ŭ	'website'
이미지 메이커	imiji meik'ŏ	'image maker'
이슈	isyu	'issue'
*인터넷 쇼핑	int'ŏnet syop'ing	'Internet shopping'
메이크업아티스트	meik'ŏp at'isŭt'ŭ	'make-up artist'
토털 뷰티살롱	to'tŏlbyut'i sallong	'total beauty salon'
스크랩	sŭk'ŭraep	'scrap'
뉴스랭킹	nyusŭraengk'ing	'news ranking'
빅뱅	pikppaeng	'big bang'
*온 오프라인	on op'ŭrain	'on-offline'
컴백	k'ŏmbaek	'comeback'
캠페인	k'aemp'ein	'campaign'
콤플렉스	k'omp'ŭleksu	'complex'
톱	t'op	'top'
포커스	p'okŏsŭ	'focus'
포토뉴스	p'ot'onyusŭ	'photo news (journalism)'
*폰트	p'ont'ŭ	'font'

In these examples, we can see a few strategies employed by Koreans in loanword adaptation. Here we discuss some of the most common strategies:

Loanword strategies:

1 For voiced obstruents (*b, d, j, g*) in word-initial positions use lax voiceless consonants (*p, t, ch, k*), as in 바베큐 [pabek'yu] 'barbecue.'
2 Use the weak [ŭ] vowel to break up an inadmissible consonant cluster into two different syllables, as in 스타 [sŭ-t'a] (← *st'a*) 'star,' or to make the syllable or word-final consonant clearer by putting it in the initial

position of the new syllable created by the insertion, as in 케이크 k'e-i-k'ŭ or 케익 k'eik (← *k'eik'*) 'cake.'

3 Since there are no off-glides other than [y] in the syllable ㅢ in Korean, original words with off-glides such as [w] in the word "down" and [y] in "sight" will become full vowels, [u] and [i] respectively, gaining a separate-syllable status, as in 다운로드 *taullodŭ* (←*taunlodŭ*) 'download' and 사이트 *sait'ŭ* 'site.'

4 Other nonexistent sounds such as [f], [v], [z], etc., are replaced by what is perceived as the closest approximation. For example, the fricative [f] is most often pronounced as an aspirated stop [p'] in initial positions as in 폰트 *p'ont'ŭ* 'font,' but in certain contexts such as before [w], [h] seems to be preferred, as in 화인 플라워 *hwain p'ullawŏ* 'fine flowers.'

Today it seems that there is no dam against the English flood to protect any language anywhere – not even in traditionally language-chauvinistic France. But in Korea the impact of English is of such magnitude that language purifiers feel they are again being colonized. To young people, however, Englishism does not connote anything like foreign domination, but they feel they are members of today's great civilization, just as their medieval ancestors regarded familiarity and facility with using literary Chinese. A good indicator of this trend is observed in the following newspaper and Web article on the opening of a new beauty salon, aimed at fashionable readers:

> 최고 스타 (sŭt'a 'star') 들의 이미지 (imiji 'image') 메이커 (meik'ŏ 'maker') 로 유명한 메이크업아티스트 (meik'ŭŏp at'isŭt'ŭ 'makeup artist')...그녀가 토털 (t'ŏt'ŏl 'total') 뷰티살롱 (pyut'isalong 'beauty salon') W퓨리피 (p'yurip'i 'purify') 를 오픈 (op'ŭn 'opening') 했다. 7월 초 오프닝 (op'ŭning 'opening') 에 참석한 아름다운 셀러브리티 (sellŏbŭrit'i 'celebrity') 5인의 메이크업 (meik'ŭŏp 'makeup') 제안 ...W퓨리피 (p'yurip'i 'purify') 의 'W' 는 'with you' 를 뜻하는 것으로 늘 고객의 입장에 서는 편안하고 친근한 서비스 (sŏbisŭ 'service') 를 나타낸다. (http://danmee.chosun.com/wdata/html/news/200608/20060829000029.html/)
>
> 'A famous makeup artist, who is famous for having created top-ranking star images with her makeup skill has opened the total beauty salon W Purify. Here are some suggestions by five beautiful celebrities who attended the opening ceremony in early July...The letter "W" in the name "W Purify" represents "with you" and means "offering comfortable and intimate service, always attentive to the customers' needs."'

Relative to Western loanwords, Koreans today exercise an interesting style of neologism. Names for products, stores, and programs are coined in such a way as to sound like loanwords from a foreign country, usually a Western nation, but also Japan. The most popular form seems to be one ending in a vowel, so that the coinages sound Spanish, Italian, or even Japanese. Sometimes the effect is achieved by using nonstandard grammar and orthographies:

Foreign-language sounding neologisms:

1 By misspelling:
누네띠네, *nunettine* ('It catches the eye!'), which sounds Italian, is a result of intentionally misspelling 눈에 <nun-e> 'to the eye' as 누네 <nu-ne>.
2 By using casual speech forms:
먹을래 사갈래 *mŏgŭllae sagallae* ('Wanna eat here or take out?') for a fast-food restaurant instead of the traditional expression, 분식점 *punsikchŏm* ('fast-food shop'), is a casual speech form that sounds French.
3 By using dialectal forms:
무까마까 *mukkamakka* ('Shall I bite/eat it or not?') rather than *hangŭl mŏkŭlkka malkka*, as a name for an eatery that indubitably sounds Japanese, is a dialectal as well as a casual form, used to communicate the intended meaning and also a humorous and intimate feeling.

As can be seen, new types of trademarks are no longer just nouns or noun phrases, but often are verbs, adverbs, or even whole sentences with foreign-sounding effect. For example, adverbial phrases such as 빼빼로 *ppaeppaero* 'in a skinny (빼빼) manner' rather than typical noun forms traditionally used for titles. The same goes with headings of newspaper articles, e.g., "5월, 문자메시지로 마술을" (*owŏl, muntcha mesiji-ro masul-ŭl*) which is a cut-off sentence meaning something like '[in the month of] May, [create your own] magic with text message,' for which the reader will supply a verb like 'create' or 'experience.'

Semantic change is a common phenomenon in borrowing. For example, the frequently used loanword 리얼 *riŏl* does not usually mean something 'real' in the sense of 'not imagined' but rather 'natural-looking,' 'realistic,' or even 'pure and unadulterated.' Likewise, 메모 *memo* means 'message.'

Innovative language dissection is also common in loanwords. For example, Americans have created *cheeseburger*, *chickenburger*, and *fishburger* from *hamburger*, which is wrongly analyzed as coming from "ham + burger." Korean examples of this sort are numerous. For instance, the first vowel of the English word *utopia* is amputated, leaving a combining form appended to another foreign or Korean word, e.g., 북토피아 *puktop'ia* ('book'-*topia*), 맛토피아 *mattop'ia* (*mat* 'taste'-*topia*).

Neologisms of this kind are particularly popular among the so-called N-generation ("Net-generation," born between the 1970s and 1990s) when they are communicating electronically. Even a quick look at a few electronic chats these days will leave the uninitiated completely lost in the new cyber-dialect of Korean. These young people find such coinages novel, chic, humorous, cute, and close to the heart, if a little silly.

Borrowing is not just lexical; it extends to syntax and discourse-pragmatics. When only a sentence structure is taken but disguised in translation – sounding like original Korean – such as 좋은 하루 되세요 *choŭn haru toeseyo* ('Have a good day'), the result is actually adopted even by purification activists, who tend to be worried mainly about lexical borrowing.

Language purists are constantly coining new pure Korean-based words to replace what they perceive as a "foreign intrusion" into the Korean language. For example, most of the professional organizations are called 연합 *yŏnhap* 'association,' 위원회 *wiwŏnhoe* 'committee,' or 협회 *hyŏphoe* 'society' – all based on Sino-Korean, but a word for 'gathering' 모임 *moim*, which used to be used only in an informal setting, is employed by many to describe a large organization or a task force. However, the purification effort seems to be mainly aimed against Sino-Korean and Japanese loanwords. Even in an advertisement for a *han'gŭl* learning kit carried in *Han'gŭl Saesosik*, a magazine engaged in a *han'gŭl*-only campaign, the very title and catchphrase of the announcement, "우리말을 게임[*keim* 'game']으로 '돌려라 한글 퍼즐 [*p'ŏjŭl* 'puzzle']" '(Learn Korean through Games: Solve it! *Han'gŭl* Puzzle),' include English loanwords (*Han'gŭl Saesosik* No. 422, October 2007). The long text of the advertisement is filled with English loanwords, even where Korean equivalents are easily available, e.g., 캐릭터 *k'aerikt'ŏ* instead of 인물 *inmul* for 'character,' 팁 *t'ip* instead of 귀띔 *kwittwim* for 'tip,' 플레이 *p'ŭllei* instead of 놀이 *nori* 'play.'

As Korea has recovered from the financial crisis of 1997 and prospered, the dynamics of cultural, academic, scientific, and commercial exchanges have changed. Korea today is like most countries of the developed world, where the populace is rapidly becoming Americanized and English is being imported uncontrollably. Korea is one of the most wired countries in the world today, and the Internet draws Koreans closer to the world of English.

There has even been a proposal to make English a second official language. Koreans are some of the most ardent travelers today, and study abroad is almost routine for whoever can afford it and even for those who cannot. Furthermore, the ascent of English no longer just involves Koreans going abroad to study. It is now possible to go to school entirely in English in Korea; at the least, many universities offer a significant proportion of their classes in English. Many native speakers of English are teaching in such institutions. Even primary school students are learning English as a required subject. Many families have relatives living abroad, whom they visit regularly and who come to see them in Korea. Koreans in the diaspora, as well as in Korea, are gaining international prominence in almost every field. Once again Koreans are borrowing foreign words in a spirit of being part of the civilization of the superpower, not as something imposed by an unwelcome occupying force.

Chapter 6

Verbs

A verb is a content word that denotes an event, i.e., an action or a state. A verb serves as the predicate of a sentence – some examples are given with the plain ending, -다 *ta*:

먹다	mŏk-ta	'eat'	쓰다	ssŭ-ta	'write'
자다	cha-ta	'sleep'	뛰다	ttwi-ta	'jump'
좁다	chop-ta	'be narrow'	깊다	kip-ta	'be deep'
–이다	–i-ta	'be (equate with, equal)'	아니다	ani-ta	'not be'
있다	iss-ta	'exist, have'	없다	ŏps-ta	'not exist, not have'

6.1 General properties of verbs

The verb is the most important part of the sentence in most languages because without a verb there is no sentence – only a fragment.

A crucial step toward mastering Korean grammar, therefore, is to understand verb nature and construction. The following are some key points to remember.

1 The verb comes last in a sentence but it is the most important part of the sentence.

So, in English one says, "I love kimch'i," but its word-by-word translation into an equivalent sentence in Korean would be 'I kimch'i love':

나는	김치를	좋아해.
na-nŭn	kimch'i-lŭl	chohahae.
I-top	kimch'i-obj	love

In English and most European languages, a verb appears right after the subject, and the hearer can tell early on what the sentence is about. So, when someone says:

"Brutus killed ..."

the hearer knows the sentence is about Brutus having killed somebody. It is a clear declarative statement of an action that Brutus committed.

As the "head" or essential element of a unit comes at the end in Korean, the main verb comes at the end of a sentence. Therefore, when someone says:

로미오가	줄리엣을 ...
romio-ka	chullies-ŭl
Romeo-Subj	Juliet-Obj

there is no telling what the sentence is about. The list of possible verbs and their forms is infinite: 'loves,' 'may love,' 'hates,' 'hated,' 'will see,' 'did not meet,' 'misunderstands,' 'is it true that Romeo loved/hates/saw/...Juliet,' etc.

Again, pay attention to what comes at the end of a sentence, i.e., the verb.

2 A verb by itself can form a sentence.

The subject and the object of a sentence are often deleted when these are considered obvious in context. Thus a verb alone can form a complete sentence. For example, the sentence:

찾았다!
ch'ach-ass-ta!
find-Past-Dec/Plain
'(I) found (it)!'

consists of only a verb; its logical subject 'I' and object 'it' are elided because the context in which this sentence would have occurred would make them obvious.

3 Verbs are inflected.

Korean is an *agglutinative* language. Words are created by "gluing" suffixes to the core or base of a word called a *stem*. A suffix is a bound form, which cannot stand by itself, but must be attached to a stem, expanding its meaning or specifying its grammatical function.

In English, *-ed*, *-s*, *-ing* are verb inflections. They are suffixes attached to the end of the base form of the verb, as shown in such forms as *cooked*, *cooks*, and *cooking*.

Korean verbs are inflected, too, but Korean verb forms are much richer and more varied than English, with many different kinds of suffixes that can follow them. A Korean word, especially a verb, can be quite long because of all the suffixes that mark grammatical contrasts. That is why Korean is called an agglutinative, polysyllabic language.

Every verb form in a Korean sentence has two parts: a *verb stem*, simple or expanded, plus a sequence of *inflectional suffixes*. The structure of a verb is as follows (where the hyphen means the item carrying it is not independent and cannot stand by itself, and the subscripted one [X_1] means 'one or more X').

$[[\quad]_{\text{Verb Stem}} - [\quad]_{\text{Suffix 1}}]_{\text{Verb}}$

A verb stem must be followed by at least one suffix. The obligatory suffix is the sentence ender with appropriate choice of speech style.

Dictionaries list verb stems with the basic plain-style sentence ender, -다 *ta*, added to the stem, because Korean speakers in effect think unbound verb forms are not even pronounceable. For example the dictionary entry for the verb 'to find' is listed as 찾다 *ch'ach-ta* instead of just the basic form 찾 *ch'ach-*. So, in order to obtain the verb stem from the dictionary entry, simply delete -다 *ta*:

Verb form in dictionary		Verb stem
찾다 ch'ach-ta	→	찾 ch'ach-

It is the general custom for Korean dictionaries to list verbs in their -다 *ta* form, called the *citation form*.

4 Verb suffixes are numerous but regular and ordered.

There are over 40 basic endings (Lee and Ramsey 2000: 221), but over 400 when the combinations of these endings are counted (Martin 1992: 244). Verb suffixes are used only when needed except for the sentence ender, which is obligatory.

Do not be threatened by the quantity of these suffixes. They are *regular* and *recurrent* in different words. The basic part of a word you should memorize is usually very short and consists of only one or two syllables, as you can see in the dictionary entries. You only have to learn them as you would learn any vocabulary item.

Grammatical categories of verb suffixes include *voice* (passive or causative), *tense* (past, present, or future), *aspect* (of an action – complete, experienced, repeated, or continuing), *honorification* (appropriate choice of suffix following language protocol), and clause-final conjunctives or sentence enders chosen from various speech styles and types of sentences such as interrogative, declarative, imperative, and suggestive.

5 The order of verb inflections is presented schematically in Figure 6.1.

Verb Stem – ①Voice – ②Subject Honorific – ③Tense/Aspect – ④Modality – ⑤Mood

Figure 6.1 Order of verb suffixes

The following is an example of a verb with all five kinds of suffixes:

잡 –	①히 –	②시–	③었–	④겠 –	④더 –	⑤라
chap –	hi –	si –	ŏss –	kess –	tŏ –	ra
catch –	Pass –	SH –	Past –	Sup –	Ret –	Dec/Plain

'(From what I observed, I tell you that) chances are (the honorable) he or she would have been arrested.'

The order of verb suffixes shows that those that are "stem-expanding" such as passives and causatives, and the subject honorification suffix, naturally occur close to the stem, and suffixes indicating modality and addressee honorification, which by definition consider the broader scope of the speaker's attitude in discourse, are found at the end. Other suffixes that are time-related, such as tense and aspect markers, are placed in between.

6.2 Types of verbs

Korean thus has four types of verbs: *action*, *stative*, *copulative*, and *existential*. Action or processive verbs involve some action or internal movement. Stative verbs simply depict situations that are static and unchanging (at least temporarily). A great portion of grammatical constructions depends on whether a verb is active or stative. Copulative and existential verbs form special classes of their own, although they are subsets of stative verbs.

6.2.1 Action verbs

Action verbs, also known as processive verbs, are dynamic verbs meaning 'do X' or 'X happens.' These include verbs denoting mental processes such as 'think' and 'love.'

Action verbs are either transitive or intransitive. Transitive verbs are directed onto, at, or toward a noun phrase, which is called an *object*. Verbs not requiring an object are intransitive.

6.2.1.1 *Transitive verbs*

Transitive verbs include:

먹-	mŏk-	'eat'
읽-	ilk-	'read'
쓰-	ssŭ-	'write'
주-	chu-	'give'
공부하-	kongbuha-	'study (do studies)'
좋아하-	chohaha-	'like'

A transitive verb is used in a sentence with an object noun, as shown below:

나는 황진이 시를 좋아한다.
na-nŭn hwang chini si-lŭl chohaha-n-ta.
I-Top Hwang Chini poem-Obj like-Pres-Dec/Plain
'I like Hwang Chini's poems.'

6.2.1.2 *Intransitive verbs*

Intransitive verbs include:

가-	ka-	'go'
자-	cha-	'sleep'
달리-	talli-	'run'
놀-	nol-	'play'
식-	sik-	'cool off, become cold'

An intransitive verb does not take an object:

국이 식었어요.
kuk-i sik-ŏss-ŏyo.
soup-Subj become cold-Past-Dec/Pol
'The soup got cold.'

6.2.2 *Stative verbs*

Stative verbs express a state or condition of the subject. For this reason they are sometimes considered as *adjectives*.

What is expressed by the sequence of *be* + adjective in English is expressed by *just a verb* in Korean. Such verbs, which require only a subject, are called *stative* or *adjectival*. Unlike English adjectives, which need a copula, Korean stative verbs do not. English speakers are warned to resist the temptation to add the copula 'be' to stative verbs, although they are often referred to as adjectival verbs or even adjectives by some linguists.

Stative verbs include:

착하-	ch'akha-	'be good'
크-	k'ŭ-	'be big'
높-	nop'-	'be high'
맑-	malk-	'be clear'
조용하-	choyongha-	'be quiet'
시끄럽-	sikkŭrŏp-	'be noisy'
깨끗하-	kkaekkŭtha-	'be clean'

Unlike English adjectives, Korean stative verbs are not modifiers of nouns, and they are never followed by nouns. They form a subset of verbs, occupying the same position as processive verbs in the sentence, i.e., at the end. Stative verbs have inflections as do all other verbs. It is useful, therefore, to view this group of words as verbs rather than adjectives.

A group of stative verbs denoting personal assessment, such as 좋 *choh-* 'be nice, good' and 슬프 *sŭlp'ŭ-* 'be sad,' belongs to a class of verbs that herein will be referred to as *emotive* or *psyche* verbs. In translating these verbs into Korean, one may use an implied phrase such as '... to me' as a mnemonic device. Here are some more examples of psyche verbs:

밉다	mip-ta	'be dislikable'
춥다	ch'up-ta	'feel cold'
고맙다	komap-ta	'feel grateful'
무섭다	musŏp-ta	'feel scary'
쉽다	swip-ta	'be easy'

Sentences with psyche verbs are always from the speaker's personal point of view. Therefore, when speaking of others' feelings or points of view, one cannot use these verbs, except when they occur in a question.

So, you can say "I am sad" or "Are you sad?" but not *"My brother is sad" or "Is he sad?" in Korean. Korean speakers, except for narrators of a novel or an essay, cannot enter the psyche of other people but can only speak for themselves.

One can, however, "report" a third person's feelings with an action verb derived from a psyche verb by adding the verb root -하 *ha-* meaning 'to do' with the union vowel vowel -어 *ŏ-* connecting them. The resulting action verb is a transitive one requiring an object.

Compare a psyche verb with its corresponding action verb:

Psyche verb	vs.	Action verb
'X is Y'		'X assesses the situation to be Y.'
슬프-		슬퍼하-
sŭlp'ŭ-		sŭlp'-ŏ-ha-
'X is sad'		'X laments...'

These verbs are used in sentences as follows:

(i) (나-는) 슬프다!
na-nŭn sŭlp'ŭ-ta!
I-Top be sad-Dec/Plain
'I am sad!'

(ii) (너-는) 슬프니?
nŏ-nŭn sŭlp'ŭ-ni?
You-Top be sad-Q/Plain
'Are you sad?'

(iii) 미나는 X-를 슬퍼한다.
mina-nŭn -lŭl sŭlp'ŏ-ha-n-ta.
Mina-Top -Obj lament-do-Pres-Dec/Plain
'Mina laments X.' [*lit.* 'Mina considers X sad.']'

If the subject is elided as in example (i) above, there is no question that the implied subject is the first-person singular. If it is an interrogative sentence as in (ii), then the absent subject will be the second person. However, when the subject is a third person, then the stative verb must become an action verb, as shown in example (iii).

Characteristics of stative verbs

While stative verbs have inflections like action verbs, they are not compatible with certain grammatical forms that action verbs allow.

This constraint is due to their inherent meaning of stativity and no action. For example:

1 Stative verbs may not have an imperative ending. Imperatives are used in commanding or requesting someone to **do** something. In Korean, one cannot order someone to **be** a certain way. So, sentences such as:

*슬퍼라! sŭlp'ŏra! * 'Be sad!' and
*슬프자! sŭlp'ŭja! * 'Let us be sad!'

are ungrammatical.

2 Stative verbs may not have a progressive ending, again because they are simply describing a stative condition or quality. So, it is impossible to say:

*미나가 착하고 있다.
mina-ka ch'akha-ko iss-ta.
Mina-Subj be good-hearted- be-Exist-
*'Mina is being good-hearted.'

3 Stative verbs may not have the plain dynamic present tense, -는 *nŭn*, which implies process. So, it is ungrammatical to say:

*미나가 크는다.
mina-ka k'ŭ-nŭn-ta.
Mina-Subj be big-Pres-Dec/Plain
*'Mina is big (at present).'

4 Stative verbs may not have a goal-oriented suffix, again because they are stative. So, it makes no sense to say a sentence like:

*슬프려고
sŭlp'ŭ-ryŏgo
-in order to
*'in order to be sad'

6.2.3 *Equational copula,* -이다 i-ta / -아니다 ani-ta *'to be' / 'not to be'*

The Korean equative verbs referred to herein as copulative are much like the English copulas ('be' verbs) which are used to predicate nouns in sentences such as "Life **is / is not** art." However Korean copulas differ from English ones in crucial ways, as shown in the sections that follow.

The affirmative form of the copula is -이다 *i-ta* 'be,' and the negative 아니다 *ani-ta* 'not be.' It is important to remember, however, that, although -이다 *i-ta* and 아니다 *ani-ta* are both copulative verbs, each requires a distinct sentence structure.

Note: Do not use the Korean copula to express existence or with an adjective complement.

1 The copula 'be' never indicates the existence of something in some location in the way the English copula *be* can.

So, never say:

*여동생이	영국에	이다/아니다.
yŏ-tongsaeng-i	yŏngguk-e	*i-ta-/ani-ta.
sister-Subj	England-Loc	*be/not be
		be-Cop

*'My sister is (not) in England.'

Instead, use existentials 있다/없다 [▶6.2.4] for this purpose as in:

여동생이 영국에 있다/없다.
iss-ta/ ŏps-ta.
be-Exist
'My sister is (not) in England.'

2 The copula can never be used with an adjective complement. So, do not look for a Korean equivalent for *be (not)* in the English sentence *'My sister is (not) smart.'

So, never say:

*여동생이	(안)	똑똑하	이다/아니다.
	(an)	ttokttokha	i-ta-/ani-ta.
	(Neg)	be smart	be-Cop/not be-Cop

*'My sister is (not) smart.'

Instead, use stative verbs, which need no copula [▶6.2.2].

여동생이	(안)	똑똑하다.
	(an)	ttokttokha-ta.
	(Neg)	is smart

'My sister is (not) smart.'

6.2.3.1 *Affirmative copula* -이다 i-ta *'to be'*

When one wants to say, 'NP_1 **is** NP_2' in English, one uses the following construction:

$[NP_1$	Cop	$NP_2]_S$
Time	is	money.

To say the same thing in Korean, use the copula -이다 *i-ta* 'be' to equate two nouns, with the second one (NP_2) identifying the first one (NP_1).

However, the copula here is part of a verb-like construction meaning 'be NP_2.' In an affirmative sentence with a copula, the first noun is marked as the subject (or topic, etc.), and the second noun is attached directly to the copula -이다 *i-ta* 'be.' The copula verb takes the following position in a typical sentential structure,

[[시간-이] $_{NP1}$ [[돈] $_{NP2}$이다]$_V$]$_S$.
sigan-i ton-*i*-ta.
time-Subj money-Cop-Dec/Plain
'Time is money.'

where both NP_1 and NP_2 are noun phrases, both of which consist of single nouns, and the hyphen between NP_2 and the copula indicates the two elements surrounding it are bound to each other, acting as one unit.

Here are more examples:

제주도-가 천국이다.
chejudo-ka ch'on'guk-i-ta.
Cheju Island-Subj paradise-Cop-Dec/Plain
'Cheju Island is a paradise.'

인생-은 꿈이다.
insaeng-ŭn kkum-i-ta.
life-Top dream-Cop-Dec/Plain
'Life is a dream.'

Although the second noun in each of the above looks like a subject complement in English, it does not carry a subject marker and is attached to the copula as if the noun and the copula are forming an extended verb stem together. The noun in this case is not a true subject complement but is part of a verbal construction. So, even though it is made of two parts, noun and copula in fact form a single unit and are pronounced as one word, i.e., without any break in between, even in slow speech. Orthographically, too, the two parts are written without a space, as one word, as shown in the above examples 돈이다, 천국이다 and 꿈이다.

Note: There may be a historical reason for the lack of a subject marker for the second noun. Today there are two kinds of subject markers, -가 *ka* after a vowel and -이 *i* after a consonant [▶8.5.1.1]. Until the late sixteenth century, however, there was only one subject marker, -이 *i*, and two identical vowels -이이 *ii* merged into a single -이 *i* when the subject marker -이 *i* and copula -이 *i-* joined. This change eventually affected the sentence structure containing the affirmative copula.

Although a copula is a verb, it has important characteristics that set it apart from other verbs.

*Some characteristics of the copula -이다 **i-ta**:*

1 In an affirmative sentence, the copula -이 *i* acts as a suffix rather than a full-fledged verb. It is obligatorily attached to the noun, while other verbs are not. Orthographically, the two units are treated as a word.
2 Unlike other verbs, which can stand by themselves to form sentences as long as the other parts are understood, the copula cannot stand by itself even if the noun it is attached to may appear redundant, thanks to its suffix-like nature.

Thus one cannot have the following sort of exchange:

한국사람 이에요?
han'guksaram i-eyo (←ŏyo)?
Korean Cop-Q/Pol
'Are you Korean?'

*네, 이에요.
Ne, i-eyo.
Yes, Cop-Dec/Pol
*'Yes, am/is/are.'

3 This copula is often dropped because of its relatively light semantic load; its meaning is easily reconstructible from the other parts of the sentence. Therefore, the copula -이 *i* is treated almost as a suffix, which explains its lack of autonomy.

A. The most common case of deletion is when the copula -이 *i* follows a noun which ends in a vowel. Compare:

학생-이에요.	vs.	친구-에요. (←친구이에요.)
haksaeng-i-eyo.		ch'in'gu-eyo.
student-Cop-Dec/Pol		friend-(Cop)-Dec/Pol
'X is a student.'		'X is a friend.'

This is also related to the tendency for Korean to avoid pronouncing two vowels in a row.

B. Careful and casual varieties:

a. In careful speech, for emphasis or clarity, the full form may be given even after a vowel-final noun.

친구-이에요.		친구-예요.
ch'in'gu-i-eyo.	→	ch'in'gu-yeyo.
Friend-Cop-Dec/Pol		
'X is a friend.'		

b. Exceptionally, the copula can be dropped in a casual speech form, 이에요 *i-eyo*, even when following a noun ending in a consonant.

대학생-에요.
taehaksang-eyo.
college student-be-Dec/Pol
'X is a college student.'

Here the sentence missing the copula -이 *i* is a possible sentence, but note that there is no such sentence as *대학생다 for 대학생이다 'X is a college student.'

6.2.3.2 *Negative copula* 아니다 ani-ta *'not to be'*

In a sentence with the negative copula, 아니 *ani-* (← 안 *an* + 이 *i*) 'not be,' the subject marker does emerge. Both the subject of the sentence and the complement of the negative copula *ani-* bear subject markers, thereby forming the so-called double-subject sentences:

NP_1	NP_2	아니다.	**'A is not B'**

돈이	약이	아니다.
ton-i	yak-i	an-i-ta.
money-Subj	medicine-Subj	Neg-Cop-Dec/Plain

'Money is not the cure.'

[The historical 안-이 sequence has come to be reanalyzed as one unit and therefore is spelled 아니 today under the principle of maximization of a CV syllable.]

자동차**가**	문제**가**	**아니다**.
chadongch'a-ka	munje-ka	ani-ta.
car-Subj	problem-Subj	not be-Dec/Plain

'The car is not the problem.'

친구**가**	화가**가**	**아니다**.
ch'in'gu-ka	hwaga-ka	ani-ta.
friend-Subj	painter-Subj	not be-Dec/Plain

'(My) friend is not a painter.'

Note that a copula in its negative form can stand by itself, forming a sentence, because the semantic load is increased, as one is saying 'something is **not** something.' Therefore, the following exchange is a completely possible and acceptable one:

미국 사람 이세요?
miguk saram-i-s-eyo?
American person-Cop-Hon-Q/Pol
'Are you American?'

아니에요.
ani-eyo.
not be-Dec/Pol
'(I) am not.'

6.2.3.3 *Alternate shapes of copulative verbs*

1 The -어요 *ŏyo* forms of the copula, 이 *i-* and 아니 *ani-*, have the following shapes:

-이 + 어요 → 이어요 iŏyo, (이)에요 (i)eyo, (이)예요 (i)yeyo 'to be'
-아니 + 어요 → 아니어요 aniŏyo, 아니에요 anieyo, 아녜요 anyeyo, 아뇨 anyo 'not to be'

2 The copula 이 *i-* is usually dropped when following a vowel-final noun except in very careful pronunciation:

누나가 의사다. [의사이다 in careful pronunciation]
nuna-ka ŭisa-(i)-ta.
elder sister-Subj doctor-(Cop)-Dec
'(My) elder sister is a doctor.'

However, the copula cannot be dropped when it is followed by a suffix beginning with the vowel 어 *ŏ*. Therefore, there are no such forms as *NP-어요, *NP-어도, or *NP-어서, etc. For example, the following sentence:

누나가 의사이어도
nuna-ka ŭisa-i-ŏdo
elder sister- Subj doctor-Cop-even if
'Even if (someone's) elder sister is a doctor...'

cannot be replaced by a sentence like *누나가 의사어도, where the copula -이 *i* is missing.

6.2.4 ***Existential* 있 iss- *'exist, have'***

The existential verb 있 *iss-* appearing in a sentence of the type,

[X-Subj 있- ...]$_S$

essentially means 'X exists' in the following two contexts:

(i) somewhere
(ii) to someone

The first, therefore, always denotes some kind of locational (either physical or psychological) existence. The second one expresses possession.

6.2.4.1 To indicate locational existence

The existential verb 있 *iss-* occurs most naturally and commonly with the locational particle used for -에 *e* 'in, on, at, over':

학교가	워싱턴에	있어요.
hakkyo-ka	wŏsingt'on-e	iss-ŏyo.
school-Subj	Washington-Loc	Exist-Dec/Pol

'The school is in Washington.'

The honorific form of 있 *iss-* is 계시 *kyesi-*. Observe:

선생님이	서울에	계세요.
sŏnsaengnim-i	sŏul-e	kyese-yo.
teacher-Subj	Seoul-Loc	Exist/Hon-Dec/Pol

'The teacher is in Seoul."

What are usually expressed by prepositions in English and other Indo-European languages are expressed in Korean by a combination of *place noun + locative particle* -에 *e*, meaning something like 'at,' 'in,' 'on,' (noun phrase). It is a little like saying 'in front of' instead of 'before' in English.

집이	극장	앞에	있어요.	'My house is
chip-i	kŭktchang	ap'-e	iss-ŏyo.	in front of a theater.'
house-Subj	theater	front-Loc	Exist-Dec/Pol	
		뒤 twi		'My house is
				in **back** of a theater.'
		옆 yŏp'		on the side of
		위 wi		on top of
		밑 mit'		on the bottom of, below
		아래 arae		on the lower part of
		안 an		inside
		바깥/밖 pakkat'/pakk		outside

6.2.4.2 To denote possession

In this usage, a dative case marker, i.e., -에게 *ege*, -한테 *hant'e*, -께 *kke*, is attached to the possessor noun overtly or covertly, literally indicating 'Something exists to/for someone.'

나한테 표가 있어요.
na-hant'e p'yo-ka iss-ŏyo.
me-Dat ticket-Subj Exist-Dec/Pol
'I have tickets.' [*lit.* 'to me tickets exist.']

When denoting possession, do not use the honorific verb 계시 *kyesi-* but simply the subject honorific suffix -으시 *ŭsi*:

선생님은 표가 있으세요.
sŏnsaengnim-ŭn p'yo-ka iss-ŭs-eyo.
teacher-Top ticket-Subj Exist/Hon-Dec/Pol
'The teacher has a ticket.' [*lit.* 'Talking of the teacher, a ticket exists (with him/her).']

Table 6.1 Summary of copula and existential verbs

	Equational		Existential			
	(= Cop 'be')		(= Exist 'be')		(= Exist 'have')	
	Neutral	Subj-Honorific	Neutral	Subj-Honorific	Neutral	Subj-Honorific
Affirmative	이다 i-ta	이시다 i-si-ta	있다 iss-ta	계시다 kye-si-ta	있다 iss-ta	있으시다 iss-ŭ-si-ta
Negative	아니다 ani-ta	아니시다 ani-si-ta	없다 ŏps-ta	안계시다 an-kye-si-ta	없다 ŏps-ta	없으시다 ŏps-ŭsi-ta

6.3 Making new verbs

6.3.1 Forming a verb by adding the suffix -하 ha to a noun

There is a very productive process in Korean which converts a noun into a verb form. This is called *denominalization* or *verbalization*. This process is achieved by adding the verbalizing suffix -하 *ha* to the noun form:

$[\text{NP} + 하\text{- ha-}]_V$

This suffix comes from the transitive verb 하 *ha-* 'do, make, perform, execute.'

Compare the following two sets of sentences.

1 a. 미나-가 요리-를 해요.
mina-ka yori-lŭl hae-yo.
mina-Subj cuisine-Obj do-Dec/Pol
'Mina does the cooking.'

b. 미나-가 생선-을 [[요리]$_{NP}$-해요]$_{V}$.
mina-ka saengsŏn-ŭl yori-hae-yo.
who-Subj fish-Obj cook-do-Dec/Pol
'Mina cooks fish.'

2 a. 아저씨-가 친구에게 칭찬을 했어요.
ajŏssi-ka ch'in'gu-ege ch'ingch'an-ŭl hae-ss-ŏyo.
uncle-Subj friend-Dat praise-Obj do-Past-Dec/Pol
'My uncle gave praise to my friend.'

b. 아저씨-가 친구-를 [[칭찬]$_{N}$했어요.
ajŏssi-ka ch'in'gu-lŭl ch'ingch'an-hae-ss-ŏyo.
uncle-Subj friend-Obj praise-do-Past-Dec/Pol
'My uncle praised my friend.'

As you can see, the nouns in the above examples are *action nouns*, and the resulting verb is an action verb. However, when *descriptive nouns or noun-like forms* are denominalized, they become stative verbs: in this case, the 하 *ha-* part is better translated into English as 'be' rather than as 'do.'

기숙사는 [[편리]$_{N}$해요]$_{V}$.
kisuksa-nŭn p'yŏlli-haeyo.
dorm-top convenient-be
'The dorm **is convenient**.'

아파트-가 [[조용]$_{N}$해요]$_{V}$.
ap'at'ŭ-ka choyong-haeyo.
apartment-Subj quiet-be
'The apartment **is quiet**.'

차-가 [[필요]$_{N}$해요]$_{V}$.
ch'a-ka p'iryo-haeyo.
car-Subj necessary-be
'A car **is necessary**.'

These suffixes may also be added to certain adverbs, especially the sound-symbolic type, to make verbs. For example:

옷이 [[알록달록]Adv-해요]$_V$.
os-i alloktallok-haeyo.
clothes-Subj in multi colors-be
'The clothes **are multi-colored**.'

눈이 [[반짝반짝]Adv -해요]$_V$.
nun-i pantchakpantchak-haeyo.
eyes-Subj with twinkles-be
'(His/her) eyes **are twinkling**.'

길이 [[질퍽질퍽]Adv -해요]$_V$.
kir-i chilp'ŏkjilp'ŏk- haeyo.
road-Subj slushily-be
'The road **is muddy**.'

Note: Foreign words are analyzed as nouns regardless of their part of speech in their original language. Observe the following example:

[[[데이트]$_N$를]$_{NP}$ [해요]$_V$]$_{VP}$?
teit'ŭ-lŭl hae-yo?
date-Obj do-Dec/Pol
'Are you going out with someone?' [*lit.* 'Do you do date?']

To obtain the verb meaning 'date, go out with,' you should add the verbalizing suffix -하 *ha* to the borrowed noun 데이트 *teit'ŭ* 'dating' as in [[데이트]$_N$하다]$_V$ 'date (someone).'

6.3.2 *Forming verbs with other suffixes*

Some other verbalizing suffixes include:

1 -답 *tap* 'is like an X (= noun) should':

[[여자 (yŏja 'woman')]$_N$답다]$_V$	'be womanly'
[[학생 (haksaeng 'student')]$_N$답다]$_V$	'be student-like'
[[한국사람 (han'guksaram 'Korean')]$_N$답다]$_V$	'be very (positively) Korean'
[[신부 (sinbu 'priest')]$_N$답다]$_V$	'be priestly'

2 -스럽 *sŭrŏp* 'be...-ish, give the aura of X (= noun)'

[[존경 (chongyŏng 'respect')]$_N$스럽다]$_V$ 'be respectful'
[[자랑 (charang 'pride')]$_N$스럽다]$_V$ 'make someone proud of...'
[[촌 (ch'on 'countryside')]$_N$스럽다]$_V$ 'be rustic'
[[수치 (such' i 'shame')]$_N$스럽다]$_V$ 'be shameful'

3 -거리 *kŏri* 'repeating the act of X (= adverb)'

[[중얼 (chungŏl 'mumbling')]$_{Adv}$거리다]$_V$ 'mumble'
[[아른 (arun 'flickering')]$_{Adv}$거리다]$_V$ 'glisten'
[[살랑 (salrang 'softly, rustling')]$_{Adv}$거리다]$_V$ 'blow gently, rustle around'
[[비틀 (bit'ŭl 'staggeringly')]$_{Adv}$거리다]$_V$ 'stagger'

6.4 Voice

Verb stems are *active*, *passive*, or *causative*. What distinguishes one from another is called *voice*. Voice indicates the relation between the subject of the sentence and the action expressed by the verb. Active verbs are not marked for voice, but passive and causative verbs are.

6.4.1 Passive voice

When the passive voice is used, the grammatical subject of the sentence is the recipient, not the source, of the action expressed by the verb, as we can see in the English passive sentence "*My car was sold by a dealer*," or in its abbreviated version "*My car was sold*." In a passive sentence, the object of the verb in an equivalent active sentence takes the subject particle, and the actual agent of the verb takes a dative form, -에 *e*, -에게 *ege*, -한테 *hant'e*, or -께 *kke* or a phrase -에 의하여 *e ŭihayŏ* 'following (the will of)..., by (the power of)...' A passive sentence, therefore, has the following structure:

[NP_2-subj $\underline{NP_1\text{-Dat.}}$ V_{Pass}]S_{Pass}
Agent Phrase

Compare passive and active sentences:

Active

[N P_1-Subj NP_2-Obj V_{Act}]S_{Act}
sun'gyŏng-i mina-lŭl chap-ass-ta
police-Subj mina-Obj catch-Past-Dec/Plain
'The police caught Mina.'

Passive

[NP_2-Subj NP_1-Dat V_{Pass}]S_{Pass}
mina-ka sun'gyŏng-hant'e chap-hy-ŏss-ta
Mina-Subj police-Dat catch-Pass-Past-Dec/Plain
'Mina was caught by the police.'

Only transitive verbs, i.e., those with an object, can be passivized by suffixation. The passive suffix has four different variants. The basic passive suffix form is -이 *i*; the other forms are its variants with extra consonants inserted to clarify the boundary between two important meaning-carrying elements (basic stem and passive suffix) within a verb stem.

The passive suffixes are -이 *i*, -리 *li*, -기 *ki*, and -히 *hi*. The choice depends on the last sound of the preceding verb stem.

Passive suffixes

1 -이 *i* when the verb stem ends in a vowel (an intervening *h* is as if it were not there):

보 po-	vs.	보이 po-i-	'see/be seen'
쌓 ssah-		쌓이 ssah-i-	'pile up/piled up'

2 -리 *li* when the verb stem ends in *l* (ㄹ).

팔 p'al-	vs.	팔리 p'alli-	'sell/be sold'
물 mul-		물리 mulli-	'bite/be bitten'

[*Note:* An extra *l* is inserted to maintain a clear boundary between stem and suffix.]

3 -기 *ki* when the verb stem ends in a nasal (an intervening *h* as if it were not there):

심 sim-	vs.	심기 sim-ki-	'plant/be planted'
끊 kkŭnh-		끊기 kkŭnk'i-	'cut/be cut'

4 -히 *hi* elsewhere:

잡 chap-	vs.	잡히 chaphi-	'catch/be caught'
읽 ilk'-		읽히 ilk'i (←ilkhi)-	'read/be read'

These suffixes turn a limited number of active verbs into passive verbs. However, it is important to remember that some passive forms do not have corresponding active forms as in English, e.g., "He was drunk."

길이 막혔다.
kil-i mak-hy-ŏss-ta.
road-Subj block-Pass-Past-Dec/Plain
'The road is congested.' [*lit.* 'The road is blocked' no real agent is known.]

Another increasingly productive way to passivize a verb is by the use of an auxiliary verb -어 지다 *ŏ chi-ta* 'become. . . .' For example:

이 책이 요새 대학생들에게 많이 읽어지고
i ch'aeg-i yosae taehaksaengdŭl-ege manhi ilg-ŏjigo
this book-Subj these days college students-Dat a lot read-Pass
있다.
iss-ta.
be/Prog-Dec/Plain
'This book is popular among many college students these days.'
[*lit.* 'This book is read a lot by college students.']

Passive sentences were not as common in Korean as they are now, and older speakers find sentences like this example unnatural. However, through Koreans' contact with foreign languages, such sentences are used more and more frequently, especially by the younger generation.

Denominalized verbs of the N +*ha-* form such as 수정하다 *sujŏngha-ta* 'revise' and 보장하다 *pojangha-ta* 'guarantee' are passivized by replacing 하 *ha-* with 되 *toe-* 'become':

[NP-하 ha]$_{\text{VActive}}$ → [NP-되 toe]$_{\text{VPassive}}$

건축사가 도안을 수정하였다.
kŏnch'uksa-ka toan-ŭl sujŏng-hay-ŏss-ta.
architect-Subj plan-Obj [revision-do]V_{Active} -Past-Dec/Plain
'The architect revised the plan.'

도안이 건축사에 의하여 수정되었다.
toan-i kŏnch'uksa-e ŭihayŏ sujŏng-toe-ŏss-ta.
plan-Subj architect-Loc by [be revised]$_{VPassive}$-Past-Dec/Plain
'The plan was revised by the architect.'

6.4.2 *Causative voice*

In Korean, as in many other languages such as English, French, and Japanese, passive and causative meanings share a basic conceptual structure from which the two forms branch out. Causative suffixes are very similar to the passive with a few variations:

Causative suffixes

1 -추 *ch'u* after ㅈ (*ch*) or ㅊ (*ch'*)

맞 mach vs. 맞추 mach-ch'u- 'be correct/fit'
늦 nŭch- 늦추 nŭch-ch'u- 'be late/postpone'

2 -이우 *iu* after a vowel with an orthographic <i>

자 cha- vs. 재우 chae-u (←cha-iu) 'sleep/put to sleep'
서 sŏ- 세우 se-u (←sŏ-iu) 'stand/establish, set straight'

3 -이 *i* when the verb stem ends in vowel other than one with an orthographic <i> or after ㄱ (*k*):

보 po- vs. 보이 poi- 'see/show'
먹 mŏk 먹이 mŏgi- 'eat/feed'

4 -리 *li* when the verb stem ends in ㄹ (*l*).

알 al- vs. 알리 salli- 'know/inform'
울 ul- 울리 ulli- 'cry/make X cry'

5 -기 *ki* when the verb stem ends in a nasal (an intervening *h* is as if it were not there) or an ㅅ (*s*) sound:

남 nam- vs. 남기 nam-ki- 'remain/leave'
벗 pŏs- 벗기 pŏt-ki- 'take off/undress'

6 -히 *hi* elsewhere

앉 anch- vs. 앉히 anch'i- (←anch-hi) 'sit down/seat'
읽 ilk'- 읽히 ilk'i (←ilk-hi) 'read/make X read'

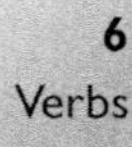

6.5 Marking event time and aspect

6.5.1 Tense

Tense locates the action, process, or state expressed by the verb of the sentence in a time scale – preceding, concurrent with, or following a reference point that usually is the time of utterance.

6.5.1.1 Present

The present tense expresses an ongoing action or phenomenon. The present tense can be used not only for a common, repeated event, but also for past or future events, given the proper context. For example, 미국에 간다 *miguk-e kan-ta* 'I am going to America now' can be uttered by someone in an airplane flying to the United States, by someone who goes to America regularly for business or pleasure, or by someone who will be going to the U.S. some time in the future.

An important point to remember is that only action verbs are marked for present tense. Stative verbs with no tense marker are understood as present tense.

The present tense marker is -(느)ㄴ *(nŭ)n*. Choose -ㄴ *n* after a vowel, but -는 *nŭn* after a consonant.

Present tense

Action verb				Stative verb	
-는 *nŭn* after C		**-ㄴ *n*** after V		**zero**	
과일이	익는다	비가	온다	옷이	작다
kwail-i	ik-**nŭn**-ta	pi-ka	o-n-ta	os-i	chak-Ø-ta
fruit-Subj	ripen-Pres-Dec	rain-Subj	come-Pres-Dec	clothes-Subj	small-Ø-Dec
'Fruits are ripening.'		'It is raining/ The rain comes.'		'The dress is (too) small.'	

6.5.1.2 Past-tense marker -었 ŏss

The past tense expresses a definite, completed event prior to a referenced point in time that is usually the present but can be another time, depending on context.

The past-tense marker is -었 *ŏss*. It usually comes just before the sentence ender.

수요일에는 날씨가 좋았어요.
suyoil-e-nŭn nalssi-ka choh-ass-ŏyo.
Wednesday-Loc-Top weather-Subj be good-Past-Dec/Pol
'The weather was good on Wednesday.'

점심에 피자를 먹었어요.
chŏmsim-e p'ija-lŭl mŏk-ŏss-ŏyo.
lunch-Loc pizza-Obj eat-Past-Dec/Pol
'I had pizza for lunch.'

The VH rule applies to -었 *ŏss*, yielding the alternate form -았 *ass* when it follows a syllable with the vowel *a* or *o* [▶2.2.2]. Two identical vowels in a row are merged into one (*ŏ-ŏss* → *ŏ-ss* / *a-ass* → *a-ss*). The various forms of the past-tense marker may be schematically presented as follows:

Different forms of past tense

-았 ***ass*** after a syllable containing ㅏ ***a*** or ㅗ ***o***	-ㅆ **ss** directly after the vowel ㅏ ***a*** or ㅓ **ŏ**	-었 **ŏss** everywhere else
서울-에 살았다 sŏul-e sal-**ass**-ta Seoul-Loc live-Past-Dec 'X lived in Seoul.'	서울-에 갔다 sŏul-e ka-**ss**-ta (← k**a**-**ass**-ta) Seoul-Loc live-Past-Dec 'X went to Seoul.'	호텔-에 묵었다 hot'el-e mug-**ŏss**-ta hotel-Loc stay-Past-Dec 'X stayed in a hotel.'

6.5.1.3 *Past-past (PP)*

When the past tense marker -었 *ŏss* is doubled, the two together are called "past-past," "double past," or "past perfect," which will be referred to in this book as past perfect (PP). Here only the first vowel of the suffix -었-었 *-ŏss-ŏss* follows the VH principle, because the second vowel is no longer following a verb stem but only another suffix. So, there is never a form such as *-았-았 *-ass-ass*.

PP in general denotes that the event expressed by the verb happened before a reference point in the past and no longer holds true.

판소리-를 배웠었어요.
p'ansori-lŭl paeu-ŏss-ŏss-ŏyo.
p'ansori-Obj learn-Past-Past-Dec/Pol
'X had studied/used to study *p'ansori*.'

PP can denote having experienced an event in the past. Compare the following two sentences:

Past 서울-에 갔다.
sŏul-e ka-**ss**-ta (←k**a**-**ass**-ta).
Seoul-Loc go-Past-Dec/Plain
'X went to Seoul.'

Past-past 서울-에 갔었다.
sŏul-e ka-**ss**-**ŏss**-ta.
Seoul-Loc go-Past-Past-Dec/Plain
'X has been to Seoul.'

In the first sentence, someone went to Seoul and whether he or she is still there is immaterial. In the second sentence, someone went to Seoul and is no longer there.

Often PP is used to emphasize the contrast between the past and present:

우리 엄마는 일을 했었는데 이제는
uri ŏmma-nŭn il-ŭl hae-**ss**-**ŏss**-nŭnde ijenŭn
us mom-Top work-Obj do-Past-Past-but now-Top
일하지 않아요.
ilha-chi anh-ayo.
do-Comp Neg-Dec/Pol
'My mom used to work, but she doesn't work anymore.'
[*lit.* 'As for our mom, (she) had done work, but as for now, (she) doesn't work.']

PP can also denote a habitual behavior before a reference point in the past.

토요일마다 다방에 갔었다.
t'oyoil-mada tabang-e ka-**ss**-**ŏss**-ta.
Saturday-every tearoom-Loc go-Past-Past-Dec/Plain
'X used to go to a tearoom every Saturday.'

6.5.1.4 Future

There are two major ways of indicating future tense: (1) by employing the volitional suffix -겠 *kess*; (2) by using the expression -을 거다 *ŭl kŏ-ta*, which simply predicts what will happen.

Future marking strategies

1 Use volitional modal suffix -겠 ***kess*** meaning 'intention.'

Korean speakers do not believe they can go into someone else's psychological sphere, which explains why this suffix with volitional meaning will be used only with a first-person subject.

(i) 오늘은 점심을 안 먹겠습니다.
onŭl-ŭn chŏmsim-ŭl an mŏk-kess-sŭpnita.
today-Top lunch-Obj Neg eat-Vol-Dec/Def
'I will not eat lunch today.'

(ii) *우리 선생님이 오늘 안 오시겠어요.
uri sŏnsaengnim-i onŭl an o-si-kess-ŏyo.
our teacher-Subj today Neg come-SH-Sup-Dec/Pol
'My teacher *will not come today.' [Ungrammatical if the intended meaning is volitional. The ungrammatical sentence for the intended meaning in example (ii) above, therefore, becomes grammatical if the intended meaning is '(I am afraid) my teacher will not come today.' See below.]

Note that when the suffix is not reporting one's own volition, it represents strong conjecture.

참 맛있겠어요.
ch'am mas-iss-kess-ŏyo.
truly taste-Exist-Sup-Dec/Pol
'It must be very delicious [– it sure looks so].'

비가 오겠어요.
pi-ka o-kess-ŏyo.
rain-Subj come-Sup-Dec/Pol
'It looks like rain [, I am afraid].'

지금쯤 도착했겠다.
chigŭmtchŭm toch'ak-hae-ss-kess-ta.
now-about arrival-do-Past-Sup-Dec/Plain
'They must have arrived by now[, I bet].'

2 Express a **simple prediction by using the expression** -을거다 ***ŭl kkŏ-ta*** 'it will be that...'

The form, -을 거다 *ŭl kŏ-ta* is derived from -을 *ŭl* + 것이다 *kŏs-i-ta*, [approximately, 'It is the thing that...'].

아마 내일 비가 올 거에요.
ama naeil pi-ka o-l kŏ-eyo.
perhaps/probably tomorrow rain-Subj come-Mod it will be
'It will probably rain tomorrow.'

그 식당은 비쌀 거에요
kŭ siktang-ŭn pissa-l kŏ-eyo
that restaurant-Top be expensive-Mod it will be
'I think/presume that restaurant is expensive.'

Note: This expression is chosen today by younger speakers even for the intentional meaning. It probably started as a politeness strategy, e.g., to indicate that something will just happen, rather than the speaker's intention to do something as a hedge, e.g.,

저는 그런 차는 안 살 거에요.
chŏ-nŭn kŭrŏn cha-nŭn an sa-l kŏ-eyo.
me-Top that sort car-Top Neg buy-Mod it will be
'I will not buy such a car.' [*lit.* 'It will probably not happen that I will buy such a car.']

6.5.2 *Aspect*

Aspect is also time-related and works closely with tense. Aspect indicates whether an event is completed, incomplete, ongoing, experienced, repeating, having an effect, reminisced, etc., rather than simply locating an event vis-à-vis a certain reference point. There are at least two ways of expressing aspect. One is by suffixation and the other is by creating a complex verb by attaching inherently aspectual verbs.

Some suffixes contain both tense and aspect because of overlapping definitions. For example, the past tense marker -었 *ŏss* denotes what occurred before the referent time like utterance time and also the fact that the event has been completed [▶6.5.1.2]. The past-perfect marker, -었-었 *-ŏss-ŏss*, can simply indicate that an event happened before another event in the past, but also can have an aspectual meaning of past experience that has no effect on today. The present can also have the aspectual meaning of repetition or habit.

Two important aspect markers are the *progressive* and the *resultative*. Both use the existential verb 있 *iss-*, which is preceded by a connective form of the verb.

6.5.2.1 *Progressive aspect* -고 있다 ko iss-ta

In English, a progressive meaning is expressed by

be V_{STEM}-ing

In Korean, progressives are formed using the pattern Verb + -고 있다/계시다 (Hon), meaning 'to be . . . ing.'

V_{STEM}-고	있-
-ko	iss-
-Conn	be

The above sequence is not a phrase but must be considered a single verbal unit with an ongoing, imperfective aspectual meaning. This pattern is used only with action verbs.

저는	영문학을	공부하고	있어요.
chŏ-nŭn	yŏngmunhak-ŭl	kongbuha-ko	iss-ŏyo.
me-Top	English literature-Obj	study-Conn	be/Prog-Dec/Pol

'I am studying English literature.'

아버지가	서울에서	일하시고	계세요
abŏji-ka	sŏul-esŏ	il-ha-si-ko	kyes-eyo
father-Subj	Seoul-Loc	work-do-SH-Conn	be/Hon/Prog-Dec/Pol

'My father is working in Seoul.'

If the tense marker for the sentence (i.e., the one immediately following the verb -있 *iss*) is the present, then the whole verb is present progressive; if it is past, then the whole verb is past progressive. Consider the following examples:

아이-가	책-을	읽-고	있다.
ai-ka	ch'aek-ŭl	ilk-ko	iss-ta.
child-Subj	book-Obj	read-Conn	be/Prog-Dec/Plain

'A child is reading a book.'

아이-가	책-을	읽-고	있었다.
ai-ka	ch'aek-ŭl	ilk-ko	iss- ŏss-ta.
child-Subj	book-Obj	read-Conn	be/Prog-Past-Dec/Plain

'A child was reading a book.'

Only active verbs can have the progressive aspect.

6.5.2.2 *Resultative aspect* -어 있다 ŏ iss-ta

The resultative, sometimes called perfective, aspect denotes completed actions. In addition, it describes the resulting state following the completion of an action. These apply to a limited number of verbs, but nevertheless are very common vocabulary items. There are two different constructions for this purpose: V-고 있 *ko iss-* and V-어 있 *ŏ iss-*.

In a limited number of cases, however, especially with verbs for wearing, V-고 있 *ko iss-* can express the resultative, stative aspect as well as the progressive. In these cases, the verb forms can be ambiguous without proper context:

> 아이-가 교복-을 입-고 있다.
> ai-ga kyobog-ŭl ip-ko iss-ta (←iss-ta).
> child-Subj uniform-Obj wear-Conn be/Prog-Dec/Plain
> 'A child is wearing a uniform.' (*Ambiguously* 'A child is putting on the uniform' or 'A child has a uniform on.')

A proper context such as the use of certain adverbs will disambiguate the sentence easily. For example, if the sentence contains the adverb 지금 *chigŭm* 'now, at this moment,' then it is a progressive sentence. If the adverb is something like 또 *tto* 'again,' then the sentence is resultative.

Here are some more examples of 'wearing' verbs with ambiguous meanings:

안경을 쓰고있다	an'gyŏng-ŭl ssŭgo iss-ta	'wear glasses'
신을 신고있다	sin-ŭl sin-ko iss-ta	'wear shoes'
모자를 쓰고있다	moja-lŭl ssŭgo iss-ta	'wear a hat'
장갑을 끼고있다	changgab-ŭl kkigo iss-ta	'wear gloves'
반지를 끼고있다	panji-lŭl kki-go iss-ta	'wear a ring'

Other, non-wearing verbs that can be ambiguous include:

가지고 있다	kaji-go iss-ta	'is holding' or 'is in possession of'
모시고/데리고 있다	mosi-go/teri-go iss-ta	'is accompanying X' or 'is in the situation of taking care of X'
놀고 있다	nolgo- iss-ta	'is playing' or 'is unemployed'
(머리를) 올리고 있다	(mŏri-lŭl) olli-go iss-ta	'is making a chignon' or 'has her hair up'
(장미를) 심고 있다	(changmi-lŭl) sim-ko iss-ta	'is planting (roses)' or 'has a (rose) garden'

> *Note*: The very common verbs of knowing / not knowing (알다 *al-ta* 'know' / 모르다 *morŭ-ta* 'now know'), being stative verbs, cannot have progressive aspect but can have resultative aspect by attaching -고 있다 *ko iss-ta*, as in 알고 있다 *al-ko iss-ta* and 모르고 있다 *morŭ-ko iss-ta* 'is aware/unaware.'

A limited set of intransitive verbs takes the V-어 있 *ŏ iss-* construction to denote a resultative state. Compare the following pairs:

Past	Resultative
미나가 섰다. mina-ka s(ŏ)- ŏss-ta. Mina-Subj stand-Past-Dec/Plain 'Mina stood up.'	미나가 서 있다. mina-ka sŏ iss-ta. Mina-Subj stand be/Prog-Dec/Plain 'Mina is standing (as a result of having stood up).'
미국에 갔다. miguk-e ka-ss-ta. America-Loc go-Past-Dec/Plain 'X went to America.'	미국에 가 있다. miguk-e ka iss-ta. America-Loc go be/Prog-Dec/Plain 'X is in America (as a result of having gone there).'
벽에 사진이 걸렸다. pyŏk-e sajin-i kŏlly-ŏss-ta. wall-Loc photo-Subj is hung-Past-Dec 'A picture was hung on the wall.'	벽에 사진이 걸려 있다. pyŏk-e sajin-i kŏllyŏ iss-ta. wall-Loc photo-Subj hang be/Prog-Dec/Plain 'A picture hangs on the wall.'

> *Note*: The Janus-faced verb 살다 *salda* 'live' is used for two different meanings of 'live': 'lead a life, make a home' and 'be alive, living.' The following two forms are illustrative:
>
> | | |
> |---|---|
> | 지금 서울에서 살고 있다.
chigŭm sŏul-esŏ sal-ko iss-ta.
now Seoul-Loc live-is living-Dec
'X is living in Seoul.' | 지금 서울에 살아 있다.
chigŭm sŏul-e sal-a iss-ta.
now Seoul-Loc be alive-Dec
'X (e.g. a criminal) is alive in Seoul.' |

6.6 Expressing speaker's attitude: Modals

An important part of the information conveyed in Korean sentences is the speaker's attitude toward: (1) an event; (2) a referent in a sentence; and (3) the relative situation of the addressee from the speaker's point of view. This is achieved through the use of modals, addressee honorific (AH) marking, or both.

A modal expresses the speaker's (the hearer's in a question sentence) attitude, judgment, and assertion beyond the simple declaration of fact. In

Korean, modals include suffixes expressing volition, conjecture, or retrospective meaning.

6.6.1 *Volitional* -겠 kess

The modal -겠 *kess* expresses the speaker's strong will to do something in the future. Therefore, modal -겠 *kess* is often called a future-tense marker. However, as mentioned above, since the volitional use of -겠 *kess* is limited to the first-person singular, one cannot speak of someone else's volition, except in a question.

나는 그 사람하고는 절대로 결혼 안
na-nŭn kŭ saram-hago-nŭn chŏltaero kyŏrhon an
me-Top that person-with-Top absolutely marriage Neg
하겠습니다.
ha-kess-sŭpni-ta.
do-Vol-Dec/Def
'I will never marry that person.' [*lit.* 'As for me, with that person I will absolutely not marry.']

6.6.2 *Suppositive or strong-prediction* -겠 kess

Modal -겠 *kess* expresses strong assertion or prediction, including the fear of the eventual realization of the fact expressed in the sentence. Consider:

아유, 우리 팀 지겠다.
ayu, uri t'im chi-kess-ta.
Int us team lose-Sup-Dec/Plain
'Oh no, (I am afraid) our team will lose!'

6.6.3 *Retrospective* -더 tŏ

The retrospective -더 *tŏ* denotes that the speaker reports what he or she actually observed, as follows:

인호가 집에 가더라.
inho-ka chip-e ka-tŏ-la.
Inho-Subj home-Loc go-Ret-Dec
'(I saw with my own eyes and am reporting to you that) Inho was going home.'

> *Note*: Declarative -다 *ta* changes to its weakened variant -라 *la* when it follows the retrospective ending -더 *tŏ*. Thus always use 하더라 *ha-tŏ-la*, never *하더다 *ha-tŏ-ta*.

When the retrospective suffix -더 *tŏ* is used with the past modifier suffix -은 *ŭn*, it acquires the meaning of habitual-past 'used to' or some ongoing event that has been interrupted or discontinued, as shown:

[[내가 살던]$_{Mod}$ [고향]$_{N}$]$_{NP}$
nae-ka sal-tŏ-n kohyang
I-Subj live-Ret-Mod/Past hometown
'the hometown I used to live in'

[[누나-가 먹던]$_{Mod}$ [밥]$_{N}$]$_{NP}$
nuna-ka mŏk-tŏ-n pap
elder sister-Subj eat-Ret-Mod/Past rice
'the leftover rice of my elder sister'

[[예쁘던]$_{Mod}$ [얼굴]$_{N}$]$_{NP}$
yeppŭ-tŏ-n ŏlgul
be pretty-Ret-Mod/Past face
'the face that used to be pretty'

6.7 Mood suffixes indicating sentence types

Verb forms determine the types of sentences they are in. Table 6.2 shows various sentence-concluding endings indicating different types of sentences and marking the expressed relationship of the speaker vis-à-vis the addressee.

Table 6.2 Sentence-concluding endings: Various forms of the verb 가 *ka-* 'go'

	Declarative (Dec)	Imperative (Imp)	Propositive (Prop)	Question (Q)
Deferential	갑니다 ka-pni-ta	가십시오 ka-si-psio	갑시다 ka-psi-ta	갑니까 ka-pnikka
Respectful/Polite	가요 ka-yo	가요 ka-yo	가요 ka-yo	가요 ka-yo
Panmal	가 ka	가 ka	가 ka	가 ka
Unguarded/Plain	간다 ka-n-ta	가라 ka-ra	가자 ka-cha	가니 ka-ni

6.8 Honorific marking

Honorific marking in Korean is most commonly and most systematically indicated through the use of an honorific suffix on a verb or a special honorific form of a verb. Honorific marking does not merely mean elevating the interlocutor but includes a variety of styles expressing the other types of recognized relative relationships between the speaker and the hearer in terms of power and intimacy. There are two basic ways of indicating interpersonal relationship from the speaker's point of view: (1) showing deference to the human subject of the sentence; and (2) expressing the speaker's attitude toward the hearer [▶10.1].

6.8.1 *Subject honorification (SH)*

The suffix -으시 *ŭsi* is attached to the verb stem to show the speaker's deference to the superior social status of the person referred to by the subject of the sentence, with respect to the hearer and the speaker. This phenomenon is called subject honorification. Subject honorification applies also to any body part or other close possession of a respected person. The first vowel 으 *ŭ-* is deleted if it is preceded by another vowel, as expected [▶3.3.1].

수고하십니다 [← 수고하- + 으시 + -읍니다].
sugo-ha-sip-ni-ta.
work hard-Dec/Def
'You are working hard.'

Each of the following sentences expresses an extra message: 'I, the speaker, express my respect to "the teacher" and assume the hearer also respects "the teacher."'

(i) 선생님이 오신다.
sŏnsaengnim-i o-si-n-ta.
teacher-Subj come-SH-Pres-Dec/Plain
'The teacher is coming.'

(ii) 선생님은 눈이 크시다.
sŏnsaengnim-ŭn nun-i k'ŭ-si-ta.
teacher-Top eye-Subj be big-SH-Dec/Plain
'The teacher has big eyes. / The teacher's eyes are big.'

(iii) 선생님은 학생이 많으시다.
sŏnsaengnim-ŭn haksaeng-i manh-ŭsi-ta.
teacher-Top students-Subj be abundant-SH-Dec/Plain
'The teacher has many students. / The teacher's students are numerous.'

In the case of (ii) and (iii), the subject of the sentence is not the target of honorification but is an entity that is very close to the honored one, if not actually belonging to him or her.

6.8.2 *Addressee honorification (AH)*

Addressee honorification is not only at the core of the Korean language protocol but an essential part of Korean grammar. While SH involves an optional marker to express deference to the subject of the sentence, AH is indicated through the choice of proper sentence enders. No one can utter even the simplest sentence without a sentence ender, and that is why a Korean speaker must first consider his or her relationship to the hearer or reader and the communicative situation before speaking.

The following sentence has the ending -습니다 *supni-ta*, which denotes the speaker's expressed deference for the hearer's elevated status and consequently the speaker's self-humbling approach.

그 때는 몰랐습니다.
ku ttae-nŭn moll-ass-**sŭpni-ta**.
that time-Top not know-Past-Dec/Def
'I didn't know at that time.'

Besides -습니다 *sŭpni-ta*, there are other AH forms that can be used to express different relationships between the speaker and the hearer but still mean 'I didn't know at that time.' Table 6.3 is a schematic representation of seven different AH forms that exist in Korean.

As far as AH is concerned, the forms given in Table 6.3 are only declarative forms. Other sentence-enders of equivalent honorific style exist of course, e.g., questions, propositives, commands, etc.

Table 6.3 Addressee-honorific endings

a.	(-**C**)-습니다 **sŭp-ni-ta** (-**V**)-ㅂ니다-**p-ni-ta**	(H>S) (DEF)	Self-humbling/Addressee-elevating
b.	-나이다 **nai-ta**	(H>>S) (S-DEF)	Self-humbling/Addressee-deifying
c.	-으오 **ŭo**	(S≥H) (AUTH-1)	Self-elevating/Addressee-respecting
d.	-네 **ne**	(S≥H) (AUTH-2)	Self-elevating/Addressee-elevating
e.	-다 **ta**	(S≥H) (PLN)	Self-unguarded/Addressee-unfeared
f.	-어 **ŏ**	(S-H) (Panmal)	Self-neutral/Addressee-indeterminate
g.	-어요 **ŏ-yo**	(S-H) (RES)	Self-neutral/Addressee-indeterminate but respecting

Note 1: Power relationships between the Hearer (H) and the Speaker (S) are given in parentheses, where > means 'of greater power than,' >> 'of much greater power than,' ≥ 'of equal or greater power than,' and – 'in unspecified power relationship with.'
Note 2: Some forms were made of more than one suffix historically, and their boundaries are indicated by hyphens, but the whole string is understood as one unit in contemporary Korean. That is why -습니다 is romanized as a unit as *-sŭmnida*, although written *-sŭp-ni-ta*, where the part indicating the plain declarative ending *-ta* is shown.
Note 3: Remember the vowel -으 *ŭ* is dropped when following another vowel or a verb-final *l*, and -어 *ŏ* becomes -아 *a* after a yang vowel (*a* or *o*).

6.9 Compound verbs

Sometimes more than one verb can be combined into a long verb by putting a union or connective vowel -어 *ŏ* between them. These are usually put in chronological order:

사자가 코키리를 잡아죽여먹었다.
saja-ka k'okkiri-lul chap-a-chuk-i-ŏ-mŏk-ŏss-ta.
lion-Subj elephant-Obj catch-ŏ-kill-Caus-ŏ-eat-Past-Dec/Plain
'The lion caught-killed-ate an elephant.'

Where the complex verb 잡아죽여먹다 consists of three verb stems 잡 *chap-* 'catch,' 죽이 *chuk-i* 'kill,' and 먹 *mŏk-* 'eat,' all three having been combined by the union vowel -어 *ŏ*. (This vowel follows the VH principle, so *ŏ-* becomes *a-* when the preceding vowel is either 아 *a* or 어 *ŏ*.)

Other examples include:

삶아먹다 salm-a-mŏk-ta (삶다 'boil' + 먹다 'eat')
때려죽이다 ttaery-ŏ-chuk-i-ta (때리다 'hit' + 죽이다 'kill')
만들어팔다 mandŭl-ŏ-p'al-ta (만들다 'make' + 팔다 'sell')
써보내다 ss-ŏ-ponae-ta (쓰다 'write' + 보내다 'send')
뜯어고치다 ttŭt-ŏ-koch'i-ta (뜯다 'take apart' + 고치다 'mend, fix')

6.10 Auxiliary verbs

Another verb-stem extension uses an auxiliary verb. The number of auxiliary verbs in Korean is estimated at about 50; most of these can serve as main verbs. So the main verb + auxiliary verb sequence may be considered a kind of compound verb, although not all constructions use the same connective as in the usual complex-vowel formation.

Some examples will illustrate how auxiliary verbs contribute to the meaning of the verb complex:

1 V + -어 버리다 *ŏ pŏri-ta*

This expression is attached to an action verb stem to make a complex verb indicating some kind of **finality of action**. 버리다 *pŏri-ta* means 'throw away,' so the complex verb means 'do something and throw it away'; i.e., 'do something completely and be done with it.' As an extended meaning, speakers can use this expression to get rid of some psychological burden or indicate regret at the finality of something.

다 잊어버렸기 때문에요.
ta ich-ŏ-pŏry-ŏss-ki ttaemun-eyo.
all forget away-Past-Nom because-Cop-Dec/Pol
'It's because I forgot it all.'

다 먹어버렸어요.
ta mŏk-ŏ-pŏry-ŏss-ŏyo.
all eat away-Past-Dec/Pol
'I ate up all [the food].'

자동차를 팔아버렸어요.
chadongch'a-lŭl p'al-a-pŏry-ŏss-ŏyo.
car-Obj sell away-Past-Dec/Pol
'I sold the car off [maybe because it kept breaking down].'

2 V + -어 주다/드리다 *ŏ chu-ta/tŭri-ta*

The verb 주다 *chu-ta*/드리다 *tŭri-ta* (Hon) means 'to give.' When it follows another verb, connected by the union vowel -어 *ŏ* and forming a complex verb, it imparts a meaning to the other verb that one is doing it as a favor to someone else.

내일 전화 해 (← 하 + 어) 드리겠어요.
naeil chŏnhwa hae tŭri-kess-ŏyo.
tomorrow telephone do give(OH)–Vol-Dec/Pol
'I will call you [for your sake].'

차 한 잔 사 주세요.
ch'a han chan sa chu-s-eyo.
tea one cup buy-SH-Dec/Pol
'Please buy me a cup of coffee.'

3 Some more examples of common auxiliary verbs:

Main verb	Connective	Auxiliary verb	Verb + auxiliary verb	Meaning
사 sa 'buy'	아 a	두 tu 'put away'	사두다 sa-tu-ta	'buy X for later use'
주 chu 'give'	고 ko	말 mal 'stop'	주고말다 chu-ko-mal-ta	'end up giving…and can't do anything about it'
읽 ilk 'read'	어 ŏ	보 po 'see'	읽어보다 ilk-ŏ-po-ta	'try to read, have the experience of reading'
가 ka 'go'	고 ko	싶 sip 'want'	가고싶다 ka-ko-sip'-ta	'want to go'

6.11 Conjunctives

Clausal conjunctives are attached to the verbs and together form a word. Some conjunctives start with consonants, but many conjunctives start with the vowel 어 *ŏ* or the vowel 으 *ŭ*. The vowel 어 *ŏ* changes to 아 *a* following the VH principle [▶3.3.3]. 으 *ŭ* is a weak vowel that gets deleted when meeting another vowel [▶3.3.1].

> *Note*: A subordinate sentence that carries a conjunctive always comes first. This again follows the principle by which the most important items come last.

1 The sequential suffix -어서 *ŏsŏ* '...and so'

When two clauses are linked by the conjunctive -어서 *ŏsŏ*, there is a clear sequential relationship between the first clause and the second one. This relationship can be simply temporal, or one of cause and effect.

몸이 아파서 (← 아ㅍ + 아서 ← 아프 + 어서) 학교에 못 갔어요.
mom-i ap'asŏ hakkyo-e mot k-ass-ôyo.
body-Subj ache-so school-Loc Neg go-Past-Dec/Pol
'I could not go to school because I was sick.'
[*lit.* 'My body ached and so I could not go to school.']

나는 아침에 일어나서 샤워해요.
(←일어나 + 아서
←일어나 + 어서)
na-nŭn ach'im-e irŏn-asŏ syawŏ-hae-yo.
I-Top morning-Loc getup-and shower-do-Dec/Pol
'I get up in the morning and take a shower.'

The -서 *sŏ* in -어서 *ŏsŏ* is sometimes dropped. In this case – especially if there is no pause between the two verbs – the verbs form a compound verb with a much more closely knit semantic relationship between them.

나는 기숙사에 살기 때문에 음식을 안 하고 사(서)먹어요.
na-nŭn kisuksa-e sal-ki ttaemune ŭmsik-ŭl an ha-ko sa-(sŏ)-mŏk-ŏyo.
I-Top dorm-Loc live-Nom because food-Obj Neg do-and buy-(and)-eat-Dec/Pol
'Because I live in a dorm, I don't cook, but eat out.'
[*lit.* 'Because I live in a dorm, I don't make food, but buy and eat it.']

Note: -어서 *ŏsŏ* can never be preceded by a past tense marker. Therefore, there is no such sentence as 비가 *왔어서 등산 못 갔어요 *pi-ka *w-ass-ŏsŏ tŭngsan mot k-ass-ŏyo*. In order to say 'Because it rained, we could not go on a hike,' choose 비가 와서 등산 못 갔어요 *pi-ka wasŏ tŭngsan mot k-ass-ŏyo*.

2 The affix -으니까 *ŭnikka* 'because/since/as'

When the cause is generally accepted and legitimate, one links the two clauses using -으니까 *ŭnikka*:

눈이 오니까 자동차가 없어요.
nun-i o-nikka chadongch'a-ka ŏps-ŏyo.
snow-Subj come-since car-Subj not exist-Dec/Pol
'Since it is snowing, there are no cars.'

일요일에는 안 바쁘니까 일요일에 가요.
iryoir-e-nŭn an papp-ŭnikka iryoir-e ka-yo.
Sunday-on-Top Neg be busy-since Sunday-Loc go-Dec/Pol
'Let's go on Sunday, as we are not busy on Sunday.'

-으니까 *ŭnikka* is also used to indicate a discovery that leads to a natural consequence, where it often takes on the English translation of 'Upon…ing…'

집에 가니까 친구가 와있었어요.
chip-e ka-nikka ch'in'gu-ka wa-iss-ŏss-ŏyo.
home to go-as friend-Subj come-exist-Past-Dec/Pol
'Upon arriving home, (I found out) my friend had come.'

3 The affix -기 때문에 *ki ttaemune* 'because/since/as'

The basic meaning of -때문 *ttaemun* is 'cause,' 'reason,' or '(bad) cause.' With the locative particle -에 *e*, the conjunctive means 'because [*lit.* 'with the reason/cause/excuse of'].' Use of -때문 *ttaemun* always indicates a reason from the speaker's subjective point of view. When we say 'because (of)...' in Korean, we use either the pattern NP + -때문에 *ttaemune* or the pattern V + -기 때문에 *ki ttaemune*, where '-기 *kï*' is a nominalizer turning the whole sentence into a noun (i.e., **V** + -기 = **N**).

한국말이 재미있기 때문에 공부해요.
han'guk-mal-i chaemi-iss-ki ttaemune kongbu-hae-yo.
Korean-Subj interest-exist-Nom because of study-do-Dec/Pol
'Because Korean is interesting, I study it.'

비가 왔기 때문에 안 갔어요.
pi-ka w-ass-ki ttaemune an k-ass-ŏyo.
rain-Subj come-Past-Nom because of Neg go-Past-Dec/Pol
'Because it rained, I didn't go.'

Note: **'Because' in Korean**

Having introduced -어서 *ŏsŏ*, -으니까 *ŭnikka*, and -때문에 *ttaemune*, take a moment to compare all three patterns.

1 -어서 *ŏsŏ*

In clauses linked by -어서 *ŏsŏ*, there is a clear relation between the first clause and the next one. The relation can be simply temporal, or one of cause and effect.

눈이 와서 학교에 안 갔어요.
nun-i w-asŏ hakkyo-e an k-ass-ŏyo.
snow-Subj come-and so school-Loc Neg go-Past-Dec/Pol
'I did not go to school because it snowed.' (giving a simple excuse)

2 -으니까 *ŭnikka*

A clause with -으니까 *ŭnikka* expresses the reason for the event or situation in the main clause. Note that this reason is one that is generally accepted or can be publicly acknowledged.

눈이 오니까 학교에 못 갔어요.
nun-i o-nikka hakkyo-e mot k-ass-ŏyo.
snow-Subj come-as school-Loc Neg go-Past-Dec/Pol
'[As you know] it snowed, so I could not go to school.' (Giving an excuse that cannot be challenged; therefore, the sentence could sound rude.)

3 -때문에 *ttaemune*

Here, again, a reason is given, only the reason is a more subjective (often apologetic) excuse.

눈이 왔기 때문에 학교에 못 갔어요.
nun-i w-ass-ki ttaemune hakkyo-e mot k-ass-ŏyo.
snow-Subj come-Past-Nom because of school-Loc Neg go-Past-Dec/Pol
'I did not come to school because it had snowed.' (There is a slight sense of blaming the snow here.)

4 Conditional -으면 *ŭmyŏn* 'if/when'

The conditional -으면 *ŭmyŏn* is attached to a verb stem and has the meaning 'if and when.' -으면 *ŭmyŏn* means 'if' in the conditional sense and is never used in the sense of the English word 'whether.'

봄이 오면 캠퍼스가 아주 예뻐요.
pom-i o-myŏn k'aempŏsŭ-ka aju yepp-ŏyo.
spring-Subj come-if campus-Subj very be pretty-Dec/Pol
'When the spring comes, the campus is very pretty.'

공부 안 하고 술만 먹으면 나쁜
kongbu an ha-ko sul-man mŏk-ŭmyŏn napp-ŭn
study Neg do-and alcohol-only consume-if be bad-Mod
학생이에요.
haksaeng-i-eyo.
student-Cop-Dec/Pol
'If one does not study and only drinks liquor, one is a bad student.'

여름방학이 빨리 왔으면 좋겠어요.
yŏrŭm-panghak-i ppalli w-ass-ŭmyŏn choh-kess-ŏyo.
summer-vacation-Subj quickly come-Past-if be good-Sup-Dec/Pol
'I wish summer vacation would come quickly.'
[*lit.* 'If summer vacation came quickly, it would be good.']

5 The conjunctive -으려고 *ŭryŏgo* 'in order to…'

-으려고 *ŭryŏgo* means 'in order to…' when used by itself, as in the following:

친구를 만나려고 식당에 갔어요.
ch'in'gu-lŭl manna-ryŏgo siktang-e k-ass-ŏyo.
friend-Obj meet-in order to restaurant-to go-Past-Dec/Pol
'I went to a restaurant to meet a friend.'

에이를 다 받으려고 열심히 공부했어요.
ei-lŭl ta pat-ŭryŏgo yŏlsimhi kongbu-hae-ss-ŏyo.
A-Obj all receive-in order to zealously study-do-Past-Dec/Pol
'In order to get all *A*s, I studied hard.'

Note that with a verb of coming and going, -으러 *ŭrŏ* is usually used.

한국에 무엇을 하러 가세요?
han'guk-e muŏs-ŭl ha-rŏ ka-s-eyo?
Korea-Loc what-Obj do-in order to go-SH-Q/Pol
'Why are you going to Korea?'
[*lit.* 'In order to do what are you going to Korea?']

내 병원에 있는 친구를 방문하러 가요.
nae pyŏng'wŏn-e iss-nŭn ch'in'gu-lŭl pangmun-ha-rŏ k-ayo.
my hospital-Loc be-Mod friend-Obj visit-do-in order to go-Dec/Pol
'I'm going to visit my friend in the hospital.'

6 The conjunctive -는데 *nŭnde* 'but' or 'and'

-는데 *nŭnde* (-은데 *ŭnde* after a stative verb in the present tense, except for the existential copula) is essentially a conjunctive ending that is attached to the end of the first sentence, and is often translated as 'but' or 'and.'

시간은 있는데 돈이 없어요.
sigan-ŭn iss-nŭnde ton-i ŏps-ŏyo.
time-Top have-but money-Subj not have-Dec/Pol
'I have time, but no money.'

날씨는 좋은데 시간이 없어요.
nalssi-nŭn choh-ŭnde sigan-i ŏps-ŏyo.
weather-Top be good-but time-Subj not have-Dec/Pol
'The weather is nice, but I have no time.'

Note: When -는데 *(n)ŭnde* is used, it indicates that there is something else to say about that clause. When a sentence ends with -는데 *(n)ŭnde*, it is up to the listener to infer what would have followed. Therefore, such usage is often a politeness strategy.

학교가 바쁜데요.
hakkyo-ka papp-ŭnde-yo.
school-Subj be busy-but-Dec/Pol
'The school is busy, ...'

맥주는 없는데요.
maekchu-nŭn ŏps-nŭnde-yo.
beer-Top not exist-but-Dec/Pol
'There's no beer ...' or '(We) have no beer ...'

7 The contrastive conjunctive -지만 *chiman* '..., but'

The affix -지만 *chiman* means something like 'granted that..., but...' The clause in -지만 *chiman* is introduced as fact, then the concluding clause states or implies some other fact in contrast to the first. Thus, -지만 *chiman* can also be used in a politeness strategy.

나도 가고 싶지만 숙제가 너무 많아서
na-to ka-ko sip'-chiman sukche-ka nŏmu manh-asŏ
me-too go-want to-but homework-Subj too much-and so
가지 못해요.
ka-chi mot hae-yo.
go-cannot-Dec/Pol
'I want to go too, but I have too much homework, so I can't go.'

방학은 짧지만 수업이 없고 파티가
panghak-ŭn ccalp-chiman suŏp-i ŏp-ko p'at'i-ka
vacation-Top be short-but class-Subj lack-and party-Subj
많아서 좋아요.
manh-asŏ choh-ayo.
be many- so be good-Dec/Pol
'The vacation is short, but there are no classes and we have many parties, and so I like it.'

Note: **How are -지만 *chiman* and -는데 *(n)ŭnde*, which can both be translated as 'but,' different?**

Contrast the following examples with -지만 and -는데:

날씨가 좋지만 집에 있겠어요.
nalssi-ka choh-chiman chip-e iss-kess-ŏyo.
weather-Subj be good-but home-Loc stay-Vol-Dec/Pol
'Granted the weather is good, nevertheless I will stay home.'

날씨가 좋은데 왜 안 가요?
nalssi-ka choh-ŭnde wae an k-ayo?
weather-Subj be good-but why Neg go-Q/Pol
'The weather is fine, so why aren't you going?'

The first example recognizes that the weather is good, but there may be other things that do not make going out a natural consequence. Here the connective -지만 *chiman* provides that contrast. In the second example, we again state that the weather is good, only this time using -는데 *(n)ŭnde*. The difference here is that -는데 introduces the fact about the weather as contextual information, and then asks, within that context, why the listener is not doing what is naturally expected. That is why the connectives in the above sentences cannot be interchanged.

8 -어도 *ŏdo* 'even if, even though...'

When two sentences are linked by the conjunctive -어도 *ŏdo*, the subordinate clause also gets a contrastive meaning in the sense that 'even if it is the case that...(X will do something unexpected)':

죽어도 눈물 안 흘리겠어요.
chuk-ŏdo nunmul an hŭlli-kess-ŏyo.
die-even if tears Neg shed-Vol-Dec/Pol
'Even if I die, I won't shed any tears.'

비가 와도 등산을 가요.
pi-ka w-ado tŭngsan-ŭl ka-yo.
rain-Subj come-even though hiking-Obj go-Dec/Pol
'Even if it rains, we will go hiking.'

6.12 Irregular verbs

A number of Korean verbs are called "irregular" because they do not seem to follow the general phonological rules during conjugation. However, these are not random exceptions to the grammar, and many are explainable by assuming different forms as basic. Some of the true exceptions are the result of historical change. Furthermore, most of the "irregular" verbs belong to the basic, common vocabulary, and it is important to learn to which class a verb belongs to from the beginning.

ㅂ *p*-, ㄷ *t*-, and ㅅ *s*- irregular verbs are among the most common types.

Recall that lax consonants are voiced in voiced surroundings [▶3.4.2]. A group of verbs that end in ㅂ *p*, ㄷ *t*, ㅅ *s* do not voice their final consonants but undergo further weakening when followed by a vowel-initial suffix. The three groups of verbs are discussed below.

1 ㅂ *p*-irregular verbs

The final consonant ㅂ *p* of this group of verbs weakens to a semivowel [w] when followed by a vowel-initial affix. The [w] gains a full vowel status when it cannot form a single nucleus with the following vowel.

쉽 swip [→swiw]	+ 은 ŭn	ㅂ becomes [w]
쉬우 swiu	+ 은 ŭn	w vocalization [w→u]
쉬우 swiu	+ ㄴ n	으 **ŭ** deletion
쉬운 swiun		syllable merge

The [w] sound combines with the following vowel under the VH principle to form a single nucleus, e.g., 쉽 + 어 → 쉬워.

Table 6.4 lists examples of *p*-irregular verbs and their conjugations.

A great number of verb stems ending in ㅂ *p* are *p*-irregular verbs, but the following verbs are regular, in which the ㅂ *p* is simply voiced as [b] between vowels, which are voiced in Korean.

잡 *chap*- 'hold, take, catch, grab,' 집 *chip*- 'pick up, take up,' 수줍 *suchup*- 'be shy, timid,' 뽑 *ppop*- 'take out, pull out, pluck,' 좁 *chop*- 'be narrow,' 접 *chŏp*- 'fold,' 입- *ip*- 'wear, receive, suffer,' etc. Verbs with more than one final consonant are all regular: e.g., 짧다 *tch'alp-ta* 'be short,' and 넓다 *nŏlp-ta* 'be broad, wide.'

Table 6.4 Various forms of *p*-irregular verbs

-다 -ta	-어요 -ŏyo	-은 -ŭn	
쉽다 swip-ta	쉬워요 swi-wŏyo	쉬운 swi-un	'be easy'
어렵다 ŏryŏp-ta	어려워요 ŏryŏ-wŏyo	어려운 ŏryŏ-un	'be difficult, hard'
덥다 tŭp-ta	더워요 tŭ-wŏyo	더운 tŭ-un	'be hot/warm'
춥다 ch'up-ta	추워요 c'hu-ŏyo	추운 c'h-un	'be cold'
아름답다 arŭmdap-ta	아름다워요 arŭmta-wŏyo	아름다운 arŭmda-un	'be beautiful'
곱다 kop-ta	고와요 ko-wayo	고운 ko-un	'be fine/lovely'

p-regular verbs	vs.	*p*-irregular verbs
뽑-아도 ppop-ado [ppob-ado] 'even if one selects'		돕-아도 top-ado [tow-ado] 'even though one helps'

Here are some more examples:

p-regular verbs	vs.	*p*-irregular verbs
잡- chap- 'catch'		줍- chup- 'pick up'
접- chŏp- 'fold'		덥- tŏp- 'be warm'
입- ip- 'wear'		눕- nup- 'lie down'
씹- ssip- 'chew'		깁- kip- 'mend'
굽- kup- 'bend'		굽- kup- 'bake'

2 ㄷ *t*-irregular verbs

In the case of *t*-irregular verbs, the verb stem-final ㄷ *t* becomes [l] and then [r] instead of regularly becoming a [d]:

t-regular verbs	vs.	*t*-irregular verbs
닫-아도		깨닫-아도
tat-ado		kkaedat-ado
[tadado]		[kkaedarado]
'even if one closes...'		'even if one understands deeply'

Here is a sample conjugation of *t*-irregular verbs:

Dictionary form	Dec/Pol		
-다 -ta	-어요 -ŏyo	-은 -ŭn	
듣다 tŭt-ta	들어요 tŭl-ŏyo	들은 tŭl-ŭn	'listen'
묻다 mut-ta	물어요 mul-ŏyo	물은 mul-ŭn	'ask'
걷다 kŏt-ta	걸어요 kŏl-ŏyo	걸은 kŏl-ŭn	'walk'
싣다 sit-ta	실어요 sil-ŏyo	실은 sil-ŭn	'load'
긷다 kit-ta	길어요 kil-ŏyo	길은 kil-ŭn	'draw (water)'

Here are some more examples:

t-regular verbs	vs.	*t*-irregular verbs
묻 mut- 'bury'		듣 tŭt- 'hear'
믿 mit- 'believe'		묻 mut- 'ask'
쏟 ssot- 'pour'		걷 kŏt- 'walk
얻 ŏt- 'get'		싣 sit- 'load'
딛 tit- 'tread'		긷 kit- 'draw (water)'

3 ㅅ *s*-irregular verbs

In the case of *s*-irregular verbs, the verb stem-final ㅅ *s* is deleted instead of staying unchanged as in regular verbs. In this case, the disappearing ㅅ *s* leaves its trace by lengthening the preceding vowel:

s-regular verbs	vs.	*s*-irregular verbs	
빼앗-아도		낫-아도	
[ppaeas-ado]		nas-ado	[na:-ado]
'even if one takes away...'		'even if one gets better'	

Here are some more examples:

s-regular verbs	vs.	*s*-irregular verbs
씻 ssis- 'wash'		잇 is- 'connect'
솟 sos- 'rise (above)'		붓 pus- 'pour'
벗 pŏs- 'take off'		짓 chis- 'build'
빗 pis- 'comb'		긋 kŭs- 'draw a line'
줏 chus- 'pick up'		젓 chos- 'row'

4 르 *lŭ*-irregular verbs

In the case of 르 *lŭ*-irregular verbs, the verb stem-final -르 *lŭ* first loses its weak vowel 으 *ŭ* as it meets another vowel and the -ㄹ *l* is doubled, as shown in Figure 6.2:

르 **lŭ**-irregular verbs:
-르 + 어 → -V_1ㄹ 라 [V_1 = ㅗ or ㅏ] e.g., 올라 olla
-V_2ㄹ 러 [V_2 = all vowels other than V_1] 불러 pullŏ

Figure 6.2 Conjugation of ㄹ *l*- or 르 *lŭ*-irregular verbs

Here is how it works:

빠르 +	어	
빠ㄹ	어	으-deletion before a vowel
빠ㄹ ㄹ	어	ㄹ-doubling
빠ㄹ ㄹ	아	VH
빨	라	Syllable adjustment

Compare the regular and irregular conjugations:

lŭ-regular verbs	vs. *lŭ*-irregular verbs
따르-어도	고르-어도
ttarŭ-ŏdo	korŭ-ŏdo
[ttarado]	kol-ŏdo
'even if one follows'	kol-ado
	kollado
	'even if one selects'

There are many more examples of 르 *lŭ*-irregular verbs:

다르-	(달라)	tarŭ-talla	'be different'
부르-	(불러)	purŭ-pullŏ	'call'
짜르-	(짤라)	tcharŭ-tchalla	'cut'
기르-	(길러)	kirŭ-killŏ	'raise'
가르-	(갈라)	karŭ-kallŏ	'divide'
모르-	(몰라)	morŭ-molla	'not know'
찌르-	(찔러)	tchirŭ-tchillŏ	'stab'
지르-	(질러)	chirŭ-chillŏ	'scream'

but only a handful of *lŭ*-regular verbs:

치르-	(치러)	ch'irŭ-ch'irŏ	'pay back'

5 ㄹ *l*-deletion

Verb stem-final *l*-deletion is not really a case of verb "irregularity," but applies to all *l*-final verb stems when one joins a suffix beginning with 으, 오, ㄴ, or ㅅ. They are called irregular because /l/ does not get deleted in these idiosyncratic environments elsewhere in the grammar:

살-으니까 sal-ŭnikka
사-으니까 sa-ŭnikka
사-니까 sa-nikka
'as X lives'

Here is a sample conjugation:

Table 6.5 *l*-irregular verbs and their conjugation

-다 -ta	-고 -ko	-어요 -ŏyo	-은 ŭn	-네 -ne	-세요 -seyo	
알다 al-ta	알고 al-ko	알아요 al-ayo	안 an	아네 a-ne	아세요 a-seyo	'know'
살다 sal-ta	살고 sal-ko	살아요 sal-ayo	산 san	사네 sa-ne	사세요 sa-seyo	'live'
울다 ul-ta	울고 ul-ko	울어요 ul-ŏyo	운 un	우네 u-ne	우세요 u-seyo	'cry'
놀다 nol-ta	놀고 nol-ko	놀아요 nol-ayo	논 non	노네 no-ne	노세요 no-seyo	'play'
갈다 kal-ta	갈고 kal-ko	갈아요 kal-ayo	간 kan	가네 ka-ne	가세요 ka-seyo	'be beautiful'

6 The irregularity of 하다 *ha-ta* 'do, be'

A sequence of two vowels in a row is avoided as much as possible. Avoidance strategies include deleting one of them, merging the two into one, changing the sequence into a single new vowel, or inserting a semivowel between the two. When the verb stem 하 *ha-* 'do' or a verbalizing suffix 하 *ha-* meets a suffix-initial -어 ŏ, two such strategies involve two different kinds of conjugation:

(i) Merge the two syllables into a new syllable 해 *hae-*, as the following examples show:

하 ha + 어 ŏ	→	해 hae	(Conj/Dec)
하 ha + 어야 ŏya	→	해야 haeya	'only if...'
하 ha + 어도 ŏdo	→	해도 haedo	'even though...'
하 ha + 어서 ŏsŏ	→	해서 haesŏ	'... and so'
하 ha + 어라 ŏra	→	해라 haera	(Imp/Plain)

(ii) Insert a semivowel *y* between the two syllables. In this case, the insertion blocks VH. For this reason, Koreans call this phenomenon the "여 *yŏ*- anomaly." Observe the following examples:

하 ha + 어 ŏ	→	하여 hayŏ	(Conj/Dec)
하 ha + 어야 ŏya	→	하여야 hayŏya	'only if...'
하 ha + 어도 ŏdo	→	하여도 hayŏdo	'even though...'
하 ha + 어서 ŏsŏ	→	하여서 hayŏsŏ	'...and so'
하 ha + 어라 ŏra	→	하여라 hayŏra	(Imp/Plain)

Note: 하여 *hayŏ* is allowed only as a conjunctive, and not as a sentence ender.

The two coexisting forms are not completely optional. The first group is much more commonly used, especially in spoken Korean today. The second group sounds a bit more formal and old-fashioned.

7 ㅎ *h*-irregular verbs

We have seen that the suffix-initial 어 *ŏ*- vowel together with the verb 하 *ha*- merge into one syllable 해 *hae*-. A group of verb stems, which derive their full or partial forms from the verb 하 *ha*- 'do, be' – including all basic color words such as 빨갛다 *ppalkah-ta*, 노랗다 *norah-ta*, 파랗다 *p'arah-ta*, and 까맣다 *kkamah-ta*, and some other descriptive verbs such as 어떻다 *ŏttŏh-ta* and 그렇다 *kŭrŏh-ta* – undergo a similar change when they meet an 어 *ŏ*-initial affix. These verbs, although manifesting only the ㅎ *h* part of their historical origin, 하 *ha*- 'do,' show the vowel's trace in the conjugation. When the vowel 어 *ŏ* follows this ㅎ *h* sound, it changes to 애 *ae* and the ㅎ *h* is deleted in the process. These details are no longer important, but useful for understanding the formula shown in Table 6.6:

Table 6.6 Verb-final ㅎ *h* anomaly

X-ah + ŏ- → X-ae-
X-ŏh + ŏ- → X-ae-

Table 6.7 includes a sample conjugation for the 하 *ha*-irregular verbs:

Table 6.7 하 *ha*-irregular verbs and their conjugation

-다 -ta	-고 -ko	-어요 -ŏyo	-어도 -ŏto	-어서 -ŏsŏ
하다 ha-ta	하고 ha-ko	해요/하여요 hae-yo/hayŏyo	해도/하여도 hae-to/hayŏto	해서/하여서 hae-sŏ/ha-yŏsŏ
빨갛다 ppalkah-ta	빨갛고 ppalkah-ko	빨개요 ppalkae-yo	아도/빨개도 a-to/ppalkae-to	빩아서/빨개서 ppalk-asŏ/ppalkae-sŏ
어떻다 ŏttŏh-ta	어떻고 ŏttŏh-ko	어때요 ŏttae-yo	어때도 ŏttae-to	어때서 ŏttae-sŏ

8 되다 **toe-ta** 'become' is a class by itself.

Like most of the irregular verbs, the verb 되다 *toe-ta* 'become' belongs to the basic vocabulary. In addition to its common meaning of 'become,' it is used in passivization and also as an honorific replacement for equational copula -이다 *i-ta*. The irregular verb 되다 *toe-ta* shows the same kind of conjugation as that of 하 *ha*-irregular verbs, as shown in Table 6.8:

Table 6.8 Conjugation of 되다 *toe* 'become'

되다 toe-ta	되고 toe-ko	돼요/되어요 toae-yo/toe-ŏyo	돼도/되어도 toae-to/toe-ŏto	돼서/되어서 toae-sŏ/toe-ŏsŏ

Chapter 7

Negation

In Korean, negative (Neg) constructions have four main uses. They indicate:

1 the absence of certain characteristics (lexical negation)
2 factual denial (*ani*)
3 impossibility or inability (*mot*)
4 prohibition (*mal*)

Of these, (1) involves a *morphological* process, the addition of a prefix to turn a positive term into its antonym. The other types of negation are *syntactic* processes that are systematic and highly prevalent. We will call type (1) *lexical negation*; the others, *sentential negation*.

7.1 Lexical negation

Most languages have pairs of words that contrast in the presence or absence of certain characteristics. For example, in English, there are such parallels as *normal/abnormal*, *productive/counterproductive*, *honest/dishonest*, *familiar/unfamiliar*, *governmental/nongovernmental*, *possible/impossible*, *dependent/independent*, *credible/incredible*, *logical/illogical*, etc., where the prefixes *ab-*, *counter-*, *dis-*, *un-*, *non-*, *im-*, *in-*, *il-* all express the absence of some characteristic. Just as most English negative prefixes are borrowed from Latin, Korean negative prefixes are borrowed from Chinese. Table 7.1 lists some Sino-Korean negative prefixes that are still productive, with examples.

Table 7.1 Negative prefixes in negative words

Negative prefix	Meaning	Example	Gloss	Meaning without the prefix
무 mu 無-	absence	무소속 musosok	Independent (party)	소속 'affiliation'
미 mi 未-	unattaining	미완성 miwansŏng	unfinished	완성 'completion'
몰 mol 沒	demise	몰상식 molsangsik	ignorance	상식 'common sense'
비 pi 非	counter	비정상 pijŏngsang	abnormality	정상 'normality'
불 pu 不[a]	absence	불필요 pulp'iryo	unnecessary	필요 'necessity'
부 pul 不[a]	absence	부자유 pujayu	lack of freedom	자유 'freedom'

[a] 불 and 부 are different pronunciations for the same Sino-Korean character 不. This is a result of historical change, where the final -ㄹ [l] sound dropped before a consonant pronounced at the same site in the mouth, e.g., ㄷ [t], ㅅ [s], and ㅈ [ch].

Native vocabulary does not participate in this class of lexical parallels. One notable exception is demonstrated by copulative and existential verbs. The two very basic *be-* verbs in Korean, equational 이다 *i-ta* and existential 있다 *iss-ta*, have idiosyncratic negative forms, as shown in Table 7.2.

Table 7.2 Negative forms of '*be*' and '*have*' verbs

		Plain		With honorific subject	
	English	Affirmative	Negative	Affirmative	Negative
Equational copula	to be	이다 i-ta	아니다 ani-ta	이시다 i-si-ta	아니시다 ani-si-ta
	to be	있다 iss-ta	없다 ŏps-ta	계시다 kye-si-ta	안 계시다 an kye-si-ta
Existential	to have	있다 iss-ta	없다 ŏps-ta	있으시다 iss-ŭsi-ta	없으시다 ŏps-ŭsi-ta

Compare the example affirmative and negative sentences below. The sentences in (B) show two different negative forms of the existential verb 있다 *iss-ta* used for a subject of the sentence whose referent is a respected person, the first with the possessive, and the second with the existential, meaning.

(A) Affirmative

회장님은 오늘 약속이 있으시다.
hoejangnim-ŭn onŭl yaksok-i iss-ŭsi-ta.
CEO-Top today appointment-Subj Exist-SH-Dec
사무실에 계시다.
samusil-e kyesi-ta.
office-Loc Exist(Hon)-Dec/Plain
'The CEO has no appointment today. (He/She) is not in (his/her) office.'

(B) Negative

회장님은 오늘 약속이 없으시다.
hoejangnim-ŭn onŭl yaksok-i ŏps-ŭsi-ta.
CEO-Top today appointment-Subj not Exist-SH-Dec
사무실에 안 계시다.
samusil-e an kyesi-ta
office-Loc Neg Exist(SH)-Dec/Plain
'The CEO has no appointment today. (He/She) is not in (his/her) office.'

7.2 Sentential negation

Negative constructions vary depending on the types of sentences that are negated. Negation in declarative and question sentences with the general negative adverb 안 *an* [← 아니 *ani*] generally expresses denial or nonoccurrence of facts. When the adverb 안 is replaced by another negative adverb 못 *mot*, the inability or impossibility of reaching an ideal, an affirmative situation is connoted. Negative imperative and propositive sentences, however, indicate prohibition, in which case another negative word, 말 *mal*, is used. In English all these different types of negation are constructed with the negative adverb *not* or determiner *no*, but in Korean these distinctions are indicated by different kinds of Neg markers as discussed above.

7.2.1 *Two kinds of negative construction*

There are basically two types of negation in Korean, a short (S) and long (L) form. Both of these constructions use the negative (Neg) marker 안 *an*, etymologically from 아니 *ani*.

7.2.1.1 *Short-form (preverbal) negation*

In S-type negation, Neg is preverbal; in L-type, postverbal. In S negation, the negative adverb 안 *an* is put right before the verb:

안 + Verb

Here are some examples:

일요일에는 안 가.
ilyoil-e-nŭn an ka.
Sunday-Loc-Top Neg go-Dec/*panmal*
'I don't go on Sundays.'

날씨가 안 좋다.
nalssi-ka an choh-ta.
weather-Subj Neg be good-Dec/Plain
'This weather is not good.'

With verbs containing the verbalizing suffix -하 *ha*, Neg can be put either before the entire verb or before the -하 *ha* suffix. Whether the Neg marker can intervene between the suffix -하 *ha* and the pre-하 *ha* element depends on the nature of the latter.

When the pre-하 *ha* element is an action noun, Neg appears between the noun and 하 *ha*. When the verb consists of **a stative verb** + *ha*, then the Neg marker is placed before the entire verb. Compare:

요새는 운동 안 한다. [?* 안 운동한다]
yosae-nŭn undong an ha-n-ta.
these days-Top exercise Neg do-Pres-Dec/Plain
'These days, I do not exercise.'

아파트가 안 깨끗하다. [?* 깨끗 안 하다]
ap'at'ŭ-ka an kkaekkŭsha-ta.
apartment-Subj Neg be clean-Dec/Plain
'The apartment is not clean.'

In negative constructions, action verbs ending in -하 *ha* are consistently split into two sections, because they are paraphrasable into very similar expressions with different structures:

[운동 한다]$_V$ 'exercise'
exercise do-Pres-Dec/Plain

[[운동을]$_{NP}$ [한다]$_V$]$_{VP}$ 'do exercise'
exercise-Obj do-Pres-Dec/Plain

This kind of split is obviously easier when the noun is an action word, because the 하 *ha* suffix can gain an independent meaning 'to do' in the new structure, and the pre-하 *ha* element automatically becomes an object of that verb. It was mentioned that the 하 *ha* part can be translated either as 'do' or 'be' depending on the kind of noun that it verbalizes [▶6.3.1]. When the pre-하 *ha* element is descriptive, e.g., 씩씩 *ssikssik* 'vigor,' 뚱뚱 *ttungttung* 'fat,' it does not become a natural kind of complement of the verb meaning 'do.'

7.2.1.2 *Long-form (postverbal) negation*

Long-form negation attaches the expression 'not do X' (where X is the corresponding sentence) to the verb stem of the affirmative sentence:

[Verb]$_S$ + -지 않다 (← 아니 하다). -chi anhta (← aniha-ta)

Note the difference in spelling between the two kinds of Negs in S-type and L-type negative constructions. The ㅎ *h* in the post-verbal negative marker -않 *anh* is due to its etymological origin in the form containing the verb 하 *ha-* 'do.'

Koreans use the two negative forms interchangeably with no obvious semantic distinction. However, two distinct linguistic forms are really never identical in meaning. Long-form negation has a wide scope, whereas the short form has narrow scope. That is, the L form negates the whole sentence rather than just the verb. This becomes clear when considering negative sentences with words expressing quantity. Compare the following two negative sentences:

(i) 모두 안 왔어요.
modu an o-ass-ŏyo.
all Neg come-Past-Dec/Pol
'All did not come [= No one came].'

(ii) 모두 오지 않았어요.
modu o-ji anh-ass-ŏyo.
all come-Comp Neg-Past-Dec/Pol
'It is not the case that all came [= Some came].'

Both of these sentences contain the idea 'All did not come.' The difference in meaning results from the fact that, in the narrow scope in example (i), Neg becomes part of the verb, as it were, and 모두 *modu* 'all' acts as the unique subject of that verb. So, the sentence means 'All (every one of them all) did not come,' and therefore 'No one came.' In example (ii), what is being negated is the truthfulness of what the listener may believe. So the listener may think that all came, and the sentence is saying that 'It is not true that all did not come,' and therefore 'Some came.'

> *Note*: The verb 않다 *anh-ta* takes the processive marker -는 *-nŭn* in the present tense, when the verb of the affirmative sentence is an action verb:
>
> 그 사람은 아버지 앞에서 담배를 피지 않는다.
> kŭ saram-ŭn abŏji ap'-esŏ tambae-lŭl p'i-chi anh-nŭn-ta.
> that person-Top father front-Loc cigarette-Obj smoke-Comp Neg-Pres-Dec/Plain
> 'That person does not smoke in front of his father.'

7.2.2 *Unattainable negative constructions*

Sometimes one cannot do something either because one does not have the ability or because the circumstances do not allow it. In such a case, the negative adverb 못 *mot* is used. Syntactically this Neg appears in the same slots as 안 *an* but with a little modification, because in *an*-negation, the original verb 하 *ha-* is not visible, due to the use of a contracted form even in normal speech style and speed; but the full form is still used for a special, somewhat archaic, effect. Table 7.3 shows the two Neg markers in the two related long negative constructions:

Table 7.3 못 (*mot*) and 안 (*an*) negations

	못 mot	안 an
Short form	못 + Verb	안 + Verb
Long form	Verb stem + -지]$_N$ 못하다 chi mot-ha-ta	Verb stem + -지]$_N$ 않다/아니하다 chi anh-ta/ani-ha-ta

Compare the following pairs of sentences:

1 a. 돈이 없어서 여행 못 한다.
ton-i ŏps-ŏsŏ yŏhaeng mot ha-n-ta.
money-Subj not have-Conj travel Neg do-Pres-Dec/Plain
'I do not have money, so I cannot travel.'

b. 방학동안 집에 있고 싶어서
panghak-tong'an chip-e iss-ko sip'-ŏsŏ
vacation-during home-Loc Exist-Conj want to-Conj
여행 안 한다.
yŏhaeng an ha-n-ta.
travel Neg do-Pres-Dec/Plain
'I want to be at home during vacation, so I do not travel.'

2 a. 지금 수영복이 없어서 수영을
chigŭm suyŏngbok-i ŏps-ŏsŏ suyŏng-ŭl
now bathing suit-Subj not Exist-Conj swim do-Comp
하지 못한다.
ha-chi mot-ha-n-ta.
do-Comp Neg-do-Pres-Dec/Plain
'I can't swim because I don't have my swimsuit.'

b. 나는 호텔에서는 수영을 하지
na-nŭn hot'el-esŏ-nŭn suyŏng-ŭl ha-chi
me-Top hotel-Loc-Top swimming-Obj do-Comp
않는다.
anh-nŭn-ta.
Neg-Pres-Dec/Plain
'I do not swim at a hotel.'

The choice of short- vs. long-form 못 *mot* negation also reflects the speaker's attitude toward the listener. Compare the following short- and long-form constructions:

a. 돈이 없어서 모두 대학에 못 갔다.
ton-i ŏps-ŏsŏ modu taehak-e mot ka-ss-ta.
money not Exist-Conj all college-Loc Neg go-Past-Dec/Plain
'Because all had no money everybody could not go to college [None could go to college].'

b. 모두 대학에 가지 못 했다.
modu taehak-e ka-chi mot hae-ss-ta.
all college-Loc go-Comp Neg do-Past-Dec/Plain
'It is not the case that everybody went to college [Some of them did].'

Here again, example (a) expresses a statement that is not necessarily constrained by the external forces that the second sentence suggests. In the second sentence, the speaker assumes that the listener might expect someone to have gone to college but tells the person it is not so, as that goal was somehow unattainable.

7.2.3 Prohibitive negative constructions

When an imperative or a propositive affirmative sentence is negated, Neg has a prohibitive meaning – something along the lines of 'You may not...'

In a prohibitive negative construction, S-type negation does not occur; only L-type negation is used. Another different characteristic of prohibitive constructions is that yet another Neg form, 말 *mal-*, is used. This form, like all ㄹ *l*-final verb stems, changes to 마 *ma-* when followed by the vowel -으 *ŭ*. Here are some examples:

노래방에 가지
noraebang-e kaji
singing room-Loc go-Comp

마십시오	ma-si-psi-o	(deferential)
마세요	ma-se-yo	(polite)
말아	mal-a	(*panmal*)
마십시다	ma-si-psi-ta	(deferential)
맙시다	ma-psi-ta	(polite)
말자	mal-ja	(plain)

말 *mal*-negation is not actually limited to imperatives and propositives. The construction can be used also in other cases indicated for blocking some planned acts:

오늘 학교에 가지 말까?
onŭl hakkyo-e ka-chi mal-kka?
today school-Loc go-Comp Neg-Q/Plain
'Shall I not go to school today [although I was planning to]?'

내일 점심은 먹지 말고 저녁을
naeil chŏmsim-ŭn mŏk-chi mal-ko chŏnyŏk-ŭl
tomorrow lunch-Top eat-Comp Neg-Conj dinner-Obj
많이 먹어야겠다.
manhi mŏk-ŏya-kess-ta.
a lot eat-have-to-Dec/Plain
'Tomorrow I must not eat lunch but eat a big dinner.'

7.2.4 Negative polarity words

Some vocabulary items occur only in negative sentences. Table 7.4 lists commonly used negative-polarity vocabulary.

Table 7.4 Negative-polarity words

Neg-polarity item	Example	Romanization	Meaning
여간 yŏgan 'a bit'	여간 어렵지 않다	. . . ŏryŏp-chi an-ta	'X is very difficult.'
아직 ajik 'yet'	아직 안 오셨어요	. . . an osyŏss-ŏyo	'X didn't come yet.'
결코 kyŏlk'o 'at all'	결코 안 우는 여자	. . . an u-nŭn yŏja	'a woman who will never cry'
도무지 tomuji 'at all'	도무지 알수 없는 일	. . . a-l su ŏpsnŭn il	'a totally incomprehensible matter'
좀체로 chomch'ero 'at all'	좀체로 물이 안 빠진다	. . . mul-i an ppaji-n-ta	'The water doesn't drain regardless of the effort.'
. . . 밖에 pakke '[nothing] but'	한국사람밖에 안 간다	. . . han'guk saram pakk-e an ka-n-ta	'Only Koreans go there.'

Chapter 8

Nouns

Nominals include nouns and noun-like categories such as numerals, classifiers, pronouns, and noun phrases. As a grammatical category nominals will be referred to as nouns.

Nouns denote both concrete elements and abstract entities, referring to objects (animate and inanimate), substances (tangible and intangible), events, states, and feelings. In sentences, nouns function as subjects, objects, and complements.

8.1 General properties of nouns

1 Any unbound noun may stand by itself without any particles, but it cannot form a full sentence by itself, only a sentence fragment, even if a full sentence could be inferred from it:

투쟁! t'ujaeng! '(Let's) fight (against X)!'

2 Nouns are commonly followed by post-positions, called *particles*. A particle indicates the grammatical function or relation of the nominal to the other elements in a sentence (e.g., Subj and Obj), or delimits its meaning (e.g., emphatic).

Note: Korean particles are *postpositions* that have functions similar to those of prepositions like *of*, *to*, *in*, *as*, and *for* in English. Unlike English prepositions, however, the nominal and its particles act as a single unit. They are pronounced with no pause (and written with no space) between them, and when a nominal is deleted any suffixes attached to it are deleted as well.

So, for example, in:

어제는	미나의	언니가	그에게도	편지를	썼다.
ŏje-nŭn	mina-ŭi	ŏnni-ka	kŭ-ege-to	p'yŏnji-lŭl	ssŏ-ss-ta.
yesterday-Top	Mina-Gen	sister-Subj	him-Dat-Emph	letter-Obj	write-Past-Dec/Plain

'(Talking about) Yesterday, Mina's sister wrote a letter to him also.'

there are six particles including -는 *nŭn*, -의 *ŭi*, -가 *ka*, -에게 *ege*, -도 *to*, and -를 *rŭl*; these show various functions of the noun they are attached to. If the context makes it clear, the noun phrase 미나의 언니 *mina-ŭi ŏnni* 'Mina's sister' may be dropped. In such a case not only the noun phrase but also the particle -가 *ka* is dropped, because in the absence of the noun phrase the particle has no reason to be there.

3 Definiteness and indefiniteness of Korean nouns are not represented using articles like English *the* or *a(n)*, but by demonstratives and the numeral 한 *han* 'one' or an indefinite prenoun such as 어느 *ŏnŭ* 'some (one of the list)' or 어떤 *ŏttŏn* 'some (what kind).'

a. 그 학교
kŭ hakkyo
'that/the school'

b. 한/어느 학교
han/ŏnŭ school
'a/some school'

4 Korean nouns do not change their forms according to gender or case as in some languages such as German. The English noun also does not vary, and only some pronouns show different forms such as *I*, *my*, *me*, *he*, *his*, *him*, *she*, and *her*. Korean employs another word or context to mark gender as need arises and particles indicating whether it is the subject, object, etc., as in 그녀를 *kŭ-nyŏ-lŭl* (that-woman-Obj) 'her.'

5 *Plurals* are not obligatorily marked, except in the case of pronouns. Plural marking is often more dependent on the sentential meaning or context than required by the grammatical structure. So, when someone says,

어제	오렌지를	샀어요.
ŏje	orenji-lŭl	sa-ss-ŏyo.
yesterday	orange-Obj	buy-Past-Dec/Pol

how many oranges were bought is not indicated.

When the plural suffix -들 *tŭl* is used, the individuality of the constituting members of the noun it is attached to are more pronounced than a general sense of unspecified quantity carried by a noun without a plural marker. For example, in the following two sentences, both of which can be translated as 'There are a lot of people':

사람이	많아요.
saram-i	manh-ayo.
person-Subj	is abundant-Dec/Pol

사람들이	많아요.
saram-tŭl-i	manh-ayo.
person-Pl-Subj	is abundant-Dec/Pol

the first sentence simply indicates there is a crowd, while the second one observes that the crowd has all kinds of people in it.

Because pronouns and demonstratives are naturally of definite reference, a pronoun or a noun preceded by a demonstrative uses the plural suffix -들 *tŭl*. So, in the following sentence:

그 학생이 왔어요.
kŭ haksaeng-i wa-ss-ŏyo.
that student-Subj come-Past-Dec/Pol
'That student came.'

it is clear only one student came. If more than one student came, then the plural marker -들 *tŭl* would have been attached to the noun as 그 학생들 *kŭ haksaeng-tŭl* 'those students.'

6 The copulative verb -이 *i* 'be' may be attached to a nominal with no pause (and written with no space) between them, thereby forming a verb-like word together. This is different from an English copular sentence, e.g., "*I am American*," where the noun *American* remains an independent entity. The Nominal + Cop sequence translates as something like 'is/equals Nominal' but the sequence acts as one unit. As Korean subjects are easily dropped when context makes them clear, a sentence may consist of only a noun + Cop, as in:

봄이다. 'It is spring.'
pom-i-ta.
spring-Cop-Dec/Plain

7 Nouns may be described by modifiers. Modifiers always precede the nominals they modify. As mentioned before, the focal element of a linguistic unit appears at its end. Therefore, modifiers – whether demonstratives, adjectives made of sentences, or other nouns – always precede the modified nominals. Observe the following examples:

이 i this	동네 tongne neighborhood	'this neighborhood'
사람이 없는 [salami ŏps-nŭn]$_S$ people lack-Mod	동네 tongne neighborhood	'deserted neighborhood'
부자 puja rich person	동네 tongne neighborhood	'rich neighborhood'

8 Korean is a *numeral classifier* language, which employs classifiers together with numerals in describing and counting objects, e.g. persons. Classifiers (CL) are words that categorize objects according to their shape, function, and other characteristics that are often culturally defined. Here is an example:

연필	일곱	자루
yŏnp'il	ilgop	charu
pencil	seven	CL

The classifier 자루 *charu* is used for objects that are long, thin, and rigid like chopsticks, candlesticks, and knives.

9 All loanwords are analyzed as nouns in Korean, regardless of the part of speech they belong to in their source language. For example, to make a Korean verb meaning 'date, go out with,' add the verbalizing suffix -하 *ha* to the borrowed noun 데이트 *teit'ŭ* 'dating' as in $[[$데이트$]_N$하다$]_V$ 'date (someone),' as shown in the sentence below:

민수씨,	요즘	$[[[$데이트$]_N$	$[$해요$]_V]_V]_{VP}$?
minsu-ssi	yojŭm	teit'ŭ	hae-yo?
Minsu-Mr.	these days	date	do-Dec/Pol

'Are you going out with someone, Minsu?' [*lit.* 'Minsu, do you do "dating"?']

10 When more than one noun come together to form a complex noun, the greatest necessary background information appears first and the most focused point appears last. This is why Korean names are written with the family name first, then the given name.

8.2 Types of nouns

As is common in most languages, in Korean many grammatical phenomena need information on the types of nouns.

Korean nouns are categorized as:

- Proper or common [▶8.2.1]
- Animate or inanimate [▶8.2.2]
- Action or description [▶8.2.3]
- Countable or non-countable [▶8.2.4]
- Free-standing or bound [▶8.2.5]
- Pronouns and quasi-pronouns [▶8.2.6]
- Numerals and noun classifiers [▶8.2.7, 8.2.8]

8.2.1 *Proper nouns and common nouns*

Most nouns are common nouns referring to general objects including people (sister, teacher, baby, gentleman), animals (dog, tiger, bird, dragon), things (books, road, car, piano), and ideas (Confucianism, love, courage, dream).

Some nouns, on the other hand, refer to the unique identity of a person, thing, or concept. They are called proper nouns. They include:

서울	sŏul	(the capital of South Korea) Seoul
임권택	im kwŏnt'aek	(a famous movie director) Im Kwon-t'aek
불국사	pulguksa	(name of a Buddhist temple) Pulguksa
한글	han'gŭl	the Korean alphabet
강원도	kangwŏndo	Kangwŏn Province
고려 왕조	koryŏ wangjo	Koryŏ dynasty
추석	ch'usŏk	(an Autumn harvest festival) Ch'usŏk
미국	miguk	America
유엔	yuen	U.N.

> *Note*: Koreans call people by their full names only in indifferent formal situations, as in a classroom roll call or at certain formal gatherings. Children address each other by their full or given names. Adults address children by their given names. Calling an adult by his or her names alone (without a title of some kind) is considered extremely inappropriate.

Some parts of proper nouns may be shared by other proper nouns. For example, the names of the days of the week all end with a bound noun -요일 *yoil* 'day of the week' [▶8.2.5 on bound nouns].

Days of the week, -요일 *yoil*:

월요일	wŏl-yoil	Monday	[월 = (bd. n.) moon]
화요일	hwa-yoil	Tuesday	[화 = (bd. n.) fire]
수요일	su-yoil	Wednesday	[수 = (bd. n.) water]
목요일	mok-yoil	Thursday	[목 = (bd. n.) wood]
금요일	kŭm-yoil	Friday	[금 = (bd. n.) gold, metal]
토요일	t'o-yoil	Saturday	[토 = (bd. n.) earth]
일요일	il-yoil	Sunday	[일 = (bd. n.) sun, daylight]

8.2.2 *Animate nouns and inanimate nouns*

Animate nouns are humans and animals. Gods and ghosts, often behaving like humans, are considered animate. All other nouns are inanimate.

Animate nouns include:

애기	aegi	'baby'
노인	noin	'old person'
강아지	kang'aji	'puppy'
호랑이	horang'i	'tiger'
귀신	kwisin	'ghost'

Inanimate nouns include:

돌	tol	'stone'
책	ch'aek	'book'
꽃	kkoch'	'flower'
호박	hobak	'pumpkin'
비행기	pihaenggi	'airplane'

8.2.3 *Action nouns and description nouns*

Action nouns include:

운동	undong	'sports, exercise'
생각	saenggak	'thought'
청소	ch'ŏngso	'cleaning'
구경	kugyŏng	'viewing a sight worth seeing, sightseeing'
지불	chibul	'payment'

Descriptive nouns include:

정직	chŏngjik	'honesty'
용감	yonggam	'bravery'
우아	ua	'elegance, grace'
피곤	p'igon	'fatigue'
행복	haengbok	'happiness'

Note: When these nouns are verbalized by attaching the verbalizing suffix -하 *ha*,

Action noun + *-ha* → active verb	'do X'
Descriptive Noun + *-ha* → stative verb	'be X'

8.2.4 *Countable nouns and non-countable nouns*

Countable nouns include:

책	ch'aek	'book'
표	p'yo	'ticket'
집	chip	'house'
친구	ch'in'gu	'friend'
나비	nabi	'butterfly'

Non-countable nouns include

용서	yongsŏ	'forgiveness'
사랑	sarang	'love'
고통	kot'ong	'suffering'
희망	hŭimang	'hope'
멋	mŏs	'(having) style, good taste'

8.2.5 *Free-standing nouns and bound nouns*

Most nouns are free-standing and can occur by themselves as sentence fragments. A limited set of nouns, most of which are native vocabulary, are neither independent nor have their own specific meaning. Nouns of this group, *bound nouns*, require a modifier to form a complete and meaningful phrase. For these reasons, bound nouns are sometimes called "defective nouns." Observe how the bound nouns, which are underlined, cannot be used without a modifier preceding them in the following examples (*indicates an ungrammatical or impossible form):

(i) a. 옛날 [[이]$_{Mod}$ 곳]$_N$에는 큰 학교가 하나
yennal i kos-e-nŭn k'ŭn hakkyo-ka hana
long ago this place-at-Top big school-Subj one
있었습니다.
iss-ŏss-sŭpni-ta.
Exist-Past-Dec/Def
'Long ago, there was a big school at this place.'

b. 장소는/*곳은 케네디센터 입니다.
changso-nŭn/*kos-ŭn k'enedi-ssent'ŏ i-pni-ta.
place-Top /*place-Top Kennedy Center Cop-Dec/Def
'The place is the Kennedy Center.'

(ii) a. [[옷 갈아입는]$_{Mod}$ 데]$_{Mod}$가 어디
os-kal-a-ip-nŭn te-ka ŏdo
clothes-change-wear-Mod(Pres) place-Subj somewhere
있어요?
iss-ŏyo?
Exist-Dec(Pol)
'Is there any place where one changes (clothes)?'

b. 상황이/*데가 안 좋습니다.
sanghwang-i/ *te-ka an choh-sŭpni-ta.
circumstances-Subj/*circ.-Subj Neg be good-Dec/Def
'The circumstances are not good.'

Some of the most commonly used bound nouns are:

-것	kŏs	'thing'
-적	chŏk	'(experienced) time'
-쪽	tchok	'direction'
-동안	tong'an	'duration of time'
-분	pun	'(honorable) person'
-이	i	'person'
-척	ch'ŏk	'faking'
-데	te	'(circumstantial) situation, point/spot, place/ground/basis'
-수	su	'way, means, possibility'
-줄	chul	'fact, knowledge'

Note: Some bound nouns are more restricted in their usage than others. For example, the first four nouns above can occur with most modifiers including a demonstrative, another noun or noun phrase, and clause. Bound noun -이 *i* cannot have a noun modifier, and the last four occur usually with verbal modifiers, never with demonstratives such as 'this' or 'that,' or another noun. The bound noun -줄 *chul* can occur only with a cognitive verb (알 *al*- 'know' or 모르 *morŭ*- 'not know'). The bound noun -수 *su* commonly occurs as the subject of an existential verb (있 *iss*- 'to exist' or 없 *ŏps*- 'not exist) to mean together 'it is possible for x to…' or 'x can…

Many honorific (not necessarily deferential, but all interpersonal) titles are bound nouns, e.g., -양 *yang* 'Young Miss' and -군 *kun* 'Young Master.'

강지미 양 '(Young) Miss Kang Chimi'
김기호 군 '(Young) Mr. Kim Kiho'

Many Sino-Korean (SK) root syllables, in spite of each representing an independent meaning, cannot stand alone but must form a word by attaching mostly to another SK root. For example, SK root 춘 (Ch. 春)

ch'un means 'spring' and can be fully pronounced with an independent meaning, but must combine with another root to become a bona fide noun. Therefore a phrase such as *춘에 *ch'un-e* ('spring-in') cannot be used to connote 'in spring.' At the expense of appearing redundant, an SK root 절 *chŏl* (season) is attached to create 춘절 *ch'un-chŏl* [*lit.* 'spring season'] for this purpose.

There is a small group of words that have to be followed by nouns in order to complete their meaning. Members of this pronominal group are called *prenouns*. Here are some examples:

Prenouns		
이	i	'this'
그	kŭ	'that'
저	chŏ	'that (over there)'
어느	ŏnŭ	'which (one)'
무슨	musŭn	'what type of'
어떤	ŏttŏn	'what sort (quality) of'
한	han	'one'

The first three examples, 이 *i* 'this,' 그 *kŭ* 'that,' and 저 *chŏ* 'that over there,' are deictic expressions specifying spatial or temporal distance from the speaker's and hearer's shared perspectives. 이 *i* refers to something/someone close to the speaker, 그 *kŭ* to something/someone close to the hearer, and 저 *chŏ* to something that is detached from both the speaker and the hearer physically or cognitively. When referring to something that has just been mentioned, 그 *kŭ* 'that' is used.

8.2.6 *Pronouns and quasi-pronouns*

At first glance the inventory of Korean pronouns, which seems open-ended, may appear prohibitive. However, the Korean pronoun system is quite impoverished and lacks simple pronouns such as 'he,' 'she,' or 'they' and must resort to a **prenoun** + **noun** structure to create quasi-pronoun forms. There are two main reasons for this strategy: one is sentential structure and the other has to do with polite-speech protocol.

First, in many European languages, sentences must have subjects. Pronouns that refer to a specific noun or nouns, such as 'she,' 'it,' and 'they,' are, therefore, extremely convenient in those languages, because they allow people to avoid repeating the nouns. In Korean, however, a nominal in subject and other positions can just be deleted rather than replaced by pronouns, when it is clearly understood, either through conventional knowledge or context of the discourse.

Even when there is a need to refer to the noun already mentioned for clarification, a pronoun tends to be avoided – especially in the second person, because an inappropriate choice of speech level could be quite damaging, as the speaker is facing the listener directly. So, even the addressee is more likely referred to by name (preferably with a title), leaving no ambiguity, rather than by a pronoun. Observe the following example:

A (인호):	이거	제가	만들었어요.
(Inho):	igŏ	che-ka	mandŭl-ŏss-ŏyo.
	this	I (humble)-Subj	make-Past-Dec/Pol
	'I made this.'		

B	인호씨가	만들었어요?
	inho-ssi-ka	mandŭl-ŏss-ŏyo?
	Inho-Mr.-Subj	make-Past-Q/Pol
	'You made it?' [*lit.* 'Inho made X?']	

Here *Inho*, a given name, is used where *you* would be used in English.

8.2.6.1 *Definite pronouns*

In contrast with the multiple interpersonal relationships that are obligatorily expressed in the language, true pronouns are sparse and limited to a few neutral forms such as 나 *na* 'me,' 너 *nŏ* 'you,' and 우리 *uri* 'us.' Where in another language a pronoun would normally be used, Koreans may simply use another noun describing a particular person or object. For example, instead of a pronoun like 'she' or 'her,' Koreans may use such nouns as 소녀 *sonyŏ* 'young girl,' 여인 *yŏin* 'young lady,' 여사 *yŏsa* 'Madam,' or 노파 *nop'a* 'old woman,' etc., especially in literary narrative. In most cases, however, Korean speakers/writers use a demonstrative, 이 *i* 'this,' 그 *kŭ* 'that,' or 저 *chŏ* 'that (over there),' followed by a noun to create a phrase referring to a particular noun. The only exception may be that 그 *kŭ* is used as a third-person (mainly masculine) singular pronoun in fictions. One of the most basic ways for a speaker to express deference to the listener is to lower himself or herself. The first-person humble pronoun is 저 *chŏ*, literally 'that (over there).' Other humble expressions for the first person exist including the one that is no longer used, 소생 *sosaeng*, literally 'a small person.'

In general, honorific pronouns are usually phrases or compounds containing an honorific noun. For example, deferential third-person pronoun 그분 *kŭ pun* is composed of 그 *kŭ* 'that' + 분 *pun* 'honored person.' Derogatory third-person (compound) pronouns 그놈 *kŭ nom* and 그년 *kŭ nyŏn* represent derogatory nouns – -놈 *nom* 'bum or common/base man' and -년 nyŏn 'common/base woman,' respectively – attached to the deictic expression 그 *kŭ*. For objects, bound nouns such as -것 *kŏs* 'thing,' -때 *ttae* 'time,' -어기 *ŏgi* 'place' combine with demonstratives. Although these forms exist and are used as pronouns in other languages, they are far less frequently used in Korean than people's names, even in written narratives where they tend to be used more often than in speech.

In Korean, kinship terms such as 'elder sister,' 'elder brother,' 'uncle,' 'aunt,' and even 'nephew/niece' are used as quasi-pronouns, including the second person. These expressions essentially denote that the person referred to as such is regarded as a family member, i.e., a person enjoying all the respect, love, and care owed to a family member. For example, a sweet middle-aged lady whom one feels (or pretends to feel) close to may be called one of the following:

a. 아주머님	ajumŏnim	'respectable aunt [aunt + honorific title -nim]'
b. 아주머니	ajumŏni	'aunt'
c. 아줌마	ajumma	'auntie'
d. 아지마	ajima	'auntie [fast/casual speech form]'

Other titles identifying a person by his or her profession, place of residence, school, etc. can in fact be used as personal pronouns, including the second person.

A schematic inventory of Korean pronouns is given in Table 8.1.

Personal pronouns thus reveal the Korean honorific system, and the interpersonal relationship in various scales of power and solidarity is specifically expressed in the choice of pronouns and verb suffixes as well as some words carrying inherently polite or rude meanings [▶10].

Note: The word 자기 *chagi* 'he/she' is used when referring to a third person who has been mentioned just before (called anaphora by linguists), as in the following sentence:

미나가	자기(의)	생각을	말했다.
mina-ka	chagi(ŭi)	saenggak-ŭl	malhae-ss-ta.
Mina-Subj	her(Gen)	thoughts-Obj	speak-Past-Dec/Plain

'Mina spoke her mind.'

Table 8.1 Korean pronouns

Pronouns	Honorific scale	Singular	Plural
1st	Plain Humble	나 na 저 chŏ [*lit.* 'that (over there)']	우리들 uri(tŭl)
2nd	Plain Respect to equals Respect to juniors Affection to equals	너 nŏ 당신 tangsin [*lit.* 'the person in question'] 자네 chane 자기 chagi [*lit.* 'self']	너희들 nŏhi (tŭl)
3rd	Varying depending on the noun chosen	이 i 'this' + (NOUN) 그 kŭ 'that' + (NOUN) 저 chŏ 'that over there' + (NOUN) 자기 chagi 'self'	이 + (NOUN) (tŭl)

자기 *chagi* is often translated as 'self' because of the Chinese characters 自己 representing it, and perhaps also because it often co-occurs with the reflexive word 자신 *chasin* that truly means 'self,' as in 자기자신 *chagi chasin* 'herself/himself.' However, it simply denotes the third person with a connotation of 'that particular person' and it cannot co-occur with other personal pronouns or nouns to mean 'X-self.' In contrast, 자신 *chasin* can occur with all the pronouns as well as other animate nouns:

나 na 'me'	자신 chasin	'myself'
너 nŏ 'you'	자신 chasin	'yourself'
그 kŭ 'he/she'	자신 chasin	'herself/himself'
우리 uri 'us'	자신 chasin	'ourselves'
미나 'Mina'	자신 chasin	'Mina herself'

8.2.6.2 *Indefinite pronouns*

In English, indefinite pronouns have different forms depending on whether they are WH-words (*who, what, which, when, where,* and *how*) as in a WH-question such as "*Where did you go last Sunday?*"; an indefinite pronoun such as *someone, something, somewhere*, etc., as in a yes-no question like "*Did you go somewhere last Sunday?*"; or an indefinite pronoun – *anyone, anything, anywhere* – in a negative sentence like "*I did not go anywhere last Sunday.*" In Korean 'where,' 'somewhere,' and 'anywhere' are all expressed by the same word, 어디 *ŏdi,* because they all share the meaning of 'some place that is not specific or definite.'

Indefinite pronouns include:

어디	ŏdi	'where/somewhere'
언제	ŏnje	'when/some time'
왜	wae	'why/some reason'
아무	amu	'who/anyone'
누구	nugu	'who/someone'
무엇	muŏs	'what/something'
얼마	ŏlma	'how much/some quantity'
얼마	ŏlma	'how many/some number of'

> *Note*: (1) 누구 *nugu* + 가 *ka* → 누가 *nuga* 'who-Subj.' This change clearly occurred in this very common noun in an effort to avoid repeating a similar syllable (ㄱ + Vowel) within a short word; (2) 무엇 *muŏs* 'what' has an informal variant 뭐 *mwŏ* and a casual variant 모 *mo*.

Note that the indefinite noun 아무 *amu* means 'anyone, any person' but can also act as a prenoun [▶9.1.1.2] as in 아무 것 *amu kŏs* 'anything' or 아무 때 *amu ttae* 'any time.' The 아무 + **Noun** sequence is almost always followed by emphatic particle -도 *to* (see below), and commonly occurs in a negative sentence, as shown in the following example:

일요일에	아무 데도	안	갔어.↓
iryoil-e	amu-te-to	an	ka-ss-ŏ.
Sunday-Loc	any-place-Emph	Neg	go-Past-Dec/*panmal*

'I did not go anywhere on Sunday.'

Other examples of indefinite noun phrases that consist of prenoun + noun [▶9.1.1.2] include:

어느 ŏnŭ 'which(ever) side' (+ Noun):	쪽 tchok 'which(ever) direction,'
	편 p'yŏn 'which(ever) side'
어떤 ŏttŏn 'what(ever) sort of' (+ Noun):	것 kŏs 'what kind of thing/something,'
	친구 ch'in'gu 'what sort of/some friend'
무슨 musŭn 'what/some' (+ Noun):	때 ttae 'what/some time/period,'
	학교 hakkyo 'what school'

Korean speakers will disambiguate the types of sentences with indefinite pronouns by the context and the accentual pattern. In general, in a WH-question the indefinite pronoun gets an accent and the sentence ender a falling pitch. In a yes-no question one does not accent the indefinite pronoun and the sentence ends in a rising pitch. The word meaning 'anywhere' in a negative sentence gets the accent and the sentence has a falling pitch. Recall that WH-words are not moved to the front of the

WH-question sentence [▶4.4.2]. Consider the following sentences (accented words bolded):

(i) 일요일에 어디 갔어? ↓
iryoil-e ŏdi ka-ss-ŏ?
Sunday-Loc where go-Past-Dec/*panmal*
'Where did you go on Sunday?'

(ii) 일요일에 어디 갔어? ↑
iryoil-e ŏdi ka-ss-ŏ?
Sunday-Loc somewhere go-Past-Q/*panmal*
'Did you go somewhere on Sunday?'

(iii) 일요일에 어디도 안 갔어. ↓
iryoil-e ŏdi-to an ka-ss-ŏ.
Sunday-Loc anywhere-Emph Neg go-Past-Dec/*panmal*
'I did not go anywhere on Sunday.'

In English, a WH-question sentence usually contains only one WH-word. So, a sentence with multiple WH-pronouns such as *"*Where when who whom did meet?*" is ungrammatical. That is because WH-pronouns occur in the beginning of a WH-question sentence, and only one can take the first spot. In Korean, WH-pronouns do not have to move to the beginning of a sentence, and therefore, a question sentence with multiple WH-pronouns such as the following is possible.

누가 언제 어디서 누구를 만났어요?
nuga ŏnje ŏdiso nugu-lŭl mannass-ŏyo?
Who when where whom-Obj meet-Past-Q/Pol
'Who did somebody meet?/ Who is that somebody?/ When did that person meet the other person?/ Where did that person meet the the other person?' [*lit.* 'Who when where whom met?']

8.2.7 Numerals

8.2.7.1 Cardinal numerals

There are two parallel ways of counting in Korean. One is of native origin, the other Chinese. Native numbers go up to 99, after which all numbers are given in Sino-Korean. Therefore, any number in a series that can extend to large numbers such as a hotel room number, prices, ID numbers, etc. is counted in Sino-Korean. Here is the list of Korean cardinal numerals:

CARDINAL NUMERALS

	Native cardinal numerals		Sino-Korean cardinal numerals		
1	하나	hana	일	一	il
2	둘	tul	이	二	i
3	셋	ses	삼	三	sam
4	넷	nes	사	四	sa
5	다섯	tasŏs	오	五	o
6	여섯	yŏsŏs	육	六	(r)yuk
7	일곱	ilkop	칠	七	ch'il
8	여덟	yŏtŏl(p)	팔	八	p'al
9	아홉	ahop	구	九	ku
10	열	yŏl	십	十	sip
11	열하나	yŏl-hana	십일	十一	sip-il
12	열둘	yŏl-tul	십이	十二	sip-i
13	열셋	yŏl-ses	십삼	十三	sip-sam
14	열넷	yŏl-nes	십사	十四	sip-sa
15	열다섯	yŏl-tasŏs	십오	十五	sip-o
16	열여섯	yŏl-yŏsŏs	십육	十六	sip-yuk
17	열일곱	yŏl-ilgop	십칠	十七	sip-ch'il
18	열여덟	yŏl-yŏdŏlp	십팔	十八	sip-p'al
19	열아홉	yŏl-ahop	십구	十九	sip-ku
20	스물	sŭmul	이십	二十	i-sip
30	서른	sŏr(h)ŭn	삼십	三十	sam-sip
40	마흔	mahŭn	사십	四十	sa-sip
50	쉰	swin	오십	五十	o-sip
60	예순	yesun	육십	六十	yuk-sip
70	일흔	irhŭn	칠십	七十	ch'il-sip
80	여든	yŏdŭn	팔십	八十	p'al-sip
90	아흔	ahŭn	구십	九十	ku-sip

Higher digits

Current way of writing (in 1,000 increments)				Traditional way of writing (in 10,000 increments)
100	백	百	paek	100
1,000	천	千	ch'ŏn	1000
10,000	만	萬	man	1,0000
100,000	십만	十萬	sip-man	10,0000
1,000,000	백만	百萬	paek-man	100,0000
10,000,000	천만	千萬	ch'ŏn man	1000,0000
100,000,000	억	億	ŏk	1,0000,0000
1,000,000,000,000	조	兆	cho	1,0000,0000,0000

As noted above, native numbers only go up to 99. Native Korean numbers are used most often with native Korean classifiers such as -자루 *charu* 'stick,' -마리 *mari* 'head (of animals),' and -명 *myŏng* 'persons.' [▶8.2.8]: As a rule, use SK numbers when the series includes large numbers. Use SK numerals in the following cases, as well.

1 When telling time, use native numbers for the hours (because it is limited to a small number set of 12), and SK numbers for minutes and seconds (because the number goes to the higher 60, even though 60 is less than 99).

오전	열 한시	삼십오분	사십이초
ojŏn	yŏl-han-si	samsip-o-pun	sasip-i-ch'o
a.m.	11(Native K)-o'clock	35(SK)-minutes	42(SK)-seconds

'11:35:42 a.m.'

2 Days of the month, -일 *il* 'day,' which can go up to 31:

28일
isip-p'al-il
'the 28th day'

3 Months of the year, -월 *wŏl* 'moon, month (of),' however, take SK numbers, because they are not used as modifiers as in the case of counting hours but are parts of proper nouns, referring to a specific name of a month. (*Note*: SK nouns combine most easily with other SK nouns.)

The name of a month, therefore, is formed by adding the SK number for the month (1–12) to the bound noun -월 *wŏl*.

일월	il-wŏl	January (*lit.* 'the first moon/moon one')
이월	i-wŏl	February
삼월	sam-wŏl	March
사월	sa-wŏl	April
오월	o-wŏl	May
유월	yu-wŏl	June (the ㄱ *k* at the end of the first syllable 육 *yuk* is dropped)
칠월	ch'il-wŏl	July
팔월	p'al-wŏl	August
구월	ku-wŏl	September
시월	si-wŏl	October (the ㅂ *p* at the end of the first syllable 십 *sip* is dropped)
십일월	sip-il-wŏl	November
십이월	sip-i-wŏl	December

The number of months as duration is also expressed by putting the Sino-Korean numbers and the bound noun -개월 *kaewŏl* together. Here the SK root -개 *kae* 'individual, separate' is inserted to prevent confusion:

이개월 i-kaewŏl '(the period/expanse of) two months'
(*lit.* 'two individual months')

4 Loanwords used as measurement classifiers take SK numerals, e.g.,

시속 80 (팔십)키로 '80 km per hour'
sisok p'alsip-k'iro

키 1 (일) 미터 85 (팔십오)센티미터 '1 meter 85 cm in height'
k'i il-mit'ŏ p'alsip-o-sent'imit'ŏ

우유 2 (이)리터 '2 liters of milk'
uyu i-rit'ŏ

5 Mathematical formulae and other precision reading, including account numbers, ID numbers, and police tickets, are read in SK:

삼분 의 이 'two-thirds'
sambun ŭi i
divide by three-Gen two

영점 이삼 '0.23'
yŏng-chŏm-i-sam
zero-point-two-three

6 Cite proper numbers such as phone numbers, ID numbers, house and room numbers in SK:

325 (삼백이십오)호 실 'Room (No.) 325'
sambaekisipo-ho-sil

7 The year (-년 *nyŏn*) is also counted using SK numbers:

1446년 'the year 1446'
(일)천사백사십육년
(il)ch'ŏn-sabaek-sasip-yuk-nyŏn
(1) 1,000-400-40-6-year

8 Any official day of commemoration is read using isolated SK numbers, reading the first syllable of proper nouns referring to the month, day, etc.:

팔일오 'August 15 (Independence Day)'
p'al-il-o
8-1-5

육이오 'June 25 (Korean War Memorial Day)'
yuk-i-o
6-2-5

8.2.7.2 *Ordinal numerals*

Korean ordinals are very much like cardinals, except that the suffix -번째 *pŏntchae* is added to native words. *Note*: (1) -번 *pŏn* literally means 'time,' so use the prenominal forms of numerals before this bound noun; (2) The first syllable -번 *pŏn* is optional for numbers up to nine, but is less often deleted for bigger numbers; (3) In the case of 'the first,' the base word comes not from 하나 *hana* 'one' but from 처음 *ch'ŏŭm* 'the beginning state.'

For SK ordinal numerals, the formula is 제 *che-* + **SK cardinal number followed by a classifier** such as -회 *hoe*, -차 *ch'a*, -급 *kŭp*, -등 *tŭng*, -착 *ch'ak*, -과 *kwa* ('Xth number in a series of...,' 'Xth anniversary,' 'Xth grade,' 'Xth ranking', 'Xth arrived,' and 'Xth lesson,' respectively).

제 오십회 동창회
che osip-hoe tongch'anghoe
50 alumni-meeting
'The 50th alumni meeting'

제 이차 세계대전
che i-ch'a segye-taejŏn
2 world-great war
'World War II [*lit.* The Second Great World War]'

In most cases, the prefix 제 *che-* is easily dropped. In fact, in such common expressions as (제)일등 *(che) iltŭng* 'first (prize),' (제)이차 대전 *(che) ich'a taejŏn* 'World War II [*lit.* Second Great World War],' and (제) 삼과 *(che) samgwa* 'Lesson 3,' the prefix -제 *che* occurs only in formal ceremonies, publications, and certificates.

Here is the list of Korean ordinal numerals:

ORDINAL NUMERALS

	Native ordinal numerals		Sino-Korean ordinal numerals		
1st	첫 (←처음) (번)째	ch'ŏtts(pŏn)tchae	(제) 일	(第) 一	(che) il
2nd	둘째/두번째	tultschae/tubŏntchae	(제) 이	(第) 二	(che) i
3rd	셋째/세번째	ses-tschae/sebŏntchae	(제) 삼	(第) 三	(che) sam
4th	넷째/네번째	nes-tschae/nebŏntchae	(제) 사	(第) 四	(che) sa
5th	다섯(번)째	tasŏs(pŏn)tchae	(제) 오	(第) 五	(che) o
6th	여섯(번)째	yŏsŏs(pŏn)tchae	(제) 육	(第) 六	(che) (r)yuk
7th	일곱(번)째	ilkop(pŏn)tchae	(제) 칠	(第) 七	(che) ch'il
8th	여덟(번)째	yŏtŏl(pŏn)tchae	(제) 팔	(第) 八	(che) p'al
9th	아홉(번)째	ahop(pŏn)tchae	(제) 구	(第) 九	(che) ku
10th	열(번)째	yŏl(pŏn)tchae	(제) 십	(第) 十	(che) sip
11th	열한(번)째	yŏl-han(pŏn)tchae	(제) 십일	(第) 十一	(che) sip-il
12th	열두(번)째	yŏl-tu(pŏn)tchae	(제) 십이	(第) 十二	(che) sip-i
13th	열세(번)째	yŏl-se(pŏn)tchae	(제) 십삼	(第) 十三	(che) sip-sam
14th	열네(번)째	yŏl-ne(pŏn)tchae	(제) 십사	(第) 十四	(che) sip-sa
15th	열다섯(번)째	yŏl-tasŏs(pŏn)tchae	(제) 십오	(第) 十五	(che) sip-o
16th	열여섯(번)째	yŏl-yŏsŏs(pŏn)tchae	(제) 십육	(第) 十六	(che) sip-yuk
17th	열일곱(번)째	yŏl-ilgop(pŏn)tchae	(제) 십칠	(第) 十七	(che) sip-ch'il
18th	열여덟(번)째	yŏl-yŏdŏlp(pŏn)tchae	(제) 십팔	(第) 十八	(che) sip-p'al
19th	열아홉(번)째	yŏl-ahop(pŏn)tchae	(제) 십구	(第) 十九	(che) sip-ku
20th	스무(번)째	sŭmu(pŏn)tchae	(제) 이십	(第) 二十	(che) i-sip
30th	서른(번)째	sŏr(h)ŭn(pŏn)tchae	(제) 삼십	(第) 三十	(che) sam-sip
40th	마흔(번)째	mahŭn(pŏn)tchae	(제) 사십	(第) 四十	(che) sa-sip
50th	쉰(번)째	swin(pŏn)tchae	(제) 오십	(第) 五十	(che) o-sip
60th	예순(번)째	yesun(pŏn)tchae	(제) 육십	(第) 六十	(che) yuk-sip
70th	일흔(번)째	irhŭn(pŏn)tchae	(제) 칠십	(第) 七十	(che) ch'il-sip
80th	여든(번)째	yŏdŭn(pŏn)tchae	(제) 팔십	(第) 八十	(che) p'al-sip
90th	아흔(번)째	ahŭn(pŏn)tchae	(제) 구십	(第) 九十	(che) ku-sip

Numbers, as nouns, are often used as noun modifiers, as with any other noun.

[일곱]$_{\text{NP=Modifier}}$ [사람]$_{\text{NP}}$]$_{\text{NP}}$
ilgop saram
'seven persons'

Note, however, that the numbers *1*, *2*, *3*, *4*, and *20* have alternate forms in a prenoun position. These are formed from regular numeral nouns by dropping the final sound. Compare the following pairs:

	Prenoun variant		Basic form	
1	[[한]$_{NP}$ [사람]$_{NP}$]$_{NP}$		[하나]$_{NP}$	
	han	saram	hana	
	one	person	one	
	'one person'		'one'	
2	두 tu (Noun)		둘	tul
3	세 se (Noun)		셋	ses
4	네 ne (Noun)		넷	nes
20	스무 sŭmu (Noun)		스물	sŭmul

8.2.8 *Noun classifiers*

Classifiers, many of which are bound forms, are nouns that categorize objects according to certain (often culturally defined traits), such as shape, function, and other semantic features of countable or measurable objects. They are suffixed to numerals when specifying the number or measure of a corresponding object. Thus, noun and classifier must always agree. For example, when referring to people, one cannot use the classifier used for counting animals and vice versa, although both are animate nouns:

개 세 마리/*명
kae se mari/*myŏng
dog three head/*people
'three dogs'

학생 네 명/*마리
haksaeng ne myŏng/*mari
student four people/*head
'four students'

Below is the list of classifiers with example nouns. Of all these the most generic classifier for all inanimate objects is -개 *kae* 'individual item.' Just make sure you do not use this classifier when referring to persons or animals.

Noun categories	Classifiers	Example
human-beings	-명 myŏng	인구 in'gu 'population'
	-사람 saram 'person'	청중 ch'ŏngjung 'audience'
	-인 in [SK-plain]	참석자 ch'amsŏkja 'participant'
	-분 pun[hon.]	손님 sonnim 'guest'
animals	-마리 mari	고양이 koyang'i 'cat'

Noun categories	Classifiers	Example
inanimate objects	-개 kae	사과 sagwa 'apple'
mechanical objects	-대 tae	자동차 chadongch'a 'car'
		전화기 chŏnhwagi 'telephone'
buildings	-채 ch'ae	집 chip 'house'
volumes	-권 kwŏn	책 ch'aek 'book'
sheets	-장 chang	우표 up'yo 'stamp,'
		표 p'yo 'ticket'
glass/cup	-잔 chan	커피 k'ŏp'i 'coffee'
bottle	-병 pyŏng	맥주 maekju 'beer'
pack	-갑 kap	담배 tambae 'cigarette'
stick (long, thin, rigid)	-자루 charu	연필 yŏnp'il 'pencil'
set	-벌 pŏl	양복 yangbok 'suit'
hand/footwear	-켤레 k'yŏlle	구두 kudu 'shoes,'
		장갑 changgap 'gloves'
bundle	-단 tan	시금치 sigŭmch'i 'spinach'
egg	-알 al	포도 p'odo 'grape (individual)'
cluster, bunch	-송이 songi	꽃 kkoch 'flower,'
		포도 p'odo 'grape (bunch)'
grain, nut	-톨 t'ol	쌀 ssal 'rice,' 밤 pam 'chestnut'

There are four ways of indicating numbers and measures. Here, different relative positions of the noun call for different structures. Observe the following examples showing four ways of saying 'two puppies.'

A. Put the noun first and specify its number or quantity with a classifier as if an afterthought. This most common structure is putting the noun first and then a classifier as a kind of apposition, as in N, *so many of this type*, as shown in the following schema:

Noun	**Numeral modifier**	**Classifier**
강아지	두	마리
kang'aji	tu	mari
puppy	two	(animal) head
[*lit.* 'puppy, two animals']		

B. Put the noun last and use the classifier with numerals as a modifier. The genitive marker -의 *ŭi*, which usually indicates possession ('of'), is used in this case to express another way of apposition, as in the English expression "Queen of Mean."

Numeral modifier	Classifier	Gen.	Noun
두	마리	의	강아지
tu	mari	ŭi	kang'aji
two	(animal) head	of	puppy
[*lit.* 'two animals of puppy']			

C. Put the noun first, then simply a numeral, without specifying the kind of noun with a classifier. Note that the numerals will retain their full noun forms because they are not followed by any noun. So, 둘 *tul* (noun) instead of 두 *tu* (prenoun) is used in this case:

Noun	Numeral modifier
강아지	둘
kang'aji	tul
puppy	two
[*lit.* 'puppies two']	

D. Use numerals as prenouns and put the noun after the numerals:

Numeral modifier	Noun
두	강아지
tu	kang'aji
two	puppy
[*lit.* 'two puppies']	

Structure D is not very common and is usually limited to counting people. So, the sample sentence above requires a special context. For instance, in this particular example, the two puppies may have been mentioned previously and the expression may be used almost as a definite pronoun, i.e., 'those two puppies' instead of simply 'they.'

8.3 Making new nouns

8.3.1 *Making new nouns by suffixation*

Sentences, and in fact mere verbs, can also be converted into noun forms by addition of the nominalizing suffixes, -기 *ki* and -음 *ŭm*. Both forms can be applied to many verbs, but sometimes only one of these is appropriate because of differences in meaning between them. As a rule of thumb cognitive verbs such as 알다 *al-ta* 'know,' 듣다 *tŭt-ta* 'hear,' 보다 *po-ta* 'see,' and 중요하다 *chungyoha-ta* 'be important,' go well with -음 *ŭm* nominalization and the other non-cognitive verbs go well with -기 *ki*.

8.3.1.1 -기 ki *nominalizer*

The nominalizer ending -기 *ki* allows the new noun to retain the original verbal meaning strongly. Therefore, if it involves an active verb, it could be translated as 'the act of [V]ing' and if the original verb is a stative verb, the nominalized verb or sentence may be translated as 'the fact that...' Observe the following examples:

나는 [노래하-기]$_N$를 좋아한다.
na-nŭn norae-ha-ki-lŭl choha-ha-n-ta.
me-Top song-do-Nom-Obj like-do-Pres-Dec/Plain
'I like (the act of) singing.'

늘 [행복하-시-기]$_N$를 바랍니다.
nŭl haengbokha-si-ki-lŭl para-pni-ta.
always be happy-SH-Nom-Obj wish-Dec/Def
'I wish you happiness always.' [*lit.* 'I wish that you will be happy always.']

This -기 *ki* nominalization is used in forming some common expressions, where the original sense of the verb, whether action or state, is strongly borne. Some key conjunctives are composed of -기 *ki* + **postpositions**. Here are some examples:

Conjunctives containing nominalizer -기 *ki*

-기 때문에 *ki ttaemune* 'because of the fact...'

오늘은 숙제가 많기 때문에 못
onŭl-ŭn sukche-ka manh-ki ttaemune mot
today-Top homework-Subj be much-Nom-because could not
자겠어요.
cha-kess-ŏyo.
sleep-Sup-Dec/Pol
'Today, I won't be able to sleep because I have a lot of homework.'

-기는 커녕 *kinŭn k'ŏnyŏng* 'far from X being the case'

[공부하기]$_N$는 커녕
kongbu-ha-ki-nŭn k'ŏnyŏng
study-do-Nom-Top let alone
'far from studying'

-기 위하여/위해서 *ki wihayŏ/wihaesŏ* 'for the sake of X'

[부모님을 기쁘게하기]$_N$를 위하여/위해서
pumonim-ŭl kippŭgeha-ki-lŭl wihayŏ/wihaesŏ
parents (Hon)-Obj please-Nom-Obj for the sake of
'in order to please (my) parents'

In all these cases, a noun can be used in place of the nominalized sentence.

So, each of the sentences nominalized by -기 *ki* in the above examples can be replaced by a noun:

[...V$_{STEM}$ 기]$_N$ 때문에
↓
[숙제]$_N$ 때문에
sukche ttaemun-e
homework because of
'because of homework'

[...V$_{STEM}$ 기]$_N$는 커녕
↓
[공부]$_N$ 는 커녕
kongbu-nŭn k'ŏnyŏng
study-Top let alone
'far from studying'

[...V$_{STEM}$ 기]$_N$를 위하여/위해서
↓
[부모님]$_N$ 을 위하여/위해서
pumonim-ŭl wihayŏ/wihaesŏ
parents (Hon)-Obj for the sake of
'for (my) parents'

Special expressions composed of -기 *ki* + auxiliary verbs

When a 기 *ki*-nominalized form of a verb occurs before a stative verb such as 쉽다 *swipta* 'be easy' or 어렵다 ŏryŏpta 'be difficult,' these verbs act like auxiliary verbs, meaning something like '...is easy/difficult to...'

-기 *ki* (가 *ka*) + **stative verbs** 'It's...to...'

그 이름은 외우기(가) 쉽다.
kŭ irŭm-ŭn oeu-ki-(ka) swip-ta.
that name-Top memorize-Nom-(Subj) is easy-Dec/Plain
'That name is easy to remember.'

아픈 친구한테 전화하기(가)
ap'ŭ-n ch'in'gu-hant'e chŏnhwaha-ki-(ka)
be sick-Mod friend-Dat give a phone call-Nom-(Subj)
무섭다.
musŏp-ta.
be fearsome-Dec/Plain
'I dread calling the sick friend.'

Here are some more examples of common stative verbs used in this structure:

좋-	choh-	'be good/agreeable'
싫-	silh-	'be detestable/disagreeable/unpleasing'
나쁘-	nappŭ-	'be bad'
어렵-	ŏryŏp-	'be difficult'
간단하-	kandanha-	'be simple'
귀찮-	kwich'anh-	'be cumbersome'
일쑤-	ilssu-	'be customary/expected/routine'

Note: The reason for the optional presence of a subject particle, rather than an object particle, is that all these stative verbs are simple descriptive verbs, not transitive verbs requiring an object. Even though the English translation reads 'I like/hate/fear X,' the literal translation would be 'Doing X is good/disagreeable/scary (to me).' So, never say:

*피아노 치기를 좋아요.
p'iano ch'i-ki-lŭl choha-yo.
piano play-Nom-Obj be good-Dec/Pol
'[intended meaning] I love playing the piano.'

but say

피아노 치기가 좋아요.
p'iano ch'i-ki-ga choha-yo.
piano playing-Nom-Subj be good-Dec/Pol
'I like playing the piano' [*lit.* 'Playing the piano is good to me.']

or

피아노 치기를 좋아해요. (with the transitive verb 좋아하다 chohahada 'like')
p'iano ch'i-ki-lŭl choha-hae-yo.
piano playing-Nom-Obj like-Dec/Pol
'I like playing the piano.'

The -기 *ki* nominalization, when used with some special particles that are followed by the auxiliary verb -하 *ha*, accentuates the special meaning carried by the particles:

-기는 하다 ***ki-nŭn ha-ta*** (the contrastive topic meaning of -는 *nŭn* is emphasized)

집이 좋기는 해요.
chip-i choh-ki-nŭn hae-yo.
house-Subj be good-Nom-Top be-Dec/Pol
'The house is good all right, but...' [*lit.* 'As for the house being good, it is']

Note: The auxiliary verb -하 *ha* in this construction can be omitted in *panmal* style language. Observe the very common expression used in the following exchange:

한국말 잘 하시네요!
han'guk-mal chal ha-si-ne-yo!
Korean well speak-SH-Exc-Dec/Pol
'My, you speak Korean well!'

잘 하기는요!
chal ha-ki-nŭn-yo!
well do-Nom-Top-Dec/Pol
'Not at all' [*lit.* 'As for speaking well,...(you couldn't mean it!)']

-기도 하다 ***ki-to ha-ta*** (the emphatic meaning of -도 *to* is emphasized)

참 크기도 하다.
ch'am k'ŭ-ki-to ha-ta.
truly be big-Nom-Emph be-Dec/Plain
'It sure is big.'

-기만 하다 ***kiman ha-ta*** (the delimiting meaning 'only' is emphasized)

[결혼하기]$_N$만 해라
kyŏrhon-ha-ki-man hae-ra
marriage-do-Nom-only do-Imp
'(You) just get married!'

Clearly, -기 *ki* nominalization expresses the speaker's involvement (by admission, recognition, or conviction, etc.) in the truthfulness of the sentence.

8.3.1.2 -음 ŭm *nominalizer*

Verbs and sentences can be changed into noun forms by adding the suffix -음 *ŭm* indicating 'the fact of acting/being...,' as shown below:

[[나는 그 여자가 하바드를 나왔]$_S$음]$_N$을
na-nŭn kŭ yŏja-ka habadŭ-lŭl naw-ass-ŭm-ŭl
me-Top that woman-Subj Harvard-Obj come out-Past-Nom-Obj
몰랐다
moll-ass-ta
not know-Past-Dec/Plain
'I did not know she graduated from Harvard.'

This type of nominalization is usually used before a cognitive verb such as a verb of 'knowing':

알-	al-	'know'
깨닫-	kkaedat-	'comprehend, awake to...'
모르-	morŭ-	'not know'
짐작하-	chimjakha-	'guess'
확인하-	hwaginha-	'verify'
알리-	alli-	'inform'
느끼-	nŭkki-	'feel'

8.3.1.3 -이 i *nominalizer*

The suffix -이 *i* is used for making new nouns, but the meaning is usually more detached from their original sources, which are either verbs or adverbs. This type of nominalization is much less productive than the above two methods. It produces a compound construction consisting of

X + bound noun

Here are some examples:

From verbs

떡볶-이
ttŏk-pokk-i
rice cake-stir fry-Nom
'stir-fried rice cake [name of a dish]'

떠돌-이 (←뜨-어-돌-이 ttŭ-ŏ-tol-i '*lit.* float-turn around [Nom]')
ttŏdol-i
roam around-Nom
'vagrant'

From adverbs

빤짝-이
ppantchak-i
twinkling[Adv]-Nom
'sparkle [Noun]'

꿀꿀-이
kkul-kkul-i
oink-Nom
'a piggy' [*lit.* 'a guy that says "oink, oink".']

Note: Some nouns ending in -음 *ŭm*, -기 *ki*, and -이 *i*, although historically derived from verbs, are now fossilized and their original verbal nature is no longer transparent. Here are some examples:

Ending in -음 ***ŭm***

얼음 ŏl-ŭm (← 얼ŏl- 'freeze')	'ice'
믿음 midŭm (← 믿 mit- 'believe')	'faith'
기쁨 kippŭm (← 기쁘 kippŭ- 'be happy')	'joy'
삶 salm (← 살 sal- 'live')	'life'
셈 sem (← 세 se- 'count')	'calculation'

Ending in -기 ***ki***

보기 po-ki (← 보 po- 'see')	'example'
곱하기 kopha-ki (← 곱하 kopha- 'double')	'multiplication'
나누기 nanu-ki (← 나누 nanu- 'share')	'division'

Ending in -이 ***i***

먹이 mŏk-i (← 먹 mŏk- 'eat [verb]')	'feed [noun]'
놀이 nol-i (← 놀 nol- 'play')	'game'
넓이 nŏlp-i (← 넓 nŏlp- 'be wide')	'width'
길이 kil-i (← 길 kil- 'be long')	'length'
높이 nop'-i (← 높 nop'- 'be high')	'height'
옷걸이 os-kŏl-i (← 옷걸 os kŏl- 'hang clothes')	'hanger'
목걸이 mok-kŏl-i (← 목걸 mok kŏl- 'hang on the neck')	'necklace'
손잡이 son-chap-i (← 손잡 son chap- 'hold hand')	'(door)knob'

8.3.2 *Making new nouns by compounding*

New nouns are often created by combining more than one word. As a general rule, native words combine with other native words and SK words with other SK words, although some SK words are so nativized that speakers are not aware that they are of Chinese origin. Loanwords also participate in compounding and may combine with either group.

8.3.2.1 *Native compounds*

In coordinate compounding all components have equal weight as shown below:

위아래	wiarae (← wi 'upside' + arae 'low area')	'all (upper and lower) levels'
밤낮	pamnach (← pam 'night' + nach 'daytime')	'day and night'
앞뒤	ap'twi (← ap' 'front' + twi 'back')	'front and back'
손발	sonbal (← son 'hand' + pal 'foot')	'hands and feet'
물불	mulbul (← mul 'water' + pul 'fire')	'all calamities (flood and fire)'

However, in most cases the last item carries the heaviest weight, and the preceding items tend to serve as a modifier of the last one, as shown below:

길바닥	kilpadak (← kil 'road' + padak 'floor')	'the middle of a road'
벌집	pŏltchip (← pŏl 'bee' + chip 'house')	'hornets' nest'
비바람	pibaram (← pi 'rain' + param 'wind')	'rainstorm'
산나물	sannamul (← san 'mountain' + namul 'vegetable')	'wild vegetable'
곱슬머리	kopsŭlmŏri (← kopsŭl 'curling' + mŏri 'hair')	'curly hair'

In affixal compounding, in which a bound noun is attached to an independent noun either as a prefix or suffix, the main meaning is carried by the independent noun and the affix only adds a complementary meaning. Consider the following examples:

Prefix + noun

헛 hŏs 'empty, useless'	+ 고생 kosaeng 'suffering'	= 헛고생	'unfruitful effort'
덧 tŏs 'layered'	+ 버선 pŏsŏn 'socks'	= 덧버선	'outer socks/slippers'
알 al 'core, nucleus, egg'	+ 부자 puja 'rich person'	= 알부자	'truly rich guy'
홀 hol 'single, alone'	+ 몸 mom 'body'	= 홀몸	'single'
군 kun 'extra'	+ 살 sal 'flesh'	= 군살	'extra fat'

Noun + suffix

점 chŏm 'divination'	+ -쟁이 chaeng-i 'the guy who does...'	= 점쟁이	'fortune-teller'
게으름 keŭrŭm 'laziness'	+ -뱅이 paeng-i 'the bum who does...'	= 게으름뱅이	'lazy bum'
부채 puch'ae 'fan'	+ -질 chil 'the repeated act of...'	= 부채질	'fanning'
[Personal name]	+ -네 ne 'the house of...'	= X 네	'the house of X'
장사 changsa 'selling'	+ -꾼 kkun 'an expert/pro (pejorative)'	= 장사꾼	'a peddler'

8.3.2.2 SK compounds

It is estimated that Sino-Korean (SK) words make up more than 60 percent of the Korean vocabulary. However, Koreans make new words much more frequently and productively with SK roots than with native roots. Therefore, an infinite number of new vocabulary items could be created through the process in principle, and it is hard to pinpoint exactly what proportion of the Korean vocabulary is based on SK roots.

Many SK roots are bound forms, although they have independent meanings. This has to do with the preference in Korean for two-syllable words in Korean, especially in the case of SK words. Many SK roots act as if they are either prefixes or suffixes.

SK prefix type

친 親- ch'in 'intimate'	+ 형제 hyŏngje 'siblings'	= 친형제 'siblings [from the same parents]'
무 無- mu 'non, without'	+ 소속 sosok 'affiliation'	= 무소속 'independent'
미 未- mi 'not (yet)'	+ 완성 wansŏng 'completion'	= 미완성 'unfinished'
불 不- pul 'not'	+ 공평 kongp'yŏng 'fairness'	= 불공평 'unfairness'
재 再- chae 'again, re-'	+ 활용 hwaryong 'application'	= 재활용 'recycling'

SK suffix type

소설 sosŏl 'novel'	+ -가 家 ka 'an expert'	= 소설가 'novelist'
서양 sŏyang 'West'	+ -식 式 sik 'style'	= 서양식 'Western style'
인간 in'gan 'human being'	+ -적 的 chŏk '-like'	= 인간적 'humane'
언어 ŏnŏ 'language'	+ -학 學 hak 'the study of...'	= 언어학 'Linguistics'
도피 top'i 'escape, flight'	+ -자 者 cha 'person'	= 도피자 'fugitive'

As in the case of compounds involving native vocabulary, SK roots in nouns may have an appositional relationship:

SK coodinate compounds

내외 內外 naewoe (← nae-'inside' + woe-'outside')	'inside and out'
남녀 男女 namnyŏ (← nam-'male' + nyŏ-'female')	'male and female'
부모 父母 pumo (← pu-'father' + mo-'mother')	'parents'
전후 前後 chŏnhu (← chŏn-'before' + hu-'after')	'about' [*lit.* 'before or after']
생사 生死 saengsa (← saeng-'living' + sa-'death')	'life and death'

In non-coordinate SK compounding, the most important meaning is carried by the final syllable and the preceding part has the role of a modifier of that syllable:

Modifier + noun types

녹차 綠茶	nokch'a (← lok- 'green' + ch'a 'tea')	'green tea'
온수 溫水	onsu (← on- 'warm' + su 'water')	'hot water'
고목 古木	komok (← ko- 'ancient' + mok 'tree')	'a very old tree'
황금 黃金	hwanggŭm (← hwang- 'yellow' + kŭm 'gold')	'pure gold'
간식 間食	kansik (← kan- 'in between' + sik 'food')	'snack'

It is noteworthy that some fossilized SK compounds have a Chinese word order of Verb-Object:

수금	收金	sugŭm (← su 'collect' + kŭm 'gold, money')	'collection (of dues)'
등산	登山	tŭngsan (← tŭng 'climb' + san 'mountain')	'trekking/mountain' climbing
취침	就寢	ch'wich'im (← ch'wi 'take' + ch'im 'sleep')	'going to bed/sleep'
입학	入學	iphak (← ip 'enter' + hak 'learning')	'admission to a school'
구직	求職	kujik (← ku 'seek' + jik 'profession')	'(seeking) employment'

However, Korean speakers today do not analyze these words as being composed of a verb followed by an object noun, but simply as a noun with a unitary meaning.

8.3.2.3 *Loanwords and their compounds*

Compound nouns containing loanwords follow usual principles of Korean grammar. For example, the most important component occurs at the end of the unit:

콜택시	k'ol t'aeksi	'reserved taxi' [*lit.* 'call taxi']
여행 가이드	yŏhaeng kaidŭ	'travel guide'
핸드폰	haendŭ p'on	'mobile phone'
비닐 주머니	pinil chumoni	'plastic bag' [*lit.* 'vinyl pouch']
딸기 아이스크림	ttalgi aisŭk'ŭrim	'strawberry ice-cream'
냉커피	naeng k'ŏp'i	'ice coffee'
골프장	kolp'ŭ jang	'golf course'
테니스시합	t'enisŭ sihap	'tennis game'
메모지	memoji	'note pad'

8.4 Ordering relationship in multiple nouns

In identifying a person, place, time, or organization, the most specific point appears last.

Korean personal names usually consist of three syllables, one syllable representing the family name and two for the given name. Family names come first followed by the given name. The order of a personal name thus follows the general Korean word order, which puts the broadest category first, and the next broadest, and the most specific last. For example, the violinist Kyung Hwa Chung's name is written as:

Family name	Given name
정	경화
chŏng	kyŏng-hwa

In the same manner, a street address will typically start with the name of the province, then the city, then the next largest administrative unit, then the street or avenue or the subsection of a neighborhood, and finally the apartment or house number if there is more than one residential unit at that address. As an example, compare the order of words in the following Korean address with the one in English shown in translation:

Professor Kim Hŭisuk's professional identification and address, listing the most specific information last, i.e., her individual name:

충청북도 청주시 내덕동
ch'ungch'ŏng-puk-to ch'ŏngju-si naedŏk-tong
-North-Province -City -Section
36 번지 청주대학교 인문대학
samsipyuk-pŏnji ch'ŏngju-taehakkyo inmun-taehak
-No. -University Humanities-College
국어국문학과 교수 김 희숙
kugŏ-kungmunhak-kwa kyosu kim hŭisuk
Korean Language and Literature Dept. professor
'Professor Kim Hŭisuk, Dept. of Korean Language and Literature, College of Humanities, Ch'ŏngju University, 36 Naedŏk-tong, City of Ch'ŏngju, Province of Ch'ungch'ŏngbukto'

Here, Professor Kim Hŭisuk's identity (based on her affiliation) starts with the name of the province where her workplace is located, then that of the city, and then the next largest administrative quarter, and the street number, followed by the university, the college, the department, the rank, and finally her family name and given name.

The larger-unit-first principle holds also for common nouns. For example, telling time works in a similar way. Give the year, the month, the day, the day of the week, a.m. or p.m., hour, minutes, seconds, etc.:

2008 년	2 월	5 일	화요일	오후	3 시	10 분
ich'ŏnp'al-nyŏn	i-wŏl	o-il	hwa-yoil	ohu	se-si	sip-pun
2008-year	2-month	5-day	Sunday	p.m.	3-hour	10-minutes

22초
isip-i-ch'o
22-seconds
'Tuesday, February 5, 2008, 3:10:22 p.m.'

8.5 Noun particles

Nouns are usually followed by postpositions called *particles*, which indicate their grammatical relationship to other elements in a sentence. So, it is useful to think that in Korean, nouns are always followed by some particles. This is a little like saying **me** + **particle** (= subject marker) where you would say *I*, and **me** + **particle** (= genitive marker) where you would say *my* in English.

Although a noun + postposition sequence is analyzable into two parts, they form and act like one entity: They are pronounced without a break between them. The postposition, unlike English prepositions (e.g., "*The house I lived* ***in***"), has no independent status, and when the noun is deleted the particle is too. That is why these grammatical markers are often called "particles," and sometimes even "suffixes."

Noun particles can be broadly divided into three different categories:

1 Particles marking the structural relationship of a noun to a predicate, independent of interpretive factors: *grammatical particles*.
2 Particles that indicate semantic relationship of a noun to a predicate: *semantic particles*.
3 Particles that consider a larger, discourse context: *discourse particles*.

8.5.1 Grammatical particles

Grammatical particles include subject -이 *i* / -가 *ka*; object -을 *ŭl* / -를 *lŭl*; and genitive -의 *ŭi*. In English, the subject of a sentence is not represented by any specific form, except for a few examples like *I*, *he*, or *they*. Whether a noun is a subject or an object is mainly indicated by its position in a sentence, as in the following two sentences:

The police killed the thief.
The thief killed the police.

In Korean, the word order is fairly free, except for one requirement that the verb appear at the end of a sentence. The subjecthood or objecthood of a noun is mainly indicated by the particles carried by nouns:

경찰이 도둑을 살렸다.
kyŏngch'al-i toduk-ŭl sal-ly-ŏt-ta.
police-Subj thief-Obj live-Caus-Past-Dec/Plain

도둑을 경찰이 죽였다.
totuk-ŭl kyŏngch'al-i sal-l-y-ŏt-ta.
thief-Obj police-Subj live-Caus-Past-Dec/Plain
'The police killed the thief.'

Grammatical particles contain information about the structural relationship of the nominals (nouns and noun-like constructions) to the predicate or another noun in the sentence.

The subject, object, and genitive particles are often called "structural" because they indicate the grammatical function of the nouns in a sentence rather than their meaning. Because they are usually predictable from context, grammatical particles are easily deleted, especially in colloquial language. When they are not deleted, they often take a "focus" interpretation.

8.5.1.1 *Subject particle (Subj)* -이/가 i/ka

The subject particle marking the nominative case is attached to the end of a noun or noun phrase, indicating that an event pertains to that noun or noun phrase. All sentences have a subject, either explicit or implicit. The subject of a sentence is often a response to a question beginning with *who* or *what* (time, place, etc.). For example, Mary is the subject of the sentence, "*Mary did*," which is in response to the question "*Who won first prize?*"

The subject marker is -이 *i* when preceded by a vowel, otherwise it is -가 *ka*:

시간이 빨리 가요.
sigan-i ppalli ka-yo.
time-Subj fast go-Dec/Pol
'Time flies.' [*lit.* 'Time goes fast']

피터가 김치를 먹어요.
p'it'ŏ-ka kimch'i-lŭl mŏk-ŏyo.
Peter-Subj kimch'i-Obj eat-Dec/Pol
'Peter eats *kimch'i*.'

For ease of pronunciation choose a consonant-initial form after a vowel and a vowel-initial one after a consonant. Also remember that the *k* of *ka* changes to *g* when it follows a vowel, sonorant, or soft voiced consonant such as *m* or *l*. So 피터가 *p'it'ŏ-ka* is actually pronounced [p'it'ŏga].

A noun or noun phrase can be a subject of an intransitive or transitive verb as shown in the above examples. A noun with a subject marker can also be the complement of an intransitive or a negative copulative verb:

아들이 소설가가 되었다.
adŭl-i sosŏlga-ka toe-ŏss-ta.
son-Subj novelist-Subj become-Past-Dec/Plain
'My son became a novelist (Comp).'

나는 소설가가 아니다.
na-nŭn sosŏlga-ka ani-ta.
me-Top novelist-Subj Neg Cop-Dec/Plain
'I am not a novelist (Comp).'

A subject particle marks an exclusive focus on the noun it is attached to. So, it is a little like highlighting the subjects in the English translations given above. Some pronouns show irregular forms when combined with the subject marker -가 *ka*.

Neutral		Subj		
나	na	내가	naega	'me'
너	nŏ	네가	nega	'you'
저	chŏ	제가	chega	'he/she'
누구	nugu	누가	nuga	'who/someone'

Notes:

1 Etymologically, 내 *nae*, 네 *ne*, and 제 *che* are contracted forms of 나 *na* + 이 *i*, 너 *nŏ* + 이 *i*, and 저 *chŏ* + 이 *i*, respectively. The subject particle -가 *ka* is a recently introduced variant form; there used to be only one form -이 *i* for the subject marker (the nominative case) in earlier Korean. Therefore, 내가 *naega*, 네가 *nega*, and 제가 *chega* include two subject markers each, etymologically speaking.

2 In listening: 내가 *naega* may be pronounced as either [naega] or [nega]. This is due to the ongoing merger of the vowels 애 *ae* and 에 *e* in Korean. It is perhaps for this reason that 네가 *nega* has a casual-speech variant pronounced 니가 *ni-ka*, where the vowel is raised in order not to be confused with the new variety of 내가 *nae-ka*. A similar change occurs with 제가 *che-ka*, which has a casual-speech variant 지가 *chi-ka*. Like many contracted forms, [niga] and [chiga] convey the speaker's intimate (and rude when inappropriate) feeling toward the interlocutor. For a discussion on related genitive markers, see below.

Note: Special uses of subject markers indicate focus.

A special construction, -고 싶다 *ko sipta* 'want to…', denotes a specific desire, usually of the speaker, although it can be used in a question sentence to ask about the volition of the interlocutor. When speaking of someone else's desire, the form **Verb** + -고 싶어하다 is used. The subject particle may replace the usual object particle, in which case the noun receives focus, and the volitional meaning of the speaker is diminished. Compare the following pairs of sentences:

나는 김치를 먹고 싶다.
na-nŭn kimch'i-lŭl mŏk-ko sip'-ta.
me-Top kimch'i-Obj eat-Conn want to-Dec/Plain
'I **want to eat *kimch'i***.' [To eat *kimch'i* is what the speaker would like to do.]

나는 김치가 먹고 싶다.
na-nŭn kimch'i-ka mŏk-ko sip'-ta.
me-Top kimch'i-Subj eat-Conn want to-Dec/Plain
'It is ***kimch'i*** that I want to eat.' [The feeling just occurs to the speaker, and the focus of the gentle desire is *kimch'i*.]

When the subject is honored use the deferential subject particle -께서 *kkesŏ*:

선생님께서 말씀하셨다.
sŏnsaengnim-kkesŏ malssŭmha-sy-ŏss-ta.
teacher-honorable-Subj(Hon) speak(Hon)-SH-Past-Dec/Plain
'The (honorable) teacher spoke.'

8.5.1.2 *Object particle (Obj) -을/를 ŭl/lŭl*

The object particle or accusative case marks a noun or noun equivalent in a verb construction with the action of a verb directed on it. As with subject markers, there are two similar forms for object particles. The choice depends on the class of the preceding sound: -을 *ŭl* after a consonant and -를 *lŭl* after a vowel. In fact *lŭl* is pronounced as *rŭl* when following a vowel.

큰	가방을	좋아해요.	'I like big purses.'
k'ŭn	kabang-ŭl	chohahae-yo.	
big	purse-Obj	like-Dec/Pol	

나도	김치를	먹어요.	'I, too, eat *kimch'i*.'
na-to	kimch'i-lŭl	mŏk-ŏyo.	
me-too	kimch'i-Obj	eat-Dec/Pol	

Note: In casual and fast speech, when following a vowel, the weak and unstable vowel -으 *ŭ* between the two identical consonants in the syllable -를 *lŭl* is "squeezed out" and the two identical consonants coalesce. Thus only the consonant -ㄹ *l* is attached :

미나를	좋아해요.	'I like Mina.'
mina-lŭl	choahae-yo.	
Mina-Obj	like-Dec/Pol	

미나ㄹㄹ
minal l
으 *ŭ*-drop

미날
mina-l
ㄹ *l*-coalescence

The object particle is often dropped in informal speech and writing. When it is used, the noun phrase gets the "focus" meaning.

Note: Some intransitive verbs of motion take quasi-objectives. In these cases, nouns and noun phrases that are usually marked with meaning-carrying particles such as directional locatives are marked with objective markers. Compare the following examples:

나는 한국교회에 간다.
na-nŭn han'gukkyohoe-e ka-n-ta.
me-Top Korea-church-to go-Pres-Dec/Plain
'I go to a Korean church.' [a simple statement]

나는 한국교회를 간다.
na-nŭn han'gukkyohoe-lŭl ka-n-ta.
me-Top Korea-church-Obj go-Pres-Dec/Plain
'I go to Korean church.' [something unusual is implied by the statement]

The two sentences basically mean the same thing, and the second sentence is a little like saying "*I run 10 miles every day*," in which an intransitive verb has been turned into a transitive verb with an object. The use of the object particle instead of the directional locative here gives the noun a stronger focus on the purpose of the verb class of '*going*.'

8.5.1.3 *Obligatory deletion of subject and object particles*

The subject or object particle cannot co-occur with the topic marker -은 *ŭn* / -는 *nŭn* or the emphatic marker -도 *to* (see below). When these combinations occur, subject and object particles are deleted obligatorily:

Subject particle deletion

오늘	날씨는	좋다.	'Talking of today's
onŭl	nalssi- nŭn	choh-ta.	weather, it is good.'
today	weather-Top	be good-Dec/Plain	
*오늘	날씨가는	좋다.	*'Talking of today's
onŭl	nalssi-ka-nŭn	choh-ta.	weather, it is good.'
today	weather-Subj-Top	be good-Dec/Plain	
오늘	날씨도	좋다.	'Today's weather
onŭl	nalssi-to	choh-ta.	also is good.'
today	weather-Emph	be good-Dec/Plain	
*오늘	날씨가도	좋다.	*'Today's weather
onŭl	nalssi-ka-to	choh-ta.	also is good.'
today	weather-Subj-Emph	be good-Dec/Plain	

Object particle deletion

학교도	세웠다.	'X founded a school also.'
hakkyo-to	sew-ŏss-ta.	
school-Emph	found-Past-Dec/Plain	
*학교를도	세웠다.	*'X founded a school also.'
hakkyo-lŭl-to	sew-ŏss-ta.	
school-Obj-Emph	found-Past-Dec/Plain	

8.5.1.4 *Genitive particle (Gen)* -의 ŭi

The genitive particle connects a nominal to a main noun or a noun equivalent and is best translated by the English preposition *of* or a possessive apostrophe + *s* (or vice versa when plural) following the noun. The most common use of the genitive particle is to mark possession:

나의 고향
na-ŭi kohyang
me-Gen hometown
'my hometown'

Other uses include:

Authorship:	김소월의 진달래 kimsowŏl-ŭi chindalae kimsowŏl-Gen azaleas 'Kim Sowŏl's "Azaleas"'
Location:	서울의 축제 sŏul-ŭi ch'ukje Seoul-Gen festival 'Seoul's festival'
Time:	오늘의 소식 onŭl-ŭi sosik today-Gen news 'today's news'
Theme:	친구의 결혼 ch'in'gu-ŭi kyŏrhon friend-Gen marriage 'my friend's marriage'
Numeral + Classifier:	한권의 책 han-kwŏn-ŭi ch'aek one-volume-Gen book 'a book'

No grammatical particles such as the subject marker and object marker may co-occur with the genitive marker, which is also a grammatical particle. However, one or more meaning-bearing particles may precede the genitive marker, turning the preceding noun phrase into a kind of modifer of the head noun at the end of the phrase. For instance:

이학년학생-만-에게-의 선물
ihangnyŏnhaksaeng-man-ege-ŭi sŏnmul
sophomore-only-to-Gen gift
'gift only to sophomores [gift that is given only to sophomores]'

Note: Some pronouns show irregular forms when combined with the genitive marker -의 *ŭi*.

Neutral + 의 ŭi [Gen]	Genitive	
나 na + 의 ŭi [Gen] =	내 nae	'my'
너 nŏ + 의 ŭi [Gen] =	네 ne	'your'
저 chŏ + 의 ŭi [Gen] =	제 che	'his/her'

[*Note*: Etymologically, 내 *nae*, 네 *ne*, and 제 *che* are contracted forms of 나 *na* + -의 *ŭi*, 너 *nŏ* + -의 *ŭi*, and 저 *chŏ* + -의 *ŭi*, respectively. Historically the weak vowel -으 *ŭ* got squeezed out between two vowels and the remaining two vowels coalesced similarly to the way colloquial subject pronoun forms did [▶8.5.1.1]. Therefore, 내 *nae*, 네 *ne* , 제 *che* are sometimes genitive pronouns and sometimes subject pronouns.]

Genitive particles are easily dropped in any situation. When the genitive particle is deleted, the result of the noun combination sounds a little like a compound noun. Thus, 친구의 결혼 *ch'in'gu-ŭi kyŏrhon* 'my friend's marriage' is more often stated as 친구 결혼 *ch'in'gu kyŏrhon*, unless the noun 'friend' gets a special emphasis.

In some exceptional cases, the genitive-particle deletion is not allowed:

1 Numeral + classifier

한	권의	책	'one book'
han	kwŏn-ŭi	ch'aek	

*한권책

2 Metaphoric expressions such as

평화의 종소리	p'yŏnghwa-ŭi chong-sori	'the bell sound of peace'
*평화 종소리		
숲속의 여왕	supsok-ŭi yŏwang	'the queen of the forest'
*숲속 여왕		

3 A genitive marker preceded by other meaning-carrying particles such as:

친구와의 약속
ch'in'gu-wa-ŭi yaksok
friend-with-of promise/appointment
'promise/appointment with a friend'
*친구와 약속

무도회로의 초대
mudohoe-ro-ŭi ch'odae
ball-to-of invitation
'invitation to dance'
*무도회로 초대

[Fragments like "친구와 약속" or "무도회로 초대" are impossible as a noun phrase but are allowed in different grammatical structures such as 친구와 약속했다 'I promised/made an appointment with a friend' or 무도회로 초대합니다 'We invite you to a ball,' in which 친구와 or 무도회로 is an adverbial phrase.]

8.5.2 *Semantic particles*

Some particles carry their own meanings regardless of their grammatical function in a sentence. Because of their semantic load, these particles usually cannot be dropped like grammatical particles. These may be called "semantic particles" for convenience.

8.5.2.1 *Two kinds of locative particles* -에 e *and* -에서 esŏ *'in, on, at'*

The particles -에 *e* and -에서 *esŏ* both denote location but the two carry different core meanings. The former indicates a point while the latter an area.

1 -에 *e*

The locative particle -에 *e* is used when referring to a specific, static point of reference in time or space. Therefore, it occurs happily with existential verbs, which by nature express non-dynamic meaning, as shown in the following example:

미나는	요새	파리에	있어요.
mina-nŭn	yosae	p'ari-e	iss-ŏyo.
Mina-Top	currently	Paris-in	be-Dec/Pol

'Mina is in Paris these days.'

Depending on the verb it occurs with, the particle -에 *e* can gain extra meaning, as shown below.

a. When the particle -에 *e* is attached to a noun that occurs with a descriptive verb, it means 'for.'

버섯이	몸에	좋아요.
posŏs-i	mom-e	choh-ayo.
mushroom-Subj	body-to	be good-Dec/Pol

'Mushrooms are good for the body.'

b. When the particle -에 *e* is attached to a noun that is the destination of a verb of directional movement, it means 'to.' Here the noun is the destination.

나는	내일	파나마에	가요.
nanŭn	naeil	p'anama-e	ka-yo.
I-Top	tomorrow	Panama-to	go-Dec/Pol

I am going to Panama tomorrow.'

비행기가 나리타 공항에 도착했다.
pihaenggi-ka narit'a konghang-e toch'ak-hae-ss-ta.
airplane-Subj Narita airport-to arrival-do-Past-Dec/Plain
'The plane arrived in/got to Narita Airport.'

c. When the particle -에 *e* is attached to a noun that is the goal of a verb of transfer like 'give' or 'go,' it means 'to' or 'for the benefit of...' The usual English translation is 'to (someone/something).' This type of particle is usually called the *dative marker* with the basic meaning of a referent point. Observe the following examples:

그 책을 영국에 보내세요.
kŭ ch'aek-ŭl yŏngguk-e ponae-se-yo.
that book-Obj England-to send-SH-Dec/Pol
'Please send the book to (X who is in) England.'

나무에 비료를 주었어요.
namu-e piryo-lŭl chu-ŏss-ŏyo.
tree-to fertilizer-Obj give-Past-Dec/Pol
'(Someone) gave fertilizer to trees.'

d. When the dative particle -에 *e* is attached to an animate noun, replace -에 *e* with one of the following particles:

(plain) -에게 **ege** 친구에게 편지를 보냈다.
chingu-ege pyŏnji-lŭl ponae-ss-ta.
friend-to letter-Obj send-Past-Dec/Plain
'(I) sent a letter to a friend.'

(honorific) -께 **kke** 사장님께 선물을 드렸다.
sajangnin-kke sunmul-ŭl tŭry-ŏss-ta.
boss-to (Hon) gift-Obj give-Past-Dec/Plain
'(I) gave a gift to the boss.'

(colloquial) -한테 **hant'e** 친구한테 부탁했다.
chin'gu-hant'e putakhae-ss-ta.
friend-to ask (a favor)-Past-Dec/Plain
'(I) asked for a favor to a friend.'

Note: When used in conjunction with the existential 'be' verb, it means something like 'one has...':

선생님한테 한국어 책이 있다.
sonsaengnim-hant'e han'gugŏ ch'aek-i iss-ta.
teacher-to Korean language book-Subj exist-Dec/Plain
'My teacher has a Korean (language) book.' [*lit.* 'To my teacher a Korean language book exists.']

Various uses of the dative marker:

The meaning of the dative marker varies, again depending on the type of verb it occurs with. In addition to the most common meaning 'to . . . ,' here are some more ways dative particles are used:

Dative markers

Verb type	Meaning (X = noun)	Example
Receiving	'from X'	학장한테 편지를 받았다. hakchanghant'e p'yŏnji-lŭl pat-ass-ta. dean-from letter-Obj receive-Past-Dec/Pol 'I received a letter from the dean.'
Passive	'by X'	개가 차에 치었다. kae-ka ch'a-e ch'i-ŏss-ta. dog-Subj car-by be run over-Past-Dec/Plain 'The dog got run over by a car.'
Causative	'[make] X [do . . .]'	손님에게 서명하게했다. sonnim-ege sŏmyŏng-hagehae-ss-ta. guest-to sign-make do-Past-Dec/Plain 'I made the guest sign.'
Experiencer	'to/for X'	나무에 비료가 필요하다. namu-e piryo-ka piryo-ha-ta tree-to fertilizer-Subj necessary-do-Dec/Plain 'The tree needs fertilizer.'

The locative particle -에 *e* indicates not only a point in space but also a point in time, which is always considered static and non-dynamic. For example:

생선은 새벽에 제일 비싸요.
saengsŏn-ŭn saebyŏk-e cheil pissa-yo.
fish-Top dawn-at the most be expensive-Dec/Pol
'Fish is most expensive in the early morning.'

잠시후에 오세요.
chamsi-hu-e o-s-eyo.
a moment-after-at come-SH-Imp/Pol
'Please come a little later.'

아침에 꼭 식사를 하세요.
ach'im-e kkok siksa-lŭl ha-s-eyo.
morning-in without fail meal-Obj take-SH-Imp/Pol
'Please take a meal in the morning without fail.'

내년에 결혼하겠어요.
naenyŏn-e kyŏrhon-ha-kess-ŏyo.
next year-in marriage-do-Vol-Dec/Pol
'I will get married next year.'

Note: Some phrase-like expressions contain the particle -에 e, whose original meaning of static point is only latent. These include:

-에 대하여	e taehayŏ	'concerning…a [*lit.* facing at…]'
-에 의하여	e ŭihayŏ	'by/according to…[*lit.* leaning on…]'
-에 따라	e ttara	'according to…[*lit.* following the position of…]'
-에 비하여	e pihayŏ	'compared to…[*lit.* compared to the position of…]'
-에 불구하고	e pulguhago	'in spite of…[*lit.* disregarding/notwithstanding the fact of…]'

2 -에서 *esŏ*

The second major locative particle, -에서 *esŏ*, is used when an area rather than a point is indicated, e.g., the domain in which an action takes place.

뉴욕에서 스페인어를 배웠다
nyuyok-esŏ sŭp'einŏ-lŭl paew-ŏss-ta
New York-at Spanish-Obj learn-Past-Dec/Plain
'X learned Spanish in New York.'

Again, the specific meaning of locative -에서 *esŏ* varies depending on the verb with which it occurs.

a. When locative -에서 *esŏ* occurs with a verb of directional movement, it means 'from…'

저는 시카고에서 왔어요.
chŏ-nŭn sik'ago-esŏ w-ass-ŏyo.
me-Top Chicago-from come-Past-Dec/Pol
'I came from Chicago.'

b. When locative -에서 *esŏ* would be attached to an animate noun, replace it with one of the following particles:

(Plain)
-에게서 **egesŏ** 친구에게서 편지를 받았다.
chingu-egesŏ pyŏnji-lŭl pat-ass-ta.
friend-from letter-Obj receive-Past-Dec/Plain
'I received a letter from my friend.'

(Honorific)
-께서 **kkesŏ** 사장님께서 선물을 주셨다.
sajangnim-kkesŏ sunmŭl-ŭl chu-shi-ass-ta.
CEO-from present-Obj give-Hon-Past-Dec/Plain
'The CEO gave him a gift.'

(Informal)
-한테서 **hant'esŏ** 친구한테서 소포가 왔다.
ch'ingu-hant'esŏ sop'o-ka w-ass-ta.
friend-from package-Subj come-Past-Dec/Plain
'A package arrived from a friend.'

Note: The particle -에서 *esŏ* and its variants meaning 'from…' can be replaced by another particle -부터 *put'ŏ*, whose core meaning is 'starting from…'; but because of their inherent meanings differ, the two are not always interchangeable. Observe the following set of examples:

(**1**) a. 두시부터 세시까지 있겠어요.
tusi-put'ŏ sesi-kkaji iss-kess-ŏyo.
two o'clock-from three o'clock-up to Exist-Vol-Dec/Pol
'I will be [here] from two to three.'

b. 두시에서 세시까지 있겠어요.
tusi-esŏ sesi-kkaji iss-kess-ŏyo.
two o'clock-from three o'clock-up to Exist-Vol-Dec/Pol
'I will be [here] from two to three.'

(**2**) a. 선생님부터 잡수세요.
sŏnsaengnim-put'ŏ chapsu-s-eyo.
teacher-from eat(Hon)-SH-Dec/Pol
'Teacher, you start/eat first.' [*lit.* 'Starting with you, the teacher, eat!']

b. 선생님*에서 잡수세요.
sŏnsaengnim-esŏ chapsu-s-eyo.
teacher-from eat(Hon)-SH-Dec/Pol
*'Teacher, you start/eat first.' [*lit.* 'Starting with you, the teacher, eat!']

In example (1) -부터 *put'ŏ* and -에서 *esŏ* are interchangeable, both meaning simply 'from…,' but in example (2), (2b) is ungrammatical because -에서 *esŏ* cannot have the meaning of 'from…,' as 잡수시다 *chapsusi-ta* 'eat (Hon)' has no natural relationship with the meaning 'from…'

Note: Some verbs can take either type of locative depending on their meaning variation. For example, 살다 *sal-ta* 'live' can mean two different things: one 'to be alive/exist' in contrast to being dead and the other 'to be actively living a life.' The latter meaning is dynamic, and therefore goes well with -에서 *esŏ* when indicating an area. Observe the following examples:

나는 서울에 살아요.
na-nŭn sŏul-e sal-ayo.
me-Top Seoul-Loc live-Dec/Pol
'I live [exist/survive – therefore am just there] in Seoul.'

나는 서울에서 살아요.
na-nŭn sŏul-esŏ sal-ayo.
me-Top Seoul-Loc live-Dec/Pol
'I live [am actively engaged in a life – therefore move around] in Seoul.'

8.5.2.2 *Comitative particles -와 wa, -하고 hago, -이랑 irang '(along/together/in company) with'*

The comitative particle indicates accompaniment and means 'together with' or 'in company with.' The three different forms of the comitative particle represent different points in the scale of formality, as the following chart shows:

Comitative particle

Form		Style	Examples
-와 *wa* -과 *kwa*	after Vowel after Consonant	Formal/ written	친구와 갔다. ch'in'gu-wa ka-ss-ta. friend-with go-Past-Dec/Plain 'I went with a friend.' 선생님과 갔다. sŏnsaengnim-kwa ka-ss-ta. teacher-with go-Past-Dec/Plain 'I went with my teacher.'
-하고 *hago*		Intimate/ spoken	친구하고 갔다. ch'in'gu-hago ka-ss-ta. friend-with go-Past-Dec/Plain 'I went with a friend.'
-이랑 *irang* -랑 *rang*	after Consonant after Vowel	Casual/ spoken	선생님이랑 갔다. sŏnsaengnim-irang ka-ss-ta. teacher-with go-Past-Dec/Plain 'I went with my teacher.' 친구랑 갔다. ch'in'gu-rang ka-ss-ta. friend-with go-Past-Dec/Plain 'I went with a friend.'

The comitative particle occurs only with animate nouns. Observe the following examples:

> 친구와 오페라에 갔다.
> ch'in'gu-wa op'era-e ka-ss-ta.
> friend-with opera-Loc go-Past-Dec/Plain
> 'I went to an opera with a friend.'
> [*cf.* *악보 (akpo 'musical score') 와 오페라에 갔다 *'I went to an opera with the musical score.']

강아지랑 공원에 갔다.
kang' aji-rang kong'wŏn-e ka-ss-ta.
puppy-with park-Loc go-Past-Dec/Plain
'I took my little puppy to the park. [*lit.* 'I went to a park with my puppy.']
[*cf.* *책 ('book') 이랑 공원에 갔다 *'I went to a park with my book.']

Note: With inanimate nouns, a phrase such as -를 가지고 *lŭl kaji-ko* 'carrying/holding/taking...' is used:

회의에 카메라를 가지-/메-/들-고 갔다.
hoeŭi-e k'amera-lŭl kaji-/me-/tŭl-ko kass-ta.
meeting-to camera-Obj take/hold/carry-and go-Past-Dec/Plain
'I took my camera to the meeting' [*lit.* 'I went to the meeting holding my camera.']

The comitative particle gains extra meaning depending on the verb it occurs with. For example, when a verb implies comparison, the particle takes on the added meaning of 'compared with...'

한국은 미국과 다르다/같다.
han'guk-ŭn miguk-kwa tarŭ-ta/kat'-ta.
Korea-Top America-with be different/be the same-Dec/Plain
'Korea is different **from/the** same **as** the U.S.'

한국차가 일본차하고 비슷합니까?
han'gukch'a-ka ilbonch'a-hago pisŭs-ha-pnikka?
Korean car-Subj Japanese car-with be similar-do-Q/Def
'Is a Korean car similar **to** a Japanese car?'

When a verb usually requires two parties, then there is a reciprocal meaning:

미자는 기수랑 결혼한다.
mija-nŭn kisu-rang kyŏron-ha-n-ta.
Mija-Top Kisu-with marriage-do-Pres-Dec/Plain
'Mija is marrying Kisu.' [*lit.* 'Mija is marrying with Kisu.]'

동생하고 또 싸웠구나!
tongsaeng-hago tto ssaw-ŏss-kuna!
younger sibling-with again fight-Past-Dec
'(Oh my), you fought **with** your younger brother again!'

When occurring between a series of nouns, the particle usually equates to English 'and.' Consider the following examples:

콜라하고 사이다 있어요.
k'olla-hago saida iss-ŏyo.
Cola-with cider Exist-Dec/Pol
'We have cola and cider (=clear soda).'

엄마하고 아빠가 오셨어요.
ŏmma-hago appa-ka o-sy-ŏss-ŏyo.
mom-with dad-Subj come-SH-Past-Dec/Pol
'Mom and dad came (Hon).'

8.5.2.3 *Topic marker -은/는 ŭn/nŭn 'as for . . . ,' 'speaking of . . .'*

Korean is a language that clearly marks the *topic* in a sentence, so it is called a "topic language."

A Korean sentence often starts with a noun or a noun phrase with the topic marker (Top), -은/는 *ŭn/nŭn*, which indicates that the noun (phrase) is what the sentence is talking about. A topic marker can be attached to any noun phrase, i.e., to a noun with or without its postposition.

Which form the topic marker takes depends on what precedes it: -은 *ŭn* after a consonant and -는 *nŭn* after a vowel:

인생은 꿈이다.
insaeng-ŭn kkum-i-ta.
life-Top dream-Cop-Dec/Plain
'Life is a dream.'

노래는 즐겁다.
norae-nŭn chŭlgŏp-ta.
song-Top be enjoyable-Dec/Plain
'Singing is enjoyable.'

In a Korean sentence, the main subject is the default topic. If some other unit than the main subject is the topic, then the topicalized element precedes the subject. If the topic-marked noun is not moved to the front, then it receives the contrastive meaning. For example in the following sentence the second topic marker is contrastive:

나는 김치는 먹는다.
na-nŭn kimch'i-nŭn mok-nŭn-ta.
me-Top kimch'i-Top/Contrast eat-Pres-Dec/Plain
'I eat *kimch'i* [but not other Korean food/vegetable/condiment, etc.].'

Multiple topics are not allowed, as one cannot talk "about" more than one thing at a time. However, multiple topics are allowable if the second and succeeding topics have contrastive meaning, as in the last example. This is why one cannot have a topic marker other than one with a contrastive meaning within a subordinate sentence. Observe the following sentence:

a. *[어머니는 쓰신]$_S$ 책은 어렵다.
*ŏmŏni-nŭn ssŭ-si-n ch'aek-ŭn ŏryŏp-ta.
mother-Top write-SH-Mod/Past book-Top be difficult-Dec/Plain

b. [어머니가 쓰신]$_S$ 책은 어렵다.
ŏmŏni-ka ssŭ-si-n ch'aek-ŭn ŏryŏp-ta.
mother-Subj write-SH-Mod/Past book-Top be difficult-Dec/Plain
'The book my mother wrote is difficult.'

Sentence (a) above, marked with an *, is ungrammatical, because the sentence modifying the noun *book* is already talking about the book, and therefore it cannot be talking about "mother" at the same time.

The topic particle is used most commonly in the following cases:

1 To introduce a topic of the sentence [translated as something like 'Talking about…']:

수미는 한국 사람이에요.
sumi-nŭn han'guk saram-i-eyo.
Sumi-Top Korea person-Cop-Dec/Pol
'Sumi is a Korean [*underlying meaning*: Let's talk about Sumi – she is a Korean.]'

학교에는 학생이 많아요?
hankkyo-e-nŭn haksaeng-i manh-ayo?
school-at-Top students-Subj be plentiful-Q/Pol
'At school, are there many students? [*underlying meaning*: Let's talk about what's in the school – are there many students?]'

2 Old information: To discuss something that is within the cognitive domain of both the speaker and the hearer. For this reason, this marker is often chosen when referring to something which has already been mentioned or understood.

짐이 어디 있어요?
chim-i ŏdi iss-ŏyo?
Jim-Subj where Exist-Q/Pol
'Where is Jim?'

짐은 집에 있어요.
chim-ŭn chip-e iss-ŏyo.
Jim-Top home-at Exist-Dec/Pol
'He is at home.'

3 A topic marker often deemphasizes the noun (phrase) it is attached to. The focus of the sentence goes to elements in the sentence other than the noun (phrase) with a topic marker. The noun phrase with a topic marker is often something which has already been mentioned or understood, and is thus frequently deleted.

짐이 어디 있어요?
chim-i ŏdi iss-ŏyo?
Jim-Subj where Exist-Q/Pol
'Where is Jim?'

집에 있어요.
chip-e iss-ŏyo.
home-at Exist-Dec/Pol
'[He] is at home.'

4 To highlight something by contrasting it with everything of the same class which is not mentioned.

불고기는 좋아요.
pulgogi-nŭn choh-ayo.
pulgogi-Top/Contrast be nice-Dec/Pol
'I like *pulgogi*, but…' [*lit.* '*pulgogi*, I like (but not *kimch'i*)']

Contrastive topic markers can be used with any noun phrases and can occur following any particle except for subject and object markers. Some examples are shown below:

기수에게만은 영화표를 두장 주었다.
Kisu-ege-man-ŭn yŏnghwap'yo-lŭl tu-chang chu-ŏss-ta.
Kisu-to-only-Top movie ticket-Obj two-CL give-Past-Dec/Plain
'(He) gave two movie tickets only to Kisu.'

여름 방학에는 놀아요.
yorŭm-panghak-e-nŭn nol-ayo.
summer vacation-on-Top play-Dec/Pol
'During the summer vacation, I do nothing [productive], but…'
[*lit.* 'During the summer vacation, I play (but not during the school year/not during the winter break).']

Note: In casual and fast speech when following a vowel, the weak and unstable vowel 으 *ŭ* in the syllable -는 *nŭn* is dropped and the identical consonants coalesce. Thus only the consonant -ㄴ *n* is attached:

미나는 학생이다. 'Mina is a student.'
mina-nŭn haksaeng-i-ta.
Mina-Top student-be-Dec/Plain
미나 ㄴ ㄴ 으 *ŭ*-drop
미나 ㄴ ㄴㄴ *n n*-coalescence
미난

The topic marker and a grammatical particle never occur together, as mentioned above. The subject or object marker cannot co-occur with a topic marker because they are logically incompatible, as the subject marker and the object marker are focus markers, while the topic marker has almost the opposite function. A topic marker never accompanies a genitive, because the genitive combines two noun phrases into a larger noun phrase, and a part of a noun phrase cannot be topicalized.

8.5.2.4 *The emphatic particle (Emph) -도 to 'also, too, even'*

-도 *to* is an emphatic particle generally translated as 'also' in an affirmative sentence and 'even' in a negative sentence. As mentioned above, the subject or object particle must be dropped when the emphatic particle -도 *to* is used.

수미도 학생이에요.
sumi-to haksaeng-i-eyo.
Sumi-Emph student-Cop-Dec/Pol
'Sumi is also a student.' [correct with no subject particle]

*수미가도 학생이에요.
sumi-**ka-to** haksaeng-i-eyo.
Sumi-Subj-Emph student-Cop-Dec/Pol
*'Sumi is also a student.' [incorrect because -가 *ka* is a subject marker which must be dropped when -도 *to* is added]

숙제도 안 했어요?
sukje-Emph an hae-ss-ŏyo?
homework-even not do-Past-Q/Pol
'You did not even do your homework?'

*숙제를도 안 했어요?
sukje-lŭl-Emph an hae-ass-eyo?
homework-Obj-even Neg do-Past-Q/Pol
*'You did not even do your homework?' [incorrect because -를 *lŭl* is an object marker which must be dropped when -도 *to* is added]

However, emphatic -도 *to* can follow the other particles or a sequence of particles:

서울에도 가요.
Sŏul-e-to ka-yo.
Seoul-Loc-Emph go-Dec/Pol
'I go also to Seoul.'

선생님이 제임스에게도 책을 주셨어요.
sŏensangnim-i cheimsŭ-ege-to ch'aek-ŭl chu-si-ŏss-ŏyo.
teacher-Subj James-to-Emph book-Obj give-SH-Past-Dec/Pol
'The teacher gave a book to James as well.'

친구한테까지도 말 못 해요.
ch'in'gu-hant'e-kkaji-to mal mot hae-yo.
friend-to-even-Emph word Neg do-Dec/Pol
'I cannot talk even to a friend.'

8.5.2.5 *Other semantic particles*

Other semantic particles include:

Directional:
-으로 ***ŭro*** 'toward...'

집으로 가세요.
chip-ŭro ka-s-eyo.
home-toward go-SH-Imp/Pol
'Go home, please.'

Instrumental:
-으로 ***ŭro*** 'by means of...with...'

택시로 가세요.
t'aeksi-ro ka-s-eyo.
taxi-by go-SH-Imp/Pol
'Please go by taxi.'

Source:
-부터 ***put'ŏ*** 'starting with ..., from ...'

오늘부터 개학이다.
onŭl-put'ŏ kaehak-i-ta.
today-from start classes-Cop-Dec/Plain
'School starts from today.' [*lit.* 'From today, it is the school opening.']

Goal/destination:
-까지 ***kkaji*** 'up to ...'

기숙사까지 갔어요.
kisuksa-kkaji ka-ss-ŏyo.
dorm-(up)to go-Past-Dec/Pol
'I went as far as the dorm.'

Duration:
-동안 ***tong'an*** 'while ... during the period of ...'

방학동안 뭐 했어?
panghak-tong'an mwŏ hae-ss-ŏ?
vacation-during what do-Past-Dec/*panmal*
'What did you do during the vacation?'

Comparison:
-보다 ***poda*** 'than ...'

피는 물보다 진하다.
p'i-nŭn mul-pota chinha-ta.
blood-Top water-than be thick-Dec/Plain
'Blood is thicker than water.'

Unlikely:
-조차 ***choch'a*** 'even ... [Neg]'

인제는 전화조차 안 한다.
inje-nŭn chŏnhwa-choch'a an-ha-n-ta.
now-Top phone-even Neg-do-Pres-Dec/Plain
'He doesn't even call anymore.'

Unexpected:
-마저 ***majŏ*** 'even ...'

콜린은 미미를 위하여 코트마저 팔았다.
k'ollin-ŭn mimi-lŭl wihayŏ k'ot'ŭ-majŏ p'al-ass-ta.
Colin-Top Mimi-Obj (caring)for coat-even sell-Past-Dec/Plain
'Colin sold even his coat for the sake of Mimi.'

Not the best choice:
-이라도 ***irado*** 'at least (if not the best)...'

편지라도 했으면!
p'yŏnji-rado hae-ss-ŭmyŏn!
letter-if nothing else do-Past-if
'If only he wrote at least a letter (if he can't come, etc.)!'

Choice:
-이나 ***ina*** '...or [something]'

점심이나 합시다.
chŏmsim-ina ha-psi-ta.
lunch-or something do-Dec/Prop
'Let's have lunch or something [there are many things we can do together, but at least let's have lunch together].'

Exclusive:
-만 ***man*** 'only'

할머니는 한국음식만 잡수신다.
halmŏni-nŭn han'guk-ŭmsik-man chapsu-si-n-ta.
grandmother-Top Korea-food-only eat(Hon)-SH-Pres-Dec/Plain
'My grandmother (Hon) eats only Korean food.'

Granted:
-야 ***ya*** 'as expected'

컴퓨터야 물론 있지요.
k'ŏmp'yut'ŏ-ya mullon iss-chi-yo.
computer-unquestionably of course Exist-understandably-Dec/Pol
'Surely, X has a computer. [No need to even ask.]'

Chapter 9

Modifiers

Elements within a sentence are frequently extended. One of the main ways to extend a sentence is by the use of modifiers.

There are two types of modifiers:

- *adnominals* that modify nouns
- *adverbs* that modify verbs and sentences

9.1 Expanding nouns with modifiers (adnominals)

In Korean, modifiers typically precede what they modify. This is because the essential part (head) of a unit appears at its end. Note that the head noun 사람 *saram* 'person,' marked in bold in the following examples of expanded noun phrases, always occurs at the end of the phrase:

[사람]$_{NP}$
saram
person
'a person'

[[인도]$_{NP=Mod}$ [사람]$_{NP}$]$_{NP}$
[[indo]$_{NP=Mod}$ **[saram]**$_{NP}$]$_{NP}$
India person
'an Indian'

[[인도가 만든]$_{S=Mod}$ [사람]$_{NP}$]$_{NP}$
indo-ka mandŭ-n **saram**
India-Subj make-Mod/Past person
'a person that India made/formed/raised'

[[인도를 좋아하는]$_{S=Mod}$ [사람]$_{NP}$]$_{NP}$
indo-rŭl choaha-nŭn **saram**
India-Obj like-Mod/Pres person
'a person that likes India'

[[인도에서 행복한]$_{S=Mod}$ [사람]$_{NP}$]$_{NP}$
indo-esŏ haengbokha-n **saram**
India-Loc be happy-mod. person
'a person that is happy in India'

[[집이 인도에 있는]$_{S=Mod}$ [사람]$_{NP}$]$_{NP}$
chip-i indo-e iss-nŭn **saram**
home-Subj India-Loc exist-Mod/Pres person
'a person whose home is in India'

Note that in English, except for the first example, the equivalent head noun *a person* always comes at the beginning of the noun phrase (optionally preceded by a determiner such as an article or a demonstrative).

As the examples above show, the expanded unit does not change the grammatical category. If a noun phrase is preceded by a modifying word or sentence, the whole expanded unit still acts as a noun phrase.

There are mainly two ways of expanding nouns with modifiers:

- prenouns
- sentential modifiers (relative clauses)

9.1.1 Prenouns

Korean does not have true adjectives like the adjectives in such English expressions as "*That's* ***fantastic****!*," "*What a* ***nice*** *child!*," "*A* ***quick*** *and* ***easy*** *recipe*," etc., all of which can stand by themselves as in "Fantastic!," "Nice!," "Quick and easy!" In Korean there is only a very limited set of inherent modifiers of nouns. Furthermore, these act almost like bound elements, as they cannot stand by themselves but must be supported by the nouns discussed below. For this reason these noun modifiers are called *prenouns* because their only function is to modify the nouns that follow them. In their function, Korean prenouns are a little like English determiners (*a*, *the*, etc.) and possessive pronouns (*my*, *his*, etc.) in that they have to be followed by a noun and they do not inflect.

There are four different subcategories of prenouns: numerical, demonstrative, possessive, and descriptive.

9.1.1.1 *Numerical*

1 Numbers

Both cardinal and ordinal numerals are nouns [▶8.2.7], as they can stand by themselves like other nouns. Numerals, as nouns, could be and often are used as modifiers of other nouns:

[[아홉]$_{NP=Mod}$ [학교]$_{NP}$]$_{NP}$
ahop hakkyo
'nine schools'

However, only five native numbers – *1*, *2*, *3*, *4*, and *20* – have prenoun forms. These are drawn from regular numeral nouns by dropping the final sound. Compare the following pairs:

	Numeral prenoun-NP	Numeral noun
1	[한 [사람]$_{NP}$]$_{NP}$ han saram one person 'one person'	[하나]$_{NP}$ hana one 'one'
2	두 tu	둘 tul
3	세 se	셋 ses
4	네 ne	넷 nes
20	스무 sŭmu	스물 sŭmul

2 Number-related pronouns include:

모든	modŭn	'all'
여러	yŏrŏ	'various'
반	pan	'half'
전	chŏn	'entire'
총	ch'ong	'total'
뭇	mut	'many, various, all kinds'
몇	myŏt	'a few, several, how many'

9.1.1.2 *Demonstrative*

Demonstrative prenouns are deictic expressions like 'this,' 'that,' and 'some,' which refer to some spatial frame of reference, either physically or psychologically. In Korean they double as discourse deictics, referring not only to concrete objects but also to what has been mentioned.

Demonstrative prenouns are either definite or indefinite.

1 Definite

Deictic expressions:

이 *i* 'this [closer to the speaker]'
그 *kŭ* 'that [closer to the hearer, or within cognition of both the speaker and hearer because something/someone has been mentioned]'
저 *chŏ* 'that over there [far from either the speaker or the hearer physically or mentally]'

> *Note*: The three deictic expressions have diminutive forms, 요 *yo* 'this,' 고 *ko* 'that,' and 조 *cho* 'that over there' – each with a bright or yang vowel, carrying a childish, cheerful, and light connotation.

In English *this* and *that* can be either noun or determiner, but in Korean demonstrative words cannot stand alone as nouns but must co-occur with a noun. Thus, the English demonstrative pronoun 'this' is translated as 이것 *i kŏt* [*lit.* 'this thing'] (not just *이 *i*), and 'that' is 저것 *chŏ kŏt* [*lit.* 'that thing over there'] (not just *저 *chŏ*).

> *Note*: In different languages deictic expressions are often used to refer to a statement that has been made. For example, in the following exchange in English:
>
> Anna went home early.
> Tom didn't like *that*.
>
> *that* does not refer to any specific object or idea but to what has been mentioned previously. In Korean a similar context will call for a noun phrase with a deictic expression such as 그 것 *kŭ kŏt* 'that,' 이 것 *i kŏt* 'that,' or 저 것 *chŏ kŏt* 'that over there,' which also doubles as a discourse expression, referring not only to concrete objects and ideas but also to the content of the previous statement.

2 Indefinite

Indefinite (question) words include:

어떤	ŏttŏn	'what/some kind of'
어느	ŏnŭ	'which/some, one'
아무	amu	'whichever/any'
무슨	musŭn	'what/some'
몇	myŏt	'a few, several, how many'

These prenouns must occur together with nouns, as in the case of deictic expressions. However, there are also a couple of independent nouns that also have inherent indefinite meanings that are preferred to prenoun + noun forms, so:

Use 아무 *amu* 'anyone'	but	**not**	?*아무 사람	**amu saram*
			?*아무 분	**amu pun*
Use 무엇 *muŏt* 'what/ something'	but	**not**	*무슨 것	**musŭn kŏt*
Use 얼마 *ŏlma* 'how much'	but	**not**	*몇 원	**myŏt wŏn*

9.1.1.3 *Possessive*

Any noun form can have a genitive particle -의 *ŭi* 'of N' or 'N's,' and the resulting noun phrase is a pronoun. Here are some examples:

부모의
pumo-ŭi
parent-of
'parent's'

상상의
sangsang-ŭi
imagination-of
'imaginary'

9.1.1.4 *Descriptive*

순	sun	'pure'
맨	maen	'bare'
갖은	kajŭn	'all kinds of'
왼	oen	'left'

오른	orŭn	'right'
헛	hŏt	'empty, without substance'
헌	hŏn	'worn-out, used'
새	sae	'new'
옛	yet	'old, from a long time ago'

Note: There is a limited set of adjectival nouns derived from nouns by adding a descriptive suffix, e.g., Sino-Korean -적 *chŏk* '-ish, -like', -식 *sik* '-style, -way', etc. with the construction *noun + descriptive suffix*.

Here are some examples:

이국적 *igukchŏk* (< 이국 *iguk* 'foreign land' + -적 *chŏk*)	'exotic'
정치적 *chŏngch'i-chŏk* (< 정치 *chŏngch'i* 'politics' + -적 *chŏk*)	'political'
미국식 *miguk-sik* (< 미국 *miguk* 'America' + -식 *sik*)	'American-style'
서구식 *sŏgu-sik* (< 서구 *sŏgu* 'the West' + -식 *sik*)	'Western-style'

Because a descriptive suffix is more conducive to adjectival usage, these forms are more often used as prenouns than as nouns:

이국적 분위기
igukchŏk punwigi
exotic atmosphere
'exotic atmosphere'

서구식 생각
sŏgu-sik saenggak
Western-style thoughts
'Western way of thinking'

While these forms are adjectives in the source language, Chinese, and are predominantly used in Korean as adjectives and translated as such in English, they are actually noun forms, as they can occupy noun slots, as the following examples demonstrate:

그 집은 편리한 미국식이다.
kŭ chip-ŭn [[p'yŏllihan]$_{S=Mod}$ [miguksik]$_{NP}$]$_{NP}$ -i-ta.
that house-Top convenient-Mod American-style-Cop-Dec/Plain
'That house is (of) convenient American style.'

정치적으로 볼 때,...
chŏngch'ijŏk-ŭro pol ttae
political [aspect, angle]-by means of see-Mod the time when,...
'from a political perspective ...'

This is part of the general Korean tendency to regard all loanwords as nouns, regardless of the original parts of speech in their source languages [▶Chapter 5]. For example, in the following sentence the English verb *appeal* is borrowed as a noun and an equivalent verb is created by adding a verbalizing suffix 하 *ha-* 'do'.

재판부에 어필하겠다.
chaep'anbu-e ŏp'il-ha-kess-ta.
Dept. of Justice-Loc appeal-do-Vol-Dec/Plain
'I will appeal to the Department of Justice.'

9.1.2 Sentential modifiers (adnominal sentences)

9.1.2.1 Relative clauses

Sometimes a whole sentence rather than a word or a phrase can modify a noun. When the sentence is turned into a modifier, the phenomenon is called *relativization*. A sentence modifying a noun in a noun phrase is called a *relative clause*. In English the relative clause usually follows the noun it modifies. For example, the noun phrase "*a woman*" that occurs within the larger noun phrase "*a woman who dances*" is modified by a sentence and has the structure shown in Figure 9.1:

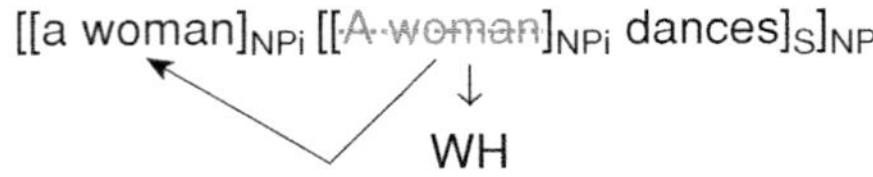

[[a woman]NPi [[A woman]NPi dances]S]NP
↓
WH

Figure 9.1 English noun phrase modified by a sentence

The embedded sentence (*a woman dances*) describes what the noun (*woman*) is like and follows the noun it describes. The repeated noun is replaced by the WH-word *who* in this case.

In Korean the relativization process is similar to that in English. In the Korean sentence that corresponds to the English one:

춤추는 여자
[[ch'umch'u-nŭn]$_S$ [yŏja]$_{NP}$]$_{NP}$
'a woman who dances'

여자 *yŏja* 'woman' is described by the embedded sentence 여자가 춤춘다 (*yŏja-ka ch'umch'u-n-ta* 'A woman dances'). In Korean, too, the identical noun in the modifier sentence is deleted. However, there are some crucial differences between the two languages.

The modified NP has the underlying structure (A), then undergoes relativization, resulting in the sentence with sentential modifier (B) as shown in Figure 9.2:

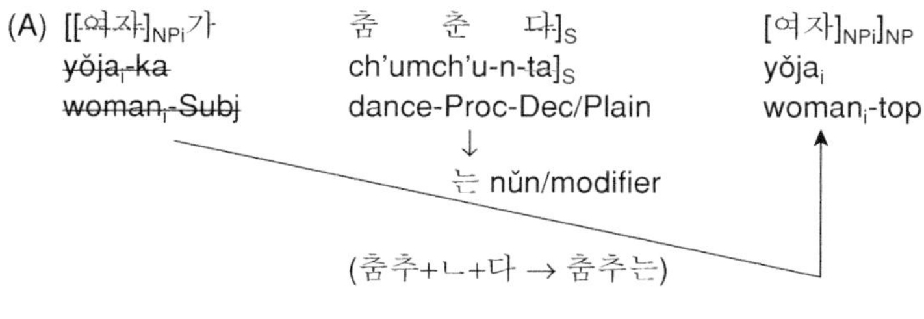

(B) [[춤추는]$_S$ [여자]$_{NPi}$]$_{NP}$
[[[ch'umch'u-nŭn]$_S$ yǒja]
dance-modifier woman
'a woman who dances'

Figure 9.2 Korean noun phrase modified by a sentence

Here is what happens when Koreans insert a sentential modifier in a noun phrase:

1 The noun that is described is placed **after** the modifying sentence (relative clause). This is due to the head-last principle in Korean [▶4]. Note that the noun 'woman' (여자 *yǒja*) follows the modifier sentence 'A woman dances (여자가 춤춘다).'
2 There is no WH-word in Korean relativization. Simply drop the repeated noun and do not replace it with anything. The particle goes with the noun that is deleted, as it would be stranded without the noun it attaches to, just as the English article is deleted along with the deleted noun.
3 The verb of the embedded sentence takes a modifier ending. In order to change the verb form into a modifier, first delete the sentence ender -다 *ta* to get the verb stem. Then add the modifier ending, which varies depending on the tense, aspect, and the kinds of verb. Table 9.1 shows sentential-modifier endings and sample verbs carrying them.

Because there are no true adjectives in Korean, Korean speakers resort to sentential modifiers when translating English adjectives into Korean. So, the English NP "*a good woman*" is rendered into Korean as something like 'a woman who is good' (착한 여자 *ch'akhan yǒja*). Here are more examples of noun phrases with sentential modifiers:

좋은 친구 choun ch'in'gu	'a good friend' (좋다 *choh-ta* 'be good,' 친구 *ch'in'gu* 'friend')

Table 9.1 Sentential-modifier endings

	Action verb	Stative verb[b]
Present[a]	-는 *-nŭn* 먹는 *mŏk-nŭn* '(N) that X eats'	-은 *-ŭn* 높은 *nop'-ŭn* '(N) that is high'
Past	-은 *-ŭn* 먹은 *mŏk-ŭn* '(N) that X ate	–
Retrospective	-던 *-tŏn* 먹던 *mŏk-tŏn* '(N) that X used to eat'	-던-*tŏn* 높던 *nop'-tŏn* '(N) that used to be high'
Future	-을 *-ŭl* 먹을 *mŏk-ŭl* '(N) that X will eat'	-을 *-ŭl* 똑똑할 *ttokttokhal* '(N) that will be smart'

[a] The existential verbs 있다 *iss-ta* and 없다 *ŏps-ta* (and increasingly 계시다 *kyesi-ta* also) take the -는 *nŭn* modifier ending, even though they are stative verbs.
[b] Stative verbs can have a past-tense modifier ending alone only in combination with the retrospective marker -더 *tŏ* (더 *tŏ* + 은 *ŭn* → -던 *tŏn*).

바쁜 사람 pappŭn saram	'a busy person' (바쁘다 *pappu-ta* 'be busy,' 사람 *saram* 'person')
어제 본 영화 oje pon yŏnghwa	'the movie I saw yesterday' (어제 *ŏje* 'yesterday,' 보다 *po-ta* 'see,' 영화 *yŏnghwa* 'movie')
내가 다니는 학교 naega taninŭn hakkyo	'the school I attend' (내가 *nae-ka* 'I-Subj', 다니다 *tani-ta* 'attend,' 학교 *hakkyo* 'school')
내일 먹을 밥 naeil mogul pap	'the rice/food I will eat tomorrow' (내일 *naeil* 'tomorrow,' 먹다 *mŏk-ta* 'eat,' 밥 *pap* 'cooked rice/food')
하와이에서 입을 옷 hawaiesŏ ibŭl ot	'the clothes that would be worn in Hawaii' (입다 *ip-ta* 'wear,' 옷 *ot* 'clothes')

An NP with a modifier sentence is like any NP and occupies any position an NP can take:

$[[$춤추는$]_S$	$[$여자$]_{NP}]_{NP}$는	위험하다.
$[[$ch'umch'u-nŭn$]_S$	$[$yŏja$]_{NP}]_{NP}$-nŭn	wihŏmha-ta.
dance-Mod/Pres	woman-Top	be dangerous-Dec/Plain

'A dancing woman is dangerous.' [*lit.* 'A woman who dances is dangerous.']

[[춤추는]$_S$ [여자]$_{NP}$]$_{NP}$를 좋아한다.
[[ch'umch'u-nŭn]$_S$ [yŏja]$_{NP}$]$_{NP}$-lŭl chohaha-n-ta.
dance-Mod/Pres woman-Obj like-Pres-Dec/Plain
'I like a dancing woman.'

9.1.2.2 *Sentential modifiers occurring with special bound nouns*

In English, a sentence can be turned into a complement by putting such words as "*the fact that*" or simply "*that*" in front of the sentence, as in "*I heard (the news) that France won the World Cup.*" The whole sentence "*France won the World Cup*" is a complement of the predicate *heard*. Korean employs relative clauses when turning the whole sentence into a noun form, in a structure where the head noun is often bound.

9.1.2.2.1 Complementation with -것 *kŏs* 'the fact that'

The most common strategy used for complementation is adding a bound noun -것 *kŏs*, 'the fact' (← 'thing') and changing the sentence into a modifier of that bound noun, as shown in Figure 9.3:

[[프랑스가	월드컵을	이기었다]$_{S=>Modifier}$	[것]$_N$]$_{NP}$
p'ŭrangsŭ-ka	wŏldŭk'ŏp-ŭl	igi-ŏss-~~ta~~	kŏs
France-Subj	World Cup-Obj	win-Past-Dec/Plain	thing
		↓	
		은]$_{Modifier}$	
		[이기은 → 이긴]	
[[프랑스가	월드컵을	이긴]$_{S=>Modifier}$	[것]$_N$]$_{NP}$
'(the fact) that France won'			

Figure 9.3 Complementation with -것 *kŏs*

9.1.2.2.2 Bound nouns with sentential modifiers in auxiliary verb-like constructions

Bear in mind that what could be expressed by one word in one language can have a large set of words in another to express the same idea. Furthermore, there may be more than one equivalent. A case in point is the English auxiliary *can*. This word has at least two meanings: (1) the inherent ability of the subject to do something; and (2) circumstances that make a certain event possible. In Korean the first case is expressed by the expression -줄 알-/모르- *-chul al-/morŭ-* [*lit.* 'know/not know the knowledge/fact']. The second one is by -울 수 있-/없- *-ŭl su iss-/ŏps-* [*lit.* 'the possibility exists/does not exist']. In both cases sentence modifiers are used.

Consider two kinds of 'can' constructions:

1 -을 줄 알-/모르- *-ŭl-chul al-/morŭ-*

The bound noun -줄 *chul* means 'the know-how, the way (how to), fact.' The sentence *X knows Y* becomes a modifier of that knowledge.

(i) 그 사람은 [[일본말을 할]$_{S=>Mod}$ 줄]$_{NP}$ 알아요.
kŭ saram-ŭn ilbonmal-ŭl ha-l **chul** al-ayo.
that person-Top Japanese-Obj speak-Mod can [*lit.* 'know the knowledge']
'He can speak Japanese [He has the knowledge of the language].'

(ii) 저는 [[운전할]$_{S=>Mod}$ 줄]$_{NP}$ 몰라요.
chŏnŭn unjŏnha-l **chul** mollayo.
I-Top drive-Mod cannot [*lit.* 'not know the knowledge']
'I cannot drive [I do not have the ability/knowledge of driving].'

(iii) [[그런 차가 있는]$_{S=>Mod}$ 줄]$_{NP}$ 몰랐어요.
kŭrŏn ch'a-ka iss-nŭn **chul** moll-ass-ŏyo.
such car-Subj Exist-Mod not know
'I did not know that such a car existed [I was ignorant of the fact/information].'

The bound noun -줄 *-chul* denotes knowledge of some fact as well as skill, competence, or ability, and therefore occurs only with cognitive verbs such as 'know' and 'not know.'

2 -을 수 있-/없- *-ŭl su iss-/ŏps-*

One may have the ability but the circumstances may allow or prevent one from doing something, in which case the expression -을 수 있-/없- *-ŭl su iss-/ŏps-* is used. This is because the noun 수 *su* means 'the way, means, solution, ability, possibility.' Here are some examples:

(i) [[비행기가 떠날]$_{S=>Mod}$ 수]$_{NP}$ 있을까요?
pihaenggi-ka ttŏna-l **su** iss-ŭlkkayo?
airplane-Subj depart-Mod can-Q/Pol
'Can planes depart [in such a snowstorm]?'

(ii) 저는 지금 운전할 수 없어요.
chŏ-nŭn chigŭm unjŏnha-l **su** ŏps-ŏyo.
I-Top now drive-do-Mod cannot-Dec/Pol
'I cannot drive now [because I have drunk too much or took some medicine].'

9.2 Expanding verbs with modifiers (adverbs)

Modifiers of verbs are called *adverbs*. Adverbs are like prenouns in that they do not inflect and precede the items they modify. However adverbs can also modify other adverbs, as in many other languages including English, such as in *very well*.

아주 잘 오셨습니다.
aju chal o-si-ŏss-sŭpni-ta.
very well come-SH-Past-Dec/Def
'You are very welcome' [*lit.* 'You (Hon) came very well.']

Even when adverbs are stacked the most important word comes last, so in the sequence 아주 잘 *aju chal* 'very well,' 잘 *chal* is the head and 아주 *aju* its modifier.

Most adverbs modify verbs, although they can also modify prenouns. Adverbs are categorized into inherent words and others derived by adding an adverbializing suffix.

9.2.1 *Inherent (lexical) adverbs*

Inherent adverbs do not inflect and they can stand by themselves. Here are some points to remember:

1 Some of the most common adverbs are inherent and not derived from other parts of speech.
2 Sound-symbolic (SS) words are inherent adverbs.

Korean is very rich in sound-symbolic (SS) words, which are inherent adverbs but can be and are manipulated for appropriately nuanced expressions. For example, the SS word 졸졸 *choljol* describes the manner in which water flows and all the visual, auditory, tactile, and emotional perception that could be connected to it. Thus the same word could

Table 9.2 Inherent (lexical) adverbs

Temporal	늘 *nŭl* 'always,' 이미 *imi* 'already,' 벌써 *pŏlssŏ* 'already,' 자주 *chaju* 'often,' 먼저 *mŏnjŏ* 'before the others,' 가끔 *kakkŭm* 'from time to time,' 이따금 *ittagŭm* 'at odd intervals,' 아직 *ajik* 'yet,' 지금 *chigŭm* 'now,' 인제 *inje* 'now (in contrast to before)'
Repetitive	또 *tto* 'again,' 다시 *tasi* 'again,' 자꾸 *chakku* 'repeatedly,' 연거푸 *yŏn'gŏp'u* 'successively'
Degree	꽤 *kkwoe* 'quite unexpectedly,' 퍽 *p'ŏk* 'quite a lot,' 참 *ch'am* 'really,' 아주 *aju* 'very,' 매우 *maeu* 'very,' 몹시 *mopsi* 'extremely,' 거의 *kŏŭi* 'almost,' 더 *tŏ* 'more,' 가장 *kajang* 'the most,' 좀 *chom* 'a little'
Qualifying	그냥 *kŭnyang* 'as is,' 부득이 *pudŭgi* 'unavoidably,' 꼭 *kkok* 'without fail,' 제발 *chebal* 'please (I entreat you),' 부디 *pudi* 'by all means, I beg you,' 기어코 *kiŏk'o* 'at all costs,' 쭉 *tchuk* 'straight'
Provisional	아마 *ama* 'perhaps,' 만약 *manyak* 'if'
Negative	안 *an* 'not,' 못 *mos* 'cannot'

modify a child following her mother in a line, the fluidity with which one recites a text, the way siblings of a family are born one after the other, etc. The intensity, force, and density of the act and the cuteness or the seriousness of the atmosphere can be conveyed by changing the consonants to a different strength scale, and/or by changing the brightness or darkness of the vowel that occurs in a typically reduplicated word.

Table 9.3 Sound-symbolic adverbs and their connotational variants

Korean sound symbolism		Consonants		
		Plain	Heavily aspirate	Tense
Vowels	Bright/yang	졸졸 *choljol* a gentle puppy following a baby	찰찰 *ch'alch'al* overflowing water from a nice jar	쫄쫄 *tcholtchol* a cowardly person following someone
	Dark/yin	줄줄 *choljol* smoothly and relaxedly reciting a verse	철철 *ch'ŏlch'ŏl* abundance of money	쭐쭐 *tchultchul* unpleasant and sticky rain

Here are some more examples of SS words:

펄펄	p'ŏlp'ŏl	'flying'
아장아장	ajangajang	'toddling'
머뭇머뭇	mŏmutmŏmut	'hesitatingly'
반짝	pantchak	'twinkling'
솔솔	solsol	'breezy'
빙글빙글	pingŭlbingŭl	'circling'
치렁치렁	ch'irŏngch'irŏng	'dangling'
올망졸망	olmangjolmang	'in small clusters'
으스스	ŭsŭsŭ	'chilly, spooky'
벌떡	pŏlttŏk	'jumping'
살살	salsal	'stealthily'

3 Nouns used as adverbs.

오늘	onŭl	'today'	[Never *오늘에]
내일	naeil	'tomorrow'	[Never *내일에]
어제	ŏje	'yesterday'	[Never *어제에]
올해	olhae	'this year'	[Never *올해에]
정말	chŏngmal	'truth'	
참말	chammal	'truth'	

4 Negative polarity adverb.

Certain adverbs require a negative element within the same sentence. We call these negative polarity adverbs. Here is an example of a negative polarity adverb in a sentence:

결코 *kyŏlk'o* 'resolutely, under no circumstances'

나의	삶은	결코	평범하지	않다.
naŭi	salm-ŭn	kyŏlk'o	p'yŏngbŏmhaji	anh-ta.
my	life-Top	resolutely	be ordinary-Comp	**Neg**-Dec/Plain

'My life is absolutely not ordinary.'

Here are some more examples of negative polarity adverbs:

절대로	chlŏtaero	'absolutely'
도무지	tomuji	'at all'
좀체로	chomch'ero	'unbudgingly'

9.2.2 *Derived adverbs*

There is a highly productive process of creating new adverbs, which includes the following:

1 Adverbial suffixes

-게 *ke* (the most common adverbializing suffix meaning 'in the manner of,' 'so that one may . . .,' etc., a little like *-ly* in English)

비싸게	pissage	'expensively'
크게	k'ŭge	'loud'
다 알게	ta alge	'openly' [*lit.* 'so that everyone knows']
늦게	nŭtke	'late'

-히 *hi* (usually for verbs ending in -하다):

공정하다	kongjŏngha-ta	→	공정히	kongjŏnghi 'fairly'
엄숙하다	ŏmsukha-ta	→	엄숙히	ŏmsukhi 'solemnly'

Other examples:

열심히	yŏlsimhi	'with zeal'
천천히	ch'ŏnch'ŏnhi	'slowly'
쓸쓸히	ssŭlssŭrhi	'in a lonely manner'
조용히	choyonghi	'quietly'

-이 *i* (for 하다 verbs when the preceding stem ends in a ㅅ (*s*) and for words that are reduplicated):

깨끗하다 kkaekkŭs-ha-ta → 깨끗이 kkaekkŭsi 'cleanly'
일일 il + 이 i → 일일이 iliri [일 il 'work, matter']
'without missing anything, in every detail'

Other examples include:

길길이	kilgiri	'in a heap'
집집이	chipchibi	'in every house'
나날이	nanari	'daily'
반듯이	pandŭsi	'straight'
따뜻이	ttattŭsi	'warmly'

-리 *li* (for ㄹ *l* or 르 *lŭ*-final verbs for ease of pronunciation):

멀리	mŏlli	'far'	(멀 mŏl- 'be far')
빨리	ppalli	'quickly'	(빠르 pparŭ- 'be fast')

-으로 *ŭro* (added to nouns and adverbs to express emphatic meaning):

참으로	ch'amŭro	(참 ch'am 'truthfulness, reality')	'truly'
억지로	ŏkchiro	(억지 ŏkchi 'unreasonable insistence')	'by force'
정말로	chŏngmallo	(정말 chŏngmal 'truth')	'truly'
날로	nallo	(날 nal 'day')	'daily'
때때로	ttaettaero	(때 ttae 'time')	'from time to time'

-상 *sang* (Sino-Korean suffix meaning 'above..., on...'): The structure is noun + 상 *sang*

위신상	wisin-sang	'in view of one's stature'
체면상	ch'emyŏn-sang	'in order to save face'
법률상	pŏmnyul-sang	'in view of rules of law'
규칙상	kyuch'ik-sang	'in light of rules and regulations'
건강상	kŏngang-sang	'for health reasons'

2 By adverbial particles

Nouns with adverbial particles act like adverbs. Most of these particles are time or place related, but others are instrumentals:

서울에	sŏul-e	'in Seoul'
서울에서	soul-esŏ	'from/in Seoul'
미국까지	miguk-kkaji	'until America'
오늘부터	onŭl-put'ŏ	'from today'
버스로	pŏsŭ-ro	'by bus'

9.3 Expanding sentences with modifiers

1 Inherent sentential adverbs include:

물론	mullon	'of course'
대개	taegae	'in general'
아마	ama	'perhaps'
하여튼	hayŏt'ŭn	'at any rate'
오히려	ohiiryŏ	'on the contrary'
다시	tasi	'again'
차라리	ch'arari	'would rather'
과연	kwayŏn	'as expected'

2 Derived sentential adverbs make interesting words in Korean.

By combining demonstrative-like words e.g. (이렇 *irŏh*, 그렇 *kŭrŏh*, 저렇 *chŏrŏh*) and the verb 하 *ha*, which are in fact pro-sentences that stand for whole sentences, and conjunctive markers, many useful adverbial expressions may be created. Table 9.4 shows these adverbs.

Table 9.4 Sentential adverbs

		이렇다 *irŏh-ta*	그렇다 *kŭrŏh-ta*	저렇다 *chŏrŏh-ta*	하다 *ha-ta*
Conjunctive	meaning	+ Conjunctive markers [▶6.11]			
-니까 *-nikka*	Since…it is this/that/that (yonder) way/so…	이러니까 *irŏnikka*	그러니까 *kŭrŏnikka*	저러니까 *chŏrŏnikka*	하니까 *hanikka*
-으면 *-ŭmyŏn*	If…it is	이러면 *irŏmyŏn*	그러면 *kŭrŏmyŏn*	저러면 *chŏrŏmyŏn*	하면 *hamyŏn*
-으나 *-ŭna*	…but, even though…	이러나 *irŏna*	그러나 *kŭrŏna*	저러나 *chŏrŏna*	하나 *hana*
-지만 *-chiman*	…but	이렇지만 *irŏhchiman*	그렇지만 *kŭrŏhchiman*	저렇지만 *chŏrŏhchiman*	하지만 *hajiman*
-어도 *-ŏdo*	even if…	이래도 *iraedo*	그래도 *kŭraedo*	저래도 *chŏraedo*	해도 *haedo*
-어야 *-ŏya*	only if…	이래야 *iraeya*	그래야 *kŭraeya*	저래야 *chŏraeya*	해야 *haeya*
-어서 *-ŏsŏ*	…and so	이래서 *iraesŏ*	그래서 *kŭraesŏ*	저래서 *chŏraesŏ*	해서 *haesŏ*

The three demonstrative verbs, 이렇다 *irŏh-ta*, 그렇다 *kŭrŏh-ta*, 저렇다 *chŏrŏh-ta*, and the pro-verb 하다 *ha-ta* act as pro-sentences referring to the immediately preceding sentence or whatever has been mentioned before. These, combined with conjunctive suffixes, are commonly used in connecting the preceding discourse to the following sentence. Sometimes these expressions are used simply to start a narrative or as a politeness strategy. So, do not be surprised if a whole narrative begins with a connective 그래서 *kŭraesŏ* ('and then'), for example.

3 Other connectives that turn sentences into adverbial sentences include:

-으려고	ŭryŏgo	'in order to…'
-도록	torok	'so that X may…'
-을 수록	ŭlssurok	'the more…the more…'
-자마자	chamaja	'as soon as…'
-거든	kŏdŭn	'if X happens,…'

Chapter 10

Linguistic protocol

To be a well-mannered adult member of any speech community one needs to acquire the knowledge of how to speak appropriately depending on the situation. In Korean, language protocol is not just one of life's little extras – it forms an integral, indeed essential, part of the grammar. Proper grammatical forms are thus chosen according to criteria established by social convention – such as age, kinship, social status, and gender – that govern other systems of social behavior. The most significant system underlying Korean linguistic etiquette is one of *honorifics*. Honorific forms, of which deferential and polite forms are just a subset, convey the speaker's expressed attitude toward the addressee and the referent and his or her position within the interpersonal relationships at the time of utterance.

In addition to clear honorific marking, there are other strategies for appropriateness in language that reflect aspects of Korean culture and society. This chapter will consider some salient features that play a role in Korean speech protocol.

10.1 Honorification

Two focal points in Korean honorifics are *reference* and *address*. Where to place the referent or the addressee in terms of relative power and intimacy as compared with the speaker is always a concern.

10.1.1 Honorific vocabulary

All languages have a set of special vocabulary items to express the speaker's varieties of attitudes toward the addressee and the referent. For example, in English instead of simply 'X died,' one could choose to say 'X expired,' 'X passed away,' or 'X kicked the bucket.' In Korean, too, there is a limited list of inherently deferential, polite, or rude words, all of which are typically irregular and must simply be learned. Table 10.1 gives examples:

Table 10.1 Inherently honorific vocabulary

	Neutral	Deferential	
Nouns	말 mal	말씀 malssŭm	'word'
	밥 pap	진지 chinji	'rice'
	나이 nai	연세 yŏnse	'age'
	이름 irŭm	성함 sŏngham	'name'
	집 chip	댁 taek	'house, home'
Verbs	먹 mŏk-	잡수시 chapsusi-	'eat'
	자 cha-	주무시 chumusi-	'sleep'
	죽 chuk-	돌아가시 toragasi-	'die'
	아프 ap'ŭ-	편찮으시 p'yŏnch'anŭsi-	'be sick'
	배고프다 paegop' ŭ-	시장하시 sijanghasi-	'be hungry'
Particles	-가 ka /-이 i	-께서 kkesŏ	Subj
	-에게 ege	-께 kke	Dat
	Neutral	**Humble**	
Nouns	나 na	저 chŏ	'me'
	누나 nuna	누이 nui	'sister'
	어머니 ŏmŏni	에미 emi	'mother'
	아버지 abŏji	애비 aebi	'father'
	식사 siksa	소찬soch'an	'meal'
Verbs	보- po-	뵙- poep-	'to see'
	주- chu-	드리- tŭri-	'to give'
	묻- mut-	여쭈- yŏtchu-	'to ask'

When Sino-Korean and pure Korean word pairs exist, with similar meaning and no inherent honorific contrast, an SK expression – unless it has been nativized over a long period and not perceived as foreign – tends to sound more formal than a native expression. Table 10.2 lists some sample word pairs.

Table 10.2 Sino-Korean and native word pairs

	Sino-Korean	Native	
Noun	식사(食事) *siksa*	밥 *pap*	'meal'
Verb	탑승(搭昇)하- *t'apsŭngha-*	타- *t'a-*	'get on (a vehicle)'
Adverb	속(速)히 *sokhi*	빨리 *ppalli*	'quickly'
Prenoun	신 (新) *sin*	새 *sae*	'new'
Numeral + Classifier	십구세(十九歲) *sipku-se*	열아홉살 *yŏrahop-sal*	'19 years of age'

10.1.2 Honorific titles

Koreans use full names mainly for administrative or other formal identifying purposes. Given names are used only when talking to or about children, junior relatives, close childhood friends, classmates, etc. If a given name ends in a consonant, an affectionate diminutive suffix -이 *i* is usually added in a manner similar to the diminutive -*y* added to the first names in English, as in *Johnny* instead of *John*.

These terms of reference are also used as terms of address (vocatives). In some limited cases such as addressing children, the vocative suffix -아/야 *(y)a*, may be attached to the given name.

In most other circumstances, it is considered rude to call someone by his or her bare name unless it is in a completely impersonal context such as making roll calls. Instead, Koreans will talk to or about people by their names, followed by titles that refer to their occupations, places of residence, kinship, and other affiliations.

Table 10.3 Usage of diminutive -이 *i*

승만이가	웃었다
sŭngman-i-ka	us-ŏss-ta
Sŭngman-Dim-Subj	smile-Past-Dec/Plain
'[My friend/child/younger brother . . .] Sŭngman smiled.'	
수아 (*이)가	웃었다
sua(*i)-ka	us-ŏss-ta
Sua-*Dim-Subj	smile-Past-Dec/Plain
'[My friend/child/younger sister . . .] Sua smiled.'	

Two quite commonly used honorific terms of reference or address are -님 *nim* and -씨 *ssi*. A name with a title can be followed by the generic honorific suffix -님 *nim* 'a respected/beloved one.' The suffix -님 *nim* can also be attached directly to the name without any title, in which case it carries the basic meaning of respect and affection. The honorific suffix -씨 *ssi* has traditionally been used in a less intimate, formal, and neutral context, but today this form is frequently used among young colleagues or couples to show respect as well as intimacy. Table 10.4 shows the order in which the name, title, and -님 *nim* and -씨 *ssi* occur:

Table 10.4 Two honorific suffixes, -님 *nim* and -씨 *ssi*

(1) Deferential terms of address or reference
Full/family name + Title + -님 ***nim***
이(기문) 교수 님
yi (kimun) kyosu nim
professor
'Professor Yi Kimun'
Full/personal name + -님 ***nim***
(이)기문 님
(yi) kimun nim
'Mr. (Yi) Kimun'

(2) Formal/noncommittal terms of address or reference
Full name + -씨 ***ssi***
이기문 씨
yi-kimun ssi
'Mr. Yi Kimun'

While both types of terms show respect, those of type (1) express respect for the *power* of the referent, while those of type (2), the *situation*.

The power-conscious suffix -님 *nim* can be attached to any names, titled or not, but the standard polite suffix -씨 *ssi* can be directly attached only to the full or given name, and not to any other title. Thus there are no forms such as *이기문 박사씨 **yi kimun paksa-ssi* for the intended meaning of 'Mr. Dr. Yi Kimun' and *이기문씨님 **yi kimun-ssi-nim* for the intended meaning of 'Honorable Mr. Yi Kimun,' etc.

Titles such as *Chairman* or *Dr.*, representing a person's important occupational position or a particular academic or social achievement, serve as honorific suffixes. When no title can clearly be identified, the universally respected word, 선생 *sŏnsaeng* 'teacher,' is evoked. The generic honorific title, therefore, is 선생님 *songsaeng-nim*, -님 *nim* being the all-purpose title of respect. This term is used when addressing a senior person, regardless of gender or status. A speaker may address a clearly younger and junior male person with the title -군 *kun* (or -양 *yang* for a female).

An older woman with a respectable social position is often given the title -여사 *yŏsa* [*lit.* 'a lady scholar/writer']. Another general way of expressing respect is by acknowledging someone as 선배 *sŏnbae*, a senior in a school or occupational environment. Table 10.5 lists some examples.

Table 10.5 Some generic titles

심선생(님) sim-sŏnsaeng(nim) -teacher	'Mr./Ms. Sim'
심군/윤식군 sim-kun/yunsik-kun -[orig. meaning of kun]king/prince	'(young) Mr. Sim/Mr. Sim Yunsik'
심양/남지 양 sim-yang/namji-yang -unmarried woman	'(young) Ms. Sim/Ms. Sim Namji'
심선배님 sim-sŏnpae-nim -senior	'(Hon.) [School/Occupation] Senior Sim'
심여사님 sim-yŏsa-nim -madam	'(Hon.) Madam Sim'

Note: Korean women do not change their names after marriage. So, 심 *Sim* here would be her maiden name, whether she is married or not.

In addition, kinship terms such as 'elder brother,' 'elder sister,' 'uncle,' 'aunt,' and even 'nephew/niece' are used as quasi-pronouns:

형	hyŏng	elder brother (for a male)
오빠	oppa	elder brother (for a female)
언니	ŏnni	elder sister (for a female)
누나	nuna	elder sister (for a male)
아저씨	ajŏssi	uncle
아주머니	ajumŏni	aunt
할아버지	harabŏji	grandfather
할머니	halmŏni	grandmother

These expressions essentially denote that the person referred to or addressed as such is regarded as a family member, i.e., a person enjoying all the respect, love, and care a family member is expected to receive.

The Korean pronoun system looks rather complex at first glance because of various honorific variants, compared to the few forms of English, as shown in Table 10.6.

In practice, however, the Korean pronoun system is rather deficient. Pronouns are limited to a few neutral forms such as 나 *na* 'me,' 너 *nŏ* 'you,' and 우리 *uri* 'us,' and their deferential or humble counterparts such as 저 *chŏ* 'me [self-effacing],' 당신 *tangsin* 'yourself,' and 저희 *chŏhŭi* 'us [self-effacing].' For the third person where normally a pronoun would be used in another language, Koreans use combinations of a demonstrative, 이 *i* 'this,' 그 *kŭ* 'that,' or 저 *chŏ* 'that over there,' followed by a bound noun referring to a person including honorific ones such as -분 *pun* 'honored person' and regular nouns like 학생 *haksaeng* 'student' and 아이 *ai* 'child'. One exception may be the demonstrative 그 *kŭ* 'that,' which is used for 'he.' It is not clear whether this is a full-fledged pronoun or an abridged expression of phrases such as 'that person,' etc., because in spoken Korean 그 *kŭ* is never used alone.

True pronouns are limited to the first and second persons. However, despite their clear identity as pronouns, they are far from being used as frequently as pronouns in other languages. There are several reasons. First, in Korean whatever is understood is frequently dropped. The two principal participants in any dialog are the first person and the second person; thus these pronouns are easily and commonly dropped in dialog. Koreans also feel that mentioning 'I,' 'me,' and 'my' all the time makes one look self-centered. However, a more important reason for pronoun avoidance is that choosing the proper terms of reference and address can be a risky business and even if a certain interpersonal relationship is clear, expressing it as such may go against general speech protocol. The result is that speakers avoid mentioning any second-person pronoun altogether.

Koreans prefer using the name or some attribute of the person addressed, even when addressing someone directly, rather than calling the person by any pronoun referring to 'you.' Observe the following example of a teacher talking to one of her students:

> 학생은 언제 한국에 왔어?
> haksaeng-ŭn ŏnje han'guk-e o-ass-ŏ?
> student-Top when Korean-Loc come-Past-Dec/*panmal*
> [*lit.* 'When did [you] the student come to Korea?']

Table 10.6 English and Korean pronouns used as terms of reference

		English	Korean	Speech Style
First	Singular	I	나 *naŭ*	Plain
			저 *chŏ*	Humble
	Plural	we	우리(들) *uri(tŭl)*	Plain
			저희(들) *chŏhŭi(tŭl)*	Humble
Second	Singular	you	너 *nŏ*	Plain
			자네 *chane*	Speaking down/formal
			그대 *kŭdae*	Speaking slightly up/respectful
			자기 *chagi*	Respectful-equal
			댁 *taek*	Speaking down/respectful
			당신 *tangsin*	Intense (variable depending on situation)
			선생 *sŏnsaeng*	Speaking up/polite
			어른 *ŏrŭn*	Speaking up/deferential
			귀하 *kwiha*	Plain/respectful formal
	Plural	you	너희(들) *nŏhŭi(tŭl)*	Plain
			자네들 *chane(tŭl)*	Speaking down/formal
			그대들 *kŭdae(tŭl)*	Speaking slightly up/respectful
			자기들 *chagi(tŭl)*	Respectful-equal
			댁들 *taek(tŭl)*	Speaking down/respectful
			당신들 *tangsin(tŭl)*	Intense (variable depending on situation)
			귀하들 *kwiha(tŭl)*	Plain/respectful formal
Third	Singular	(s)he	Dem + -애 → 애,개,재	Speaking down/casual
		(s)he	Dem + -이 → 이이,그이,저이	Speaking equal/informal
			Dem + -분 → 이분,그분,저분	Speaking up/polite
		anyone	아무 *amu*	Indefinite
		who/	누구 *nugu*	Indefinite
		someone	애,개,재 + -들	Speaking down/casual
		they	이이,그이,저이+ -들	Equal/informal
			이분,그분,저분+ -들	Speaking up/polite

So it is understandable that some immigrant Koreans in English-speaking communities use English *you* as if it were a loanword 유 *yu* 'you,' as they intentionally avoid having to choose the pronoun that they might find a bit uncomfortable in their new living environment:

정말이야.	유도	왔으면	좋겠어.
chŏngmal-i-ya.	yu-to	w-ass-ŭmŏn	choh-kess-ŏ.
truth-Cop-Dec/*panmal*	you-Emph	come-Past-if	be good-Sup-Dec/*panmal*

'I really mean it. I would like you to come, too.'

Note that very appropriately the *panmal* style is used along with the choice of "유 yu" for the second-person pronoun [▶10.1.3.2.1].

10.1.3 *Grammatical honorification*

In Korean, the speaker is required to express his or her position toward the referent and the listener. To do this, Koreans draw on two kinds of grammatical honorification: *referent honorification* (RH) and *addressee honorification* (AH). RH includes *subject honorification* (SH) and *object* or *non-subject honorification* (OH). Traditionally, in all four types honorific markers are suffixed to verbal elements. Today OH is not productive but expressed mainly through a limited set of special vocabulary, but SH and AH are regularly and systematically applied.

RH expresses deference and respect to the subject or object of the sentence. There is no mechanism for putting down a referent grammatically. RH is increasingly considered something extra and nice by the younger generation, for whom not applying RH does not necessarily mean being disrespectful as long as other cues of respect appear elsewhere in the discourse. However, AH is different. The listener is always placed in proper perspective from the speaker's point of view, and AH is the most elaborate, as well as an obligatory, component of the entire honorific system.

10.1.3.1 *Referent honorification (RH)*

10.1.3.1.1 Subject honorification (SH): V_{stem} -으시 *ŭsi*

In order to express the speaker's deference to the superior power of the subject of the sentence, the suffix -으시 *ŭsi* is attached to the verb stem.

In such a case, the deferential subject particle -께서 *kkesŏ* instead of the usual -이 *i*/가 *ka* is used. Compare the following two sentences:

비서가	서류를	찾았다.
pisŏ-**ka**	sŏryu-lŭl	ch'ach-ass-ta.
secretary-Subj	document-Obj	find-Past-Dec/AH-Plain

'The secretary found the document.'

회장님께서	서류를	찾으셨다.
hoejangnim-**kkesŏ**	sŏryu-lŭl	ch'ach-**ŭs**-yŏss-ta (← ...**ŭsi**-ŏss-ta).
chairperson(Hon)-Subj(Hon)	document-Obj	find-SH-Past-Dec/AH-Plain

'The (honorable) chairperson found the document.'

The SH suffix -으시 *ŭsi* is attached to a verb stem to turn it into an honorific stem. Therefore, it comes after the other stem-expanding suffixes such as passives and causatives but before other suffixes that must consider larger contexts such as tense–aspect, sentence types, and addressee honorification.

Here are more examples of SH verb stems. Again, note that the suffix-initial vowel -으 *ŭ* is deleted when it joins with another vowel.

Plain	SH	Meaning
읽 ilk-	읽으시 ilk-ŭsi-	'read'
놓 noh-	놓으시 noh-ŭsi-	'put down'
입 ip-	입으시 ip-ŭsi-	'wear'
가 ka-	가시 ka-si-	'go'
주 chu-	주시 chu-si-	'give'

Some verbs use special vocabulary items rather than attaching the SH suffix. For example:

	Plain	SH		
'sleep'	자다 cha-ta	주무시다 chumusi-ta	**not** *자시다	**not** * 주무다
'be (somewhere)'	있다 iss-ta	계시다 kyesi-ta	**not** *있으시다 [▶6.2.4.1]	**not** *계다

Note that these particular words contain -으시 *ŭsi* in them, but it is not a suffix for them. There are no such words as * 주무다 *chumu-ta* for the intended meaning of honorific 'sleep' or *계다 *kye-ta* for the intended meaning of honorific 'be (somewhere).'

10.1.3.1.2 Object/non-subject honorification (OH)

Object or non-subject honorification (OH) is a historical residue of an older suffix that used to show the speaker's humility and deference toward the object of a sentence, but today it is observable mainly in a few special vocabulary items. Thus in the following example, the verb 드리 *tŭri-* is an OH word corresponding to the regular verb 주 *chu-* 'give.'

할아버님께	용돈을	드렸다 (←드리었다)
harabŏnim-kke	yongton-ŭl	tŭryŏtta (← **tŭri**-ŏss-ta)
grandfather(Hon)-Dat(OH)	pocket money-Obj	give(OH)-Past-Dec/Plain

'I gave some pocket money to my (honorable) grandfather.'

> *Note*: The choice of the proper form of the verb of 주 *chu-* 'give' requires a certain amount of calculation. Here is a schematic representation of how it works –
>
> X = someone to be honored, Y = someone for whom no special deference expressed
>
> When Y_1 = the giver, Y_2 = the receiver, use 주다 *chu-ta*
>
> | 내가 | 동생에게 | 용돈을 | 주었다. |
> |---|---|---|---|
> | nae-ka | tongsaeng-ege | yongton-ŭl | chu-ŏss-ta. |
> | I-Subj | younger brother-Dat | pocket money-Obj | give-Past-Dec/Plain |
>
> 'I gave some pocket money to my younger brother.'
>
> When X = the giver, Y = the receiver, use 주시다 *chu-si-ta*
>
> | 할아버지께서 | 나에게 | 용돈을 | 주셨다. |
> |---|---|---|---|
> | harabŏnim-kkesŏ | na-ege | yongton-ŭl | chu-sy-ŏss-ta (←chu-**si**-ŏss-ta). |
> | grandfather-Subj(Hon) | me-Dat | pocket money-Obj | give-SH-Past-Dec/Plain |
>
> 'My grandfather gave me some pocket money.'
>
> When Y = the giver, X = the receiver, use 드리다 *tŭri-ta*
>
> | 동생이 | 할아버지께 | 용돈을 | 드렸다. |
> |---|---|---|---|
> | tongsaeng-i | harabŏnim-kke | yongton-ŭl | tŭry-ŏss-ta (←**tŭri**-ŏss-ta). |
> | younger brother-Subj | grandfather-Dat (Hon) | pocket money-Obj | give(OH)-Past-Dec/Plain |
>
> 'My younger brother gave my grandfather some pocket money.'
>
> When X_1 = the giver, X_2 = the receiver, use 드리시다 *tŭri-si-ta*
>
> | 아버지께서 | 할아버지께 | 용돈을 | 드리셨다. |
> |---|---|---|---|
> | abŏji-kkesŏ | harabŏji-kke | yongton-ŭl | tŭri-sy-ŏss-ta (←tŭri-ŭsi-ŏss-ta). |
> | father-Subj (Hon) | grandfather-Dat (Hon) | pocket money-Obj | give(OH)-SH-Past-Dec/Plain |
>
> 'My father gave my grandfather some pocket money.'

Other examples of OH include:

모시다	mosi-ta	'accompany (someone honored)'
뵙다	poep-ta	'see (someone honored)'
아뢰다	aroe-ta	'tell (someone honored)'
여쭈다	yŏtchu-ta	'say (to someone honored)'

10.1.3.2 *Addressee honorification (AH)*

In Korean, there are seven distinct speech styles or "levels," which indicate power relationships between the hearer and the speaker. Table 10.7 lists addressee honorific sentence-concluding endings, according to sentence types, with the most common endings highlighted.

The -나이다 *nai-ta* style, now considered improper for usual interpersonal relationships, is used only in prayers, poetry, and rituals, although it was not infrequent as recently as the mid-twentieth century.

Three different types of endings express the speaker's respect for the addressee: the super-deferential -나이다 *nai-ta* style, the deferential -습니다 *sŭp-ni-ta* style, and the polite but informal -어요 ***ŏ-yo*** style. The deferential ending -습니다 *sŭp-ni-ta* is used most commonly for all situations that call for formality, proper distance, and respect. The most popular style for showing respect today is the polite but informal -어요 *ŏ-yo* style.

Two other forms becoming increasingly obsolete are two slightly self-elevating styles, the -으오 *ŭo* and -네 *ne* forms. The self-elevating but

Table 10.7 Addressee honorification forms

Declative	Interrogative	Imperative	Propositive
-습니다 *sŭp-ni-ta*	-습니까 *sŭp-ni-kka*	-으십시오 *ŭsi-p-si-o*	-으십시다 *ŭsi-p-si-ta*
-나이다 *nai-ta*	-나이까 *nai-kka*	-으소서 *ŭso-sŏ*	-으소서 *ŭso-sŏ*
-으오 *ŭo*	-으오 *ŭo*	-으오 *ŭo*	-세 *se*
-네 *ne*	-나 *na*	-게 *ke*	-세 *se*
-다 *ta*	-가 *ka*	-어라 *ŏra*	-자 *cha*
-어 *ŏ*	-어 *ŏ*	-어 *ŏ*	-어 *ŏ*
-어요 *ŏ-yo*	-어요 *ŏ-yo*	-어요 *ŏ-yo*	-어요 *ŏ-yo*

interlocutor respecting -으오 *ŭo* style can be used among elderly people, and also by an older person to a worker or to a younger person in a formal situation. The self-elevating and interlocutor elevating -네 *ne* form can be used by a senior to express respect to a junior, e.g., a male boss to a younger subordinate, and a mother-in-law to a son-in-law, or by childhood friends who want to show respect to each other as adults, etc. In some dialects, husbands use -네 *ne* forms to their wives, but wives may use more respectful forms. However, modern Koreans are increasingly uneasy about such self-important forms as these authoritative forms.

10.1.3.2.1 Prevalence of *panmal*

Panmal literally means 'half speech,' implying an incomplete form. *Panmal* has come about as a result of avoidance of making decisions about the relative power of the interlocutor by leaving sentences unfinished. In today's Korean society, which is more and more adopting Western-style democracy, the *panmal* -어 *ŏ* that originates from an unfinished sentence with a clausal conjunctive ending, and its polite derivative -어요 *ŏ-yo*, created by adding the polite marker -요 *yo* to *panmal*, are convenient choices exactly because these two forms are quite flexible in their use, which explains their popularity.

It is important to remember that *panmal* is neither *inherently* speaking down nor "blunt," as some claim. It is even respectful if used when addressing a person who expects to be spoken down to, but impertinent if used to a person who expects to be spoken up to. *Panmal* and other honorific forms can be and are skillfully used for the best speech-protocol effect.

Not specifying any attitude toward the power status of the interlocutor at all would not be sufficiently deferential. Thus, *panmal* is often "elevated" by the polite suffix -요 *yo*, which historically comes from ← 이 *i* 'be'+ -으오 *ŭo* meaning 'It is that....'

Panmal endings have their origin in sentence fragments, but the newly created endings have now become regular sentence enders and hold a clear place in the honorific system of contemporary Korean.

There are many other cases of sentence-concluding endings belonging to the *panmal* group, which originate from unfinished sentences. All seem to have been re-analyzed from subordinate clause final endings to become addressee-honorific endings; all seem to have resulted from a politeness strategy. The first step would have involved regular sentence fragments:

a. 부산에 가거든 전화하세요.
pusan-e ka-kŏdŭn chŏnhwa-ha-s-eyo.
Pusan-Loc go-if phone-do-SH-Imp/Pol
'When and if you go to *Pusan*, please call me.'

b. 전화하세요. 부산에 가거든...
chŏnhwa-ha-s-eyo. Pusan-e ka-kŏdŭn...
'Please call. If and when you get to *Pusan*...'

Sentences like (a) are often spoken as sentences like (b), in which the subordinate clause is presented as an afterthought. The conjunctive is then identified by some listeners as a kind of sentence-ender, opening a way toward re-analysis. In this particular case, the ending -거든 *kŏdŭn* originally meant 'if and when' with a strong presupposition that the proposition would actually happen. In the *panmal* ending the strong presupposition is the dominant meaning, and therefore this expression is used with the sense 'I am telling you, you see':

나 어제 부산에 갔거든.
na ŏje pusan-e ka-ss-kŏdŭn.
I yesterday Pusan-Loc go-Past-Dec/*panmal*
'I went to Pusan yesterday, you see...'

Similarly, the *panmal* ending -잖아 *chanha*, 'isn't it though?' which originated from the negative expression -지 않아 *chi anha*, carries an extension of meaning to give the impression of not being definite about the sentence. In Korean aesthetics, being unclear, indecisive, and hesitant represents grace and what is indirect is more dignified than what is direct. Politeness strategies resort to this subtle aesthetic sense, rather than direct power-laden flattery. Consider the following *panmal* example:

인제 돈 있잖아?
inje ton iss-chanh-a?
now money Exist-Neg-Q/*panmal*
'Look, don't you have money now, though? [You will agree with me, I think.]'

There are as many as 32 *panmal* endings, each of which has gone through a comparable re-analysis through history as in the examples discussed above. Here are some more commonly used *panmal* endings:

-지 *chi* 'X, isn't it true?'

내일 가지.
naeil ka-chi.
tomorrow go-chi (seeking approval)
'Let's go tomorrow, shall we?'

-군 *kun* '(I am surprised at) X!'

밤에 눈이 왔군.
pam-e nun-i wa-ss-kun (and that's a surprise).
night-Loc snow-Subj come-Past-kun (surprise)
'Oh, it snowed last night!'

-는데 *(n) ŭnde* '(The situation is) X (and...).'

약속이 있는데요.
yaksok-i iss-nŭnde-yo.
appointment-Subj Exist-nŭnde (but,...)
'I have an appointment (so I can't go out with you)...'

-더라고 *tŏrago* '(I am telling you, you know) X.'

그 집 참 맛있더라고.
kŭ chip ch'am mas-iss-tŏrago.
that house really taste-Exist-tŏrago(I'm telling you)
'That eatery was good (I ate there myself and am telling you that it is true).'

-게 *ke* '(I bet) X, right?'

왜 벌써 가게?
wae pŏlssŏ ka-ke?
why already go-ke (it has become that way)
'Why, you are already going – you want to?!'

-다니 *tani* '(I can't believe) X! (What do you mean by) X!'

또 이사를 가다니!
tto isa-lŭl ka-tani!
again moving go-tani (I can't believe what I hear)
'My, he is moving again!'

-데 *te* '(I observed) X (and am telling you about it).'

선생님께서 그러시데.
sŏnsaengnim-kkesŏ kŭrŏ-si-te.
teacher-Subj(Hon) say so-SH-te(I am reporting what I heard.)
'The (honorable) teacher said so (I heard with my own ears).'

As mentioned above these *panmal* endings originate from an incomplete sentence, chosen intentionally by the speaker to avoid specifying an attitude toward his or her power relationship toward the addressee using a clear sentence ender. Over the recent years the Korean honorific system has undergone significant changes reflecting rapid social transformations in Korean society. Most noticeable is the disappearance of speech styles that imply inequality in power status other than non-threatening inequalities such as seniority and kinship hierarchy.

Modern language protocol requires that speakers express themselves in a way that will promote favorable and proper interpersonal relationships and avoid power-based speech levels. However, unfinished sentences do sound as if they are not respectful enough by virtue of not having forms with appropriate grammatical markers.

The informal, polite ending -요 *yo* is often called the "*panmal* elevator" and all the *panmal* endings listed above can sound very polite by simply adding -요 *yo* to them, just as any sentence fragment would by the attachment of the same ending. Consider the following two examples:

밤에 비가 왔군요.
pam-e pi-ka wa-ss-kun-**yo**.
night-Loc rain-Subj come-Past-kun-Dec/Pol
'Oh, it rained last night!'

비가-요?
pi-ka-yo↗
rain-Subj-Q/Pol
'It rained?'

> *Note*: Terms of address, including personal and occupational titles, are also undergoing change, resulting in a wholesale introduction of new, more politically correct vocabulary such as 기사 *kisa* 'mechanic' for 운전수 *unjŏnsu* 'driver' and 가정부 *kajŏngbu* 'house-keeper' for 식모 *sik-mo* 'cook (woman).' Kinship terms are extended and applied to addressing people to whom one wants to express closeness. In contemporary Korea, the honorific system is explored more as a face-saving device and a means of satisfying various communicative needs following the premise that all humans are, in principle, allowed the same measure of dignity. While clearly identifiable, power-laden honorific forms have fallen into disuse, and various politeness strategies have created new honorific endings, especially *panmal* forms.

10.1.3.2.2 Considering the listener's point of view

In honorific marking, it is usually from the speaker's point of view. However, the speaker can choose to show empathy to the listener by putting himself or herself in the listener's position. Consider the following example, in which a mother tells her son to say goodbye to her younger sister:

인호야,	인사드려라.	이모	가신다.
inho-ya,	insa-tŭry-ŏra.	imo	ka-si-n-ta.
Inho-Voc	greeting-give (OH)-Imp/Plain	(maternal) aunt	go-SH-Pres-Dec/Plain

'Inho, say goodbye. [Your] aunt is going.'

In an ordinary situation, the mother cannot use SH and OH to her younger sister, but by putting herself in her son's position both types of honorification are not only allowed her but are actually more appropriate.

However, this kind of empathy does not apply when the speaker is also the subject of the sentence. For example in the following sentence:

오늘	저녁은	아주머니가	살께.
onŭl	chŏnyŏk-ŭn	ajumŏni-ka	sa-l-kke.
today	dinner-Top	aunt-Subj	buy-Fut-Vol/*panmal*

'Tonight's dinner is on me.' [*lit.* 'Your aunt will buy tonight's dinner.']

In this sentence, the ordinary non-honorific verb form 살께 *sa-l-kke* is used rather than 사실께 *sa-si-l-kke*, even though the speaker is taking the listener's point of view. This is because the basic honorific principle of never showing deference to oneself is applied and thus, despite the speaker's clear seniority to the listener, she does not apply SH since the subject of the sentence is herself.

10.2 Non-honorific politeness strategies

There are many situations in which simply choosing an honorific expression according to the more or less exact calculus of the power and solidarity relationship between the referent, addressee, and the speaker is not sufficient to satisfy Korean speech protocol. In this section some non-honorific politeness strategies are considered.

10.2.1 Mitigating imposition

Directing someone to do something is always a risky business. It is all right if the requested act is some kind of formal instruction or is somehow beneficial to the person to whom the command is given. For example, the following sentences are quite appropriate and non-threatening:

그 가게 앞에서 오른 쪽으로 도십시오.
kŭ kage ap'-esŏ orŭn ccok-ŭro tol-ŭsi-psio.
that store front-Loc right side-to turn-SH-Imp/Def
'Please turn right in front of that store.'

새해에 복 많이 받으십시오.
saehae-e pok manhi pat-ŭsi-psio.
new year-in blessings a lot receive-SH-Imp/Def
'Happy New Year.' [*lit.* '[Honored one], receive a lot of blessings in the New Year.']

할아버지 오래 오래 사십시오.
haraboŭji orae orae sa-si-psio.
grandfather long long live-SH-Imp/Def
'Grandfather, I wish you longevity.'

However, when the command is imposing something in a way that is not clearly beneficial to the listener, then however deferential the imperative form used may be, it will not comport with language protocol, as in most languages. Thus sentences such as the following are perfectly grammatical and deferential forms are used, but they are not permitted according to language protocol.

(A) *선생님 제 추천서를 쓰십시오.
sŏnsaengnim che ch'uch'ŏnsŏ-lŭl ssŭ-si-psio.
teacher my letter of recommendation-Obj write-SH-Imp/Def
'(Honorable)Teacher, please write my letter of recommendation.'

(B) *할머니 창문을 여십시오.
halmŏni ch'angmun-ŭl yŏ-si-psio.
Grandmother window-Obj open-SH-Imp/Def
'Grandmother, please open the window.'

More appropriate sentences for the above two sentences (A) and (B) would be like (A′) and (B′):

(A′) 선생님, 제 추천서를 써 주시겠습니까?
sŏnsaengnim che ch'uch'ŏnsŏ-lŭl ssŏ chusi-kess-sŭpnikka?
teacher my letter of recommendation-Obj write give-SH-Imp/Def
'(Honorable) Teacher, would you please write a letter of recommendation for me?'

(B′) 할머니, 창문을 열어 주시겠습니까?
halmŏni ch'angmun-ŭl yŏl-ŏ-chu-si-kess-sŭpnikka?
grandmother window-Obj open-give-SH-Vol-Imp/Def
'Grandmother, will you please open the window [for my sake]?'

The three most common strategies generally employed in these situations are:

1 Use an interrogative sentence instead of an imperative. The idea is to encourage the listener that it is his or her choice to do something. By posing the command in a question form, the speaker tries to make the listener feel that he or she, rather than the requestor, has a choice regarding the requested act.
2 Use a beneficiary auxiliary such as -어 주다 *ŏ chu-ta* 'do...for the sake of [e.g., the speaker].'
3 Use an extra-polite, entreating expression such as 제발 *chebal* 'I entreat you,' 한번만 *hanbŏnman* 'just once,' 이번만 *ibŏnman* 'just this time,' 좀 *chom* 'a little,' 미안하지만 *mianhajiman* 'I am sorry but...,' or 죄송합니다만 *choesonghamnidaman* 'I am most humbly not deserving your forgiveness but...,' to bestow full power and authority on the listener.

10.2.2 Mitigating aggressiveness

As mentioned above, sentence fragments, including many *panmal* forms, are often used as part of a politeness strategy. Koreans prefer not to appear to be cutting or so decisive that they leave no room for flexibility. *Panmal* endings coming from the clausal endings -는데 *nŭnde*, -거든 *kŏdŭn*, -어서 *ŏsŏ*, and -지 *chi* are frequently used for such purposes [▶10.1.3.2.1].

Sometimes sentences are expanded, rather than cut in the middle, for the same purpose of mitigating the unwanted appearance of aggression. This practice is common, especially when one wants to submit an opinion cautiously. The most often used sentence expanders include the following:

- Modifier ending -것 같다 *-kŏt kat'-ta* 'It seems that...'

저는	뉴욕보다	워싱턴이	더
chŏ-nŭn	nyuyok-poda	wŏsington-i	tŏ
me (humble)-Top	New York-than	Washington-Subj	more

좋은	것 같아요.
choh-ŭn	kŏt kat'ayo.
good-Mod	seems-Dec/Pol

'[*lit.* It seems to me that] I prefer Washington to New York.'

- Modifier ending -지도 모르다 *-chi-to morŭ-ta* 'It is possible that...'

  그 길이 빠르지도 몰라요.
  kŭ kil-i pparŭ-l-chi-to moll-ayo.
  that road-Subj be fast-Comp-also not know-Dec/Pol
  '[*lit.* I don't know but] that road is probably faster.'

Strategies for mitigating the impression of aggression are employed much more frequently by women than men.

10.2.3 *Other humbling devices*

As shown above, Korean, like most languages, has a set of inherently humbling vocabulary items [▶10.1.3.2.1]. Minimizing one's own possession or act is another strategy for politeness. Sentences such as the following might not make any sense to foreigners but they are almost formulaic:

누추한 집이지만 쉬다 가세요.
nuch'uha-n chip-i-chiman swi-ta ka-s-eyo.
shabby-Mod house-Cop-but rest-and go-SH-Imp/Dec
'My house is humble but please stay over.'

차린 것은 없지만 많이 드세요.
ch'ari-n kŏs-ŭn ŏps-chiman manhi tŭ-s-eyo.
prepare-Mod thing-Top not Exist-but a lot take-SH-Dec/Pol
'There is nothing I prepared, but please eat a lot.'

However there are systematic ways of humbling oneself, too. For example, consider the use of the particle -이나 *ina* (*na* after a vowel).

The basic meaning of -이나 *ina* is choice, as in sentences like

불고기나 만두를 먹겠어요.
pulgogi-na mandu-lŭl mŏk-kess-ŏyo.
pulgogi-or mandu-Obj eat-Vol-Dec/Pol
'I will eat pulgogi or mandu.'

When -이나 *ina* is used by itself with no alternative apparent, it is used as a device to minimize impact. So, when one says:

내일 점심이나 합시다
naeil chŏmsim-ina ha-psita
tomorrow lunch-or do-Prop/Def

Koreans know it is an invitation to lunch. By putting -이나 *ina* after the word for 'lunch,' the invitation is made in a humble fashion, implying that there are other (better) possibilities but they should go out together anyhow.

Trying to minimize the object or idea is not limited to the speaker alone. For example, consider the use of the particle -만 *man* 'only' in the following sentence:

천불만 빌려 주세요
1,000-pul-man pillyŏ chuseyo
1,000-dollars-only lend give-Imp/Pol
'Please lend me 1,000 dollars.'

In this sentence the particle -만 *man* is used in a larger scope than the noun it is attached to. With this, it is not that the amount of money is minimized but the act of lending. So, the sentence means something like 'Please lend me 1,000 dollars [I could have asked for more, but that's only how much I am asking from you].'

10.3 Casual speech

Another kind of speech style that participates in Korean language protocol is *fast speech*, or casual or unguarded speech. It is used in informal situations, or in literature or theater where local color or casualness is intentionally highlighted. Many casual speech forms started as fast-speech phenomena but have found their firm places in the Korean language. Sometimes there are more than two speech varieties for individual words.

By far the most common casual speech phenomena are all sorts of simplifications. In casual English, such contracted forms as "I'm gonna..." and "I wanna..." are perfectly acceptable. As people speak more quickly and pay less attention to articulating their words distinctly, they produce more contractions.

In Korean, too, certain salient characteristics in phonology apply to fast and casual speech alike. The degree of applicability simply seems to depend on the speed and care of pronunciation.

Careful speech is always considered more polite than casual speech. In careful speech, words and other important boundaries are clearly marked. Certain phonological rules apply only within the same breath group, and not across a perceivable boundary. The following two examples show essentially the same message, i.e., 'I had a drink,' in two different styles: (i) deferential style and (ii) plain/intimate style.

(i) 술 한잔 했습니다.
sul- han-chan hae-ss-sŭp-ni-ta.
liquor- one-glass take-Past-Dec/Def
[sul hanjan haessŭmnida]

(ii) 술 한 잔 했다.
sul han- chan hae-ss-ta.
[surhanjan haetta] ~ (fast/casual speech) [suranjanaetta]

In the example (i), where every word is very carefully pronounced, both the final consonant ㄹ /l/ and the initial consonant ㅎ /h/ of the phrase 'a glass of liquor' are clearly pronounced. A fast speech variety for 'one glass of liquor,' [surhanjan], is possible but less applied. In the case of (ii), however, because of the "terseness" of the speech style, the whole sentence is shorter and can be pronounced within one breath, allowing the casual/fast speech form more easily and naturally. The rules that apply here are just common general phonological ones. When a speaker is extra careful in pronunciation, they do not apply.

Casual speech is not only due to sloppy or fast talk but also due to perception. A case in point is the unreleasing of syllable-final consonants. Unreleased consonants are not as audible as released ones. In general, sounds will weaken and the weaker the sound the more easily it gets dropped. Another important characteristic in casual speech simplification is that the middle part, not the periphery, of a phonological word gets deleted, as the initial sound and the last sound generally seem to carry more semantic cues than the middle one that can be filled in, as in the following pair:

(i) 그러니까 kŭrŏnnikka 'and therefore,...'
(ii) 기잉까 kiingkka

Example (ii) shows a casual form of (i). The long middle part is deleted, and the trace of the deleted part (the sound *n* in this case) is in the nasalization of the internal vowel [i], transcribed as 잉 *ing* here.

Some widely used casual speech forms include:

1 무엇 *muŏt* → 무어 *muŏ* → 뭐 *mwŏ* → 모 *mo* (→ faster and more casual) 'what'
2 Demonstrative + 이/그/저 것 *i-kŏt* → 이/그/저 거 *i-kŏ* 'this, that, that over there (thing)'

In the second group of these words, a sequence has merged with the subject particle -이 *i* and a new grammatical group of **demonstratives + Subj** has been formed:

이게	*ige*	'this (Subj)'
그게	*kŭge*	'(Subj)'
저게	*chŏge*	'that over there (Subj)'

Vowel changes are another casual-speech phenomenon:

아버지 *abŏji* → 아부지 *abuji* → 압지 *apji*. 'father'
(→ faster and more casual)

Some other extremely common casual-speech forms include:

근데 *kŭnde* (← 그런데 *kŭrŏnde* ← 그렇-은데 *kŭrŏh-ŭnde*)	'by the way'
그치, 그지 *kŭch'i, kŭji* (← 그렇-지 *kŭrŏh-chi*)	'That's so, is that so?'
개서 *kaesŏ* (← 그래서 *kŭraesŏ* ← 그렇-어서 *kŭrŏh-ŏsŏ*)	'and so'
그래각구 *kŭraekakkku* (← 그래가지고 *kŭraekajigo* ← 그렇-어 가지고 *kŭrŏ-ŏ-kajiko*)	'with that done/said'
개도 *kaedo* (← 그래도 *kŭraedo* ← 그렇/러-어도 *kŭrŏh-[ŏ]do*)	'in spite of that...'
그치만 *kŭch'iman* (← 그렇지만 *kŭrŏh-chiman*)	'...but'

All these forms are combinations of the pro-sentence 그렇다 *kŭrŏh-ta* 'X be so' or 그러다 *kŭrŏ-ta* 'X do so' followed by conjunctive endings such as -은데 *ŭnde* '(the situation is such) and...,' -어도 *ŏdo* 'even though...,' -지만 *chiman* '(that's true) but...,' etc. It is not important to understand how these have arrived at the casual speech listed above, but it is helpful to know that in Korean, word-initial positions are strong positions and the conjunctive endings carry important meaning. So, as long as those two important semantic cues are kept, the other internal elements could be dropped, especially in such common vocabulary as the ones listed above.

Appendix 1

Romanization of Han'gŭl letters

The nature of the Korean sound system complicates romanization (its representation in the Latin alphabet). Three major competing romanization systems today are the McCune-Reischauer (M-R) system developed in the 1930s, the Yale-Martin system (1942), and the Republic of Korea Governmental system (2000). The main difference is whether the emphasis is on how sounds are written in Korean (transliteration) or how they are pronounced (transcription). Linguists prefer the Yale system for its near one-to-one correspondence between *han'gŭl* letters and the romanized forms, but these are rather detached from actual pronunciation. In the M-R system, *han'gŭl* letters are represented in Roman letters in such a way that an English-speaking reader may approximate a pronunciation that would be recognizable to Korean speakers. For example, the second syllable 글 in the name of the alphabet 한글 is romanized as <kŭl> when it occurs independently or in a word-initial position because /k/ is pronounced as [k] when there is nothing preceding it to cause it to soften. However, it is pronounced as softer [g] when it is surrounded by soft sounds such as a vowel, [n], [m], [ng], or [l], and the syllable is romanized as <gŭl>. Therefore, it is not always easy to retrieve the Korean spelling from romanized forms through this system. A slightly altered version of M-R was the official system for Korean romanization in South Korea from 1984 to 2000, and another modified version is still the official system in North Korea. The new ROK governmental system promulgated in 2000 is similar to the M-R system, but avoids the cumbersome diacritics (breve marks) and apostrophes that M-R uses. The ROK system also seems to appeal to many Koreans, who find it corresponds more to their popular individual romanizations such as *Daewoo* for 대우 and *bibimpap* for 비빔밥 rather than McCune-Reischauer's *tae-u* and *pibimpap*, respectively. Table A1.1 includes some examples of the three different systems of romanization:

Table A1.1 Examples according to three systems of romanization

English	Korean	M-R	Yale	ROK Govt
on the side	옆에	*yŏp'e*	yephey	*yeope*
end	끝	*kkŭt*	kkuth	*kkeut*
sail (Obj)	돛을	*toch'ŭl*	tochul	*docheul*
stir-fry	볶다	*pokta*	pokkta	*bokta*
outside	밖	*pak*	pakk	*bak*
writing (Subj)	글이	*kŭri*	kuli	*geuri*
in the kitchen	부엌에	*puŏk'e*	puekhey	*bueoke*
script, letter	글자	*kŭlcha*	kulqca	*geulja*
difficult	어려운	*ŏryŏun*	elyewun	*eoryeoun*
is warm	따뜻하다	*ttattŭthada*	ttattushata	*ttatteuthada*

The McCune-Reischauer system is still the most commonly used system outside Korea, having been adopted by most libraries including the Library of Congress, by Korean studies journals, academic publications, and foreign governmental publications, sometimes with modifications. However, the South Korean governmental system seems to be gaining popularity as all traffic signs in Korea have been converted to it. Western-language publications coming out of Korea are also increasingly adopting the governmental system.

This book uses the M-R system. However, original *han'gŭl* forms are given at the same time in discussing Korean throughout – partly for those who know *han'gŭl* – partly for other readers who are encouraged to learn it before reading further, because *han'gŭl* is easy to master and is a far better fit to the Korean language than any system of romanization. It certainly will be enormously helpful in reading various grammatical explanations presented in this book.

Note that in M-R romanization the apostrophe is used as a diacritic to mark aspiration in consonants (e.g., in 판소리 *p'ansori*, the initial *p* is strongly aspirated like the first consonant in English *power*). In this book an apostrophe or a hyphen is similarly used to separate two syllables in a potentially ambiguous combination of consonants (e.g., 연과 *yŏn-gwa* vs. *yŏn'gwa*, and 영와 *yŏng-wa* vs. *yŏng'wa*).

Appendix 2

A quick guide to using the Korean dictionary

Each Korean dictionary lists words in alphabetic order. The Korean alphabet as used today in South Korea consists of 14 basic consonant letters and ten basic vowel letters. Each alphabetic letter is referred to by its own name, which reflects its pronunciation. As noted in Chapter 2, sounds of the letters vary depending on the position in which they occur [▶2.1]. In the case of the consonants, each letter's name shows how the consonants are pronounced in the initial and final positions in a syllable with the help of two neutral or basic vowels, 이 *i* and 으 *ŭ*. For example, the letter ㅂ *p* is read 비읍 *piŭp*, which is pronounced as [piŭp˺] with the first consonant pronounced as a gently aspirated lax consonant, while the last one is pronounced without immediate release after articulation and with no aspiration. In North Korea all the names of the consonants follow this pattern. However, in the South, there is a slight variation in the names of the consonantal letters. For example, the letters, ㄱ *k* and ㅅ *s*, are named "기억 *ki-ŏk*" and "시옷 *si-os*," respectively.

The names of the consonants and their order of entry adopted by dictionaries published in South Korea are as follows:

Letter	Name
ㄱ	기역 [kiyŏk] ← /kiŏk/
ㄴ	니은 [niŭn]
ㄷ	디귿 [tigŭt]
ㄹ	리을 [riŭl]
ㅁ	미음 [miŭm]
ㅂ	비읍 [piŭp]
ㅅ	시옷 [siot]
ㅇ	이응 [iŭng]
ㅈ	지읒 [chiŭt]
ㅊ	치읓 [ch'iŭt]

Letter	Name
ㅋ	키읔 [k'iŭk]
ㅌ	티읕 [t'iŭt]
ㅍ	피읖 [p'iŭp]
ㅎ	히읗 [hiŭt]

The geminate consonants with two identical letters are called 쌍 **X** 'double X,' as shown below:

Letter	Name
ㄲ	쌍기역 [ssang kiyŏk]
ㄸ	쌍디귿 [ssang tigŭt]
ㅃ	쌍비읍 [ssang piŭp]
ㅆ	쌍시옷 [ssang siot]
ㅉ	쌍지읒 [ssang chiŭt]

Depending on how the doubled letters are analyzed, the doubled consonantal letters may either go right after the corresponding single letters, or at the end of all the consonants. South Korean dictionaries take the former approach, but North Korean dictionaries consider them single sounds and therefore all the doubled letters appear after all the consonants.

The names of the vowel letters are essentially their sounds. Their dictionary order is as follows:

Letter	Name
ㅏ	아 [a]
ㅑ	야 [ya]
ㅓ	어 [ŏ]
ㅕ	여 [yŏ]
ㅗ	오 [o]
ㅛ	요 [yo]
ㅜ	우 [u]
ㅠ	유 [yu]
ㅡ	으 [ŭ]
ㅣ	이 [i]

Complex vowels also receive different analyses. Graphically complex letters of the alphabet are ordered according to the first component of the letter in South Korea but in North Korea all complex vowel letters appear at the end of the basic vowels.

Compare the alphabetical orders for dictionary entries in North and South Korea:

Consonants:

North Korea: ㄱ ㄴ ㄷ ㄹ ㅁ ㅂ ㅅ ㅇ ㅈ ㅊ ㅋ ㅌ ㅍ ㅎ ㄲ ㄸ ㅆ ㅉ

South Korea: ㄱ ㄲ ㄴ ㄷ ㄸ ㄹ ㅁ ㅂ ㅃ ㅅ ㅆ ㅇ ㅈ ㅉ ㅊ ㅋ ㅌ ㅍ ㅎ

Vowels:

North Korea: ㅏ ㅑ ㅓ ㅕ ㅗ ㅛ ㅜ ㅠ ㅡ ㅣ ㅐ ㅒ ㅔ ㅖ ㅚ ㅟ ㅢ ㅘ ㅝ ㅙ ㅞ

South Korea: ㅏ ㅐ ㅑ ㅒ ㅓ ㅔ ㅕ ㅖ ㅗ ㅘ ㅙ ㅚ ㅛ ㅜ ㅝ ㅞ ㅟ ㅠ ㅡ ㅢ ㅣ

Appendix 3

Sample irregular verb conjugation

	-다 ta	-습/읍니다 (s)ŭp-ni-ta	-세요 se-yo	-어요 ŏ-yo	-어도 ŏdo	-으니 ŭni	-은 ŭn
ㅂ p-irregular	쉽다 swip-ta	쉽습니다	쉬우세요	쉬워요	쉬워도	쉬우니	쉬운
	어렵다 ŏryŏp-ta	어렵습니다	어려우세요	어려워요	어려워도	어려우니	어려운
	덥다 tŏp-ta	덥습니다	더우세요	더워요	더워도	더우니	더운
	춥다 chup-ta	춥습니다	추우세요	추워요	추워도	추우니	추운
	아름답다 arŭmdap-ta	아름답습니다	아름다우세요	아름다워요	아름다워도	아름다우니	아름다운
	곱다 kop-ta	곱습니다	고우세요	고와요	고와도	고우니	고운
ㄷ t-irregular	듣다 tŭt-ta	듣습니다	들으세요	들어요	들어도	들으니	들은
	묻다 mut-ta	묻습니다	물으세요	물어요	물어도	물으니	물은
	걷다 kŏt-ta	걷습니다	걸으세요	걸어요	걸어도	걸으니	걸은
	싣다 sit-ta	싣습니다	실으세요	실어요	실어도	실으니	실은
	긷다 kit-ta	긷습니다	길으세요	길어요	길어도	길으니	길은
ㅅ s-irregular	잇다 is-ta	잇습니다	이으세요	이어요	이어도	이으니	이은
	붓다 pus-ta	붓습니다	부으세요	부어요	부어도	부으니	부은
	짓다 chis-ta	짓습니다	지으세요	지어요	지어도	지으니	지은
	긋다	긋습니다	그으세요	그어요	그어도	그으니	그은

	kŭs-ta						
	젓다 chŏs-ta	젓습니다	저으세요	저어요	저어도	저으니	저은
ㄹ-l irregular	빠르다 pparŭ-ta	빠릅니다	빠르세요	빨라요	빨라도	빠르니	빠른
	따르다 ttarŭ-ta	따릅니다	따르세요	딸라요	딸라도	따르니	따른
	고르다 korŭ-ta	고릅니다	고르세요	골라요	골라도	고르니	고른
	다르다 tarŭ-ta	다릅니다	다르세요	달라요	달라도	다르니	다른
	부르다 purŭ-ta	부릅니다	부르세요	불러요	불러도	부르니	부른
	짜르다 tcharŭ-ta	짜릅니다	짜르세요	짤라요	짤라도	짜르니	짜른
	기르다 kirŭ-ta	기릅니다	기르세요	길러요	길러도	기르니	기른
	가르다 karŭ-ta	가릅니다	가르세요	갈라요	갈라도	가르니	가른
	모르다 morŭ-ta	모릅니다	모르세요	몰라요	몰라도	모르니	모른
	찌르다 tchirŭ-ta	찌릅니다	찌르세요	찔러요	찔러도	찌르니	찌른
	지르다 chirŭ-ta	지릅니다	지르세요	질러요	질러도	지르니	지른
ㄹ l-deletion	알다 al-ta	압니다	아세요	알아요	알아도	아니	안
	살다 sal-ta	삽니다	사세요	살아요	살아도	사니	산
	울다 ul-ta	웁니다	우세요	울어요	울어도	우니	운
	놀다 nol-ta	놉니다	노세요	놀아요	놀아도	노니	논
	갈다 kal-ta	갑니다	가세요	갈아요	갈아도	가니	간
ㅎ h-irregular	하다 ha-ta	합니다	하세요	해요	해도	하니	한
	빨갛다 bbalkah-ta	빨갛습니다	빨가세요	빨개요	빨개도	빨가니	빨간
	어떻다 ŏddŏh-ta	어떻습니다	어떠세요	어때요	어때도	어떠니	어떤
돼 'become'	되다 toe-ta	됩니다	되세요	돼요	돼도	돼니	된

Appendix 4

Glossary

active voice: a voice of a verb in which the person or thing represented by the grammatical subject performs the action represented by the verb. *cf.* **passive voice.**

adjectival verb: a Korean verb corresponding to the construction 'be' + adjective in English. A unit, considered a single word in Korean, with the semantic content of a predicate adjective.

adjective: a word that modifies a noun or pronoun.

adnominal: pertaining to an adnoun; adjectival; attached to a noun.

adverb: a word that modifies a verb, an adjective, or another adverb. Adverbs generally answer one of four questions: "how?," "when?," "where?," or "to what extent?"

adverbial clause: a subordinate clause that modifies a verb, adjective, or adverb.

agglutinative language: a language in which words are created by "gluing" suffixes one after the other to the basic part of a word called "stem."

article: a type of determiner that makes a noun either specific or indefinite. In English there are three articles: the definite article "the" and the two indefinite articles "a" and "an."

aspect: a verbal property that is time-related; works closely with tense. Aspect indicates whether an event is completed, incomplete, ongoing, experienced, repeating, having an effect, or reminisced, etc., rather than simply locating an event vis-à-vis a certain temporal reference point.

aspiration: the release of a strong burst of air after certain obstruents.

assimilation: the process of conforming one sound to another to aid in pronunciation. One sound acquires features from one next to it, either partially or completely.

auxiliary verb: a verb that combines with another verb to fully or partially mark the tense, mood, voice, or condition of the verb it combines with.

bound noun: a noun that needs a modifier to form a phrase to complete its meaning.

cardinal numeral: a numeral of the class whose members are considered basic; are used in counting; and used in expressing quantities. *cf.* **ordinal numeral.**

causative: a grammatical or lexical indication of the causal role of a referent in relation to an event or state expressed by a verb.

classifier: a word that expresses the classification of a noun. In languages that employ classifiers, they act as mandatory determiners to complete a noun phrase.

clause: a subject and verb which forms part of a sentence.

common noun: a noun whose referent is nonspecific.

complement: a word or expression that, added to a verb, completes a predicate.

complex sentence: a sentence made up of one main clause and at least one subordinate clause.

compound boundary: the boundary between two components in a compound word.

compound sentence: a sentence made up of two or more independent clauses.

compound word: a word made up of two or more words combined into a single word.

conjugation: a listing, in a conventional order, of the various inflectional forms of a verb or verb-like element.

conjunction: a word that joins sentences, clauses, phrases, or words. There are two kinds of conjunctions: coordinating conjunctions (e.g., "and" or "or") and subordinating conjunctions (e.g., "but").

consonant: one of a class of speech sounds characterized by constriction or closure at one or more points in the breath channel.

consonant cluster: more than two consecutive consonants.

coordinating conjunction: a word that joins two sentences, often "but" or "and."

copula: an intransitive verb which links a subject to a noun phrase, adjective, or other constituent that expresses the predicate. Also called *copulative verb*.

count noun: a noun whose referents are separable, *cf.* **mass noun.**

dark vowel: a vowel that belongs to a harmonic group that gives a deep, low, big impression in sound-symbolic vocabulary. *See also* **yin/ŭm vowels.**

declarative sentence: a sentence that states an idea.

deictic: expressions like "this," "that," "here," "there," "now," and "then" that refer to some spatial frame of reference either physically or psychologically, which is already present in the discourse.

demonstratives: a pronoun or adjective that points out an item.

dependent clause: *see* **subordinate clause.**

descriptive verb: a verb that describes particular situations, conditions, or states of affairs.

determiner: a word or affix that belongs to a class of noun modifiers that expresses the reference, including the quantity, of a noun.

diphthong: a gliding monosyllabic speech item that starts at or near the articulatory position for one vowel and moves to or toward the position of another.

direct object: a noun or pronoun that receives the action of a verb or shows the result of the action. It answers the question "What?" or "Whom?" after an action verb.

direct quotation: a word-for-word repetition of another's utterance. In many languages, including English and Korean, the quotation is conventionally placed within quotation marks.

ditransitive verb: a verb that requires both a direct and an indirect object.

exclamatory sentence: a sentence spoken with great emotion or intensity, usually written with distinctive punctuation.

existential verb: a verb that indicates existence or absence of some concrete object or being, including humans or animals, or an abstract idea.

fragment: a group of words that resembles a sentence but does not express a complete thought. Sometimes it lacks a subject or verb.

fricative: a sound produced through a narrow opening in the vocal tract.

function word: a word which has no lexical meaning, and whose sole function is to express grammatical relationships.

geminate: double (applies to consonants).

gerund: a verbal noun (in English, ending in *-ing*).

glide: a sound produced with little or no obstruction of the airstream that is preceded (e.g., /w/ and /j/ in *we*, *you*) or followed by a vowel (e.g., /w/ or /y/ in *say*, *grow*). *See also* **on-glide**.

***hancha*:** Chinese characters as used in Korean.

head (of a phrase): the element that determines the syntactic function of the whole phrase and is therefore essential to the phrase.

head-final language: a language in which the most important item or the **head** in every major grammatical category comes at the end of the unit.

honorific marking: indicated through the use of an honorific suffix on a verb or a special honorific form of a verb. Honorifics do not merely elevate the interlocutor but comprise a variety of styles expressing other types of recognized relative relationships between the speaker and the hearer in terms of power and intimacy.

iconic: explicable in terms of similarity between the form of the sign and what it signifies. Such words as "splash," "bang," and "cuckoo" are iconic. What is "motivated" and not arbitrary.

imperative sentence: a sentence with a verb that expresses the will to influence the behavior of another, expressive of a command, entreaty, or exhortation.

imperfect: aspect of a verb that shows, usually in the past, an action or a condition as incomplete, continuous, or coincident with another action.

indefinite pronoun: a word that replaces a noun without specifying which noun it replaces.

independent clause: a clause that is not introduced by a subordinating term.

indirect object: a grammatical object representing the secondary goal of the action of its verb.

indirect question: a sentence that describes a question but does not directly ask a question.

indirect quotation: a repetition of another's utterance, altering the pronouns to represent the point of view of the speaker repeating the utterance rather than its original utterer.

interrogative sentence: a sentence that asks a direct question.

intonational contour: the rise and fall of pitch throughout that add conventionalized meanings to the utterance, including question, statement, suggestion, surprise, etc.

intransitive verb: an action verb that does not have a direct object.

Law of Initials: Korean phonological principle. Word-initial *l* is pronounced [n]. However, word-initially the sequence *ni-* or *ny-* is avoided. The [n] sound, including one derived from /l/, drops before [i] or [y].

main clause: *see* **independent clause.**

manner of articulation: the type of closure made by the articulators and the degree of the obstruction of the airstream by those articulators.

mass noun: a noun whose referents are not separable. *cf.* **count noun.**

mimetics: sound-symbolic words.

modal: a modal expresses the speaker's (or the hearer's, in an interrogative sentence) attitude, judgment, and assertion beyond a simple declaration of fact. In Korean, modals include suffixes expressing volition, conjecture, or retrospection.

modifier: a vocabulary item that describes a word or make its meaning more specific.

modifying clause: a subordinate clause that modifies a noun or pronoun. An adjective clause often begins with the relative pronouns "that," "which," "who," "whom," or "whose."

mood: a verb property, expressed by a particular set of inflectional forms, to express whether the action or state it denotes is factual or otherwise (e.g., command, possibility, or wish).

morpheme: the smallest meaningful unit.

nasalization: a way of pronouncing sounds characterized by resonance produced through the nose.

negation: a morphosyntactic operation in which a lexical item denies or inverts the meaning of another lexical item or construction.

nominal: a word which differs grammatically from a noun but functions as one.

noun: a word that is the name of something (as a person, animal, place, thing, quality, idea, or action).

object: a noun or noun equivalent either in a prepositional phrase or in a verb construction with the action of a verb directed on or toward it. Objects can be one of two kinds in English: direct object or indirect.

object particle: a grammatical suffix that denotes the object of a sentence.

obstruent: a sound produced when the airflow is completely stopped (a stop like [p], [t], [k]) or escapes through a narrow opening (a fricative like [f], [s]) in the vocal tract.

off-glide: A glide following a vowel. *cf.* **on-glide.**

on-glide: A glide preceding a vowel. *cf.* **off-glide.**

onomatopoeia: phonetic imitation in which the sound of a word imitates the sound of a real-world object.

ordinal numeral: a numeral belonging to a class whose members designate positions in a sequence. *cf.* **cardinal numeral.**

palatalization: process in which dental stops become palatal in front of the vowel /i/ or glide /y/, both of which are pronounced in the palatal area.

***panmal*:** *lit.* cut-off speech. An addressee-honorific ending avoiding a clear-cut power-laden speech style.

particle: a unit of speech expressing certain grammatical elements; affixed (in Korean, suffixed) to a stem or other unit; unstressed and generally non-independent.

part of speech: the role a particular vocabulary item is allowed to play in syntax, such as noun, verb, etc.

passive voice: voice of a verb asserting that the person or thing represented by the grammatical subject is subjected to or affected by the action represented by the verb. *cf.* **active voice.**

past: a verb tense that expresses past, definite, completed action/phenomenon.

past past: when the Korean past tense marker -었 *ŏss* is doubled, the two together are referred to as "past-past," "double past," or "past perfect."

perfective: sometimes called resultative aspect. It denotes completed actions.

phoneme: a distinctive sound, an alphabet.

phrase: a group of one or more grammatically related words that form a sense unit expressing a thought. A phrase has the force of a single part of speech, such as a noun or adverb.

possessive particle: a grammatical suffix that denotes the possessiveness of a sentence.

possessive pronoun: a pronoun that shows ownership, control, or pertinence. Some are used alone (e.g., English "mine," "yours"), some describe a noun (e.g., "my," "your").

postposition: a particle indicating the relationship of a noun stem to which it is attached to other nouns in a sentence.

predicate: the part of a sentence or clause that expresses what is said of the subject and that usually consists of a verb with or without objects, complements, or adverbial modifiers.

prenoun: a modifier of a noun that occurs before a noun, whose only function is to modify a noun.

present: a verb tense that expresses an ongoing action or phenomenon.

progressive aspect: expressing continuous or repeated action.

pronoun: a word that is used as a substitute for a noun or noun equivalent, takes noun constructions, and refers to persons or things named or understood within context.

proper noun: the name belonging to a particular individual or place.

propositive sentence: a sentence inviting the addressee to do something together with the speaker.

prosody: rhythmic and intonational rules.

quasi-pronoun: a word of the form prenoun + noun.

reflexive pronoun: a **pronoun** that "reflects" a noun or pronoun by taking the place of that noun or pronoun (the antecedent) when the noun or pronoun is doing something to itself.

relative clause: a clause subordinate to the rest of the sentence. In English it may begin with a relative pronoun such as "that," "which," "who," "whom," or "whose."

resyllabification: carrying the final consonant of a syllable over to the next syllable.

semivowel: a non-syllabic vowel that may form diphthongs with syllabic vowels.

sentence: a meaningful linguistic unit consisting of words or a single word representing a fact or event. It usually contains an explicit or implied subject and a predicate containing a verb.

sonorant: sounds produced when air flows out with no or almost no obstruction through the mouth or nose, including vowels, nasal sounds, and liquids. Sonorants are generally voiced.

stative verb: a verb that expresses a state or condition of the subject.

stem: the basic part of a word that is common to all its inflected variants.

stop: sound produced by stopping the airflow in the vocal tract.
stop neutralization: a principle of Korean in which stop sounds are unreleased in a syllable-final position.
subject: the part of a sentence that indicates the agent of the verb. It is always a noun, noun phrase, pronoun, or noun clause.
subject particle: a grammatical suffix that denotes the subject of a sentence.
subjunctive: a mood of the verb used to represent a denoted act or state not as fact but as contingent or possible or viewed emotionally (as with doubt or desire).
subordinate clause: a non-independent clause usually introduced by a subordinating element such as a subordinating conjunction or relative pronoun. It depends on the rest of the sentence for its meaning. It does not express a complete thought, so it does not stand alone. It must always be attached to a main clause that completes the meaning.
subordinating conjunction: a word that joins a subordinate clause to a main clause: e.g., "however," "although," "even though," "because."
suffix: a grammatical morpheme that is attached at the end of a word.
superlative: the degree of grammatical comparison that denotes an extreme or unsurpassed level or extent.
syllable: a word or part of a word that can be pronounced with one impulse from the voice. A syllable always contains at least a vowel sound, and most syllables have consonants associated with that vowel.
syllable coda: the syllable-final position.

tense: indication of time in a sentence such as the present, past, or future.
tensing: process by which a lax sound becomes a tense sound.
transitive verb: an action verb that takes a direct object.

unrelease: in pronouncing a stop sound, when the oral contact is not released immediately after articulation.

verb: a word that expresses an act, occurrence, or mode of being. It is the grammatical center of a predicate.
voice: a verb inflection that indicates the relation between the subject of the sentence and the action expressed by the verb. Three voices exist in Korean: active, passive, and causative.
voicing: the act of the vocal cords vibrating to make a voiceless sound become a voiced sound.
vowel: one of a class of speech sounds in the articulation of which the oral part of the breath channel is not blocked and is not constricted enough to cause audible friction; it is the most prominent sound in a syllable.
vowel harmony (VH): a group of vowels occur only with the members of the same group sharing certain articulatory features.

yang vowels: also called bright vowels. Connotes bright, cheerful, diminutive impression. Contrasts with **yin/ŭm vowels.**

yin (**ŭm**) **vowels**: also called dark vowels. Connotes, dark, big, weighty impression. Contrasts with **Yang vowels.**

Appendix 5

Bibliography for further reading

Arguëlles, Alexander, and Jong-Rok Kim. 2000. *A Historical, Literary, and Cultural Approach to the Korean Language*. Elizabeth, NJ and Seoul: Hollym.

Chang, Suk-Jin. 1996. *Korean*. Amsterdam and Philadelphia, PA: John Benjamins.

Cho, Young-mee Yu. 1999/2001. 'Language change and the phonological lexicon of Korean.' Lauree J. Brinton, ed. *Historical Linguistics 1999: Selected papers from the 14th International Conference on Historical Linguistics, Vancouver, 9–13th August 1999*. Amsterdam: John Benjamins, pp. 89–104.

Coulmas, Florian. 1989. *The Writing Systems of the World*. Oxford: Blackwell.

Ihm, Ho Bin, Hong Kyung Pyo, and Chang Suk. 2001. *Korean Grammar for International Learners*. Seoul: Yonsei University Press.

Jun, Sun-Ah, and Mira Oh. 1996. 'A prosodic analysis of three types of wh-phrases in Korean.' *Language and Speech* 39(1): 37–61.

Jung, JaeJung. 2005. *The Korean Language: Structure, Use and Context*. London and New York: Routledge.

Kim, Chin-W. 1988 *Sojourns in Language*. 2 Volumes. Seoul: Tower Press.

Kim-Renaud, Young-Key. 1974, rev. 1995. *Korean Consonantal Phonology*. Seoul: Hanshin.

Kim-Renaud, Young-Key. 1986. *Studies in Korean Linguistics*. Seoul: Hanshin.

Kim-Renaud, Young-Key, ed. 1997. *The Korean Alphabet: Its History and Structure*. Honolulu: University of Hawai'i Press.

Ledyard, Gari Keith. 1966. *The Korean Language Reform of 1446*. Ph.D. thesis, University of California – Berkeley. Published 1998 (same title). Seoul: Sin'gu Munhwasa.

Lee, Iksop, and S. Robert Ramsey. 2000. *The Korean Language*. Albany, NY: State University of New York Press.

Lee O. Young. 1985. *Sin han'guk in* (New Koreans). Seoul: Manhak Sasangsa.

Martin, Samuel E. 1992. *Reference Grammar of Korean: A Complete Guide to the Grammar and History of the Korean Language*. Rutland, VT and Tokyo: Charles E. Tuttle Co.

Sampson, Geoffrey, 1985. *Writing Systems: A Linguistic Introduction*. Stanford, CA: Stanford University Press.

Sohn, Ho-min. 1986. *Linguistic Expeditions*. Seoul: Hanshin.

Sohn, Ho-min. 1999. *The Korean Language*. Cambridge: Cambridge University Press.

Sohn, Ho-min. 2001. *The Korean Language*. Cambridge Language Surveys. Cambridge: Cambridge University Press.

Sohn, Ho-min. ed. 2006. *Korean Language in Culture and Society*. KLEAR Textbooks in Korean Language. Honolulu: University of Hawai'i Press.

Yeon, Jaehoon. 2003. *Korean Grammatical Constructions and their Form and Meaning*. London: Saffron.

Index

Printed in Great Britain
by Amazon

36333080R00156